The Role Ethics of Epictetus

The Role Ethics of Epictetus

Stoicism in Ordinary Life

Brian Earl Johnson

LEXINGTON BOOKS
Lanham • Boulder • New York • Toronto • Plymouth, UK

Published by Lexington Books
A wholly owned subsidiary of The Rowman & Littlefield Publishing Group, Inc.
4501 Forbes Boulevard, Suite 200, Lanham, Maryland 20706
www.rowman.com

10 Thornbury Road, Plymouth PL6 7PP, United Kingdom

British Library Cataloguing in Publication Information Available

Library of Congress Cataloging-in-Publication Data

ISBN 978-0-7391-7967-3 (cloth : alk. paper) -- ISBN 978-0-7391-7968-0 (electronic)
ISBN 978-1-4985-5083-3 (pbk : alk. paper)

For my parents, who lovingly balanced so many roles

Contents

Preface

Why Epictetus? Throughout much of Western history, that question would have surprised a literate adult because Epictetus was held in high esteem as a popular spokesman for Stoicism. In turn, Stoicism enjoyed wide recognition for its ethics, one that was seen as both an alternative and complement to Christian ethics. As Thomas Jefferson wrote to a friend in 1819, "Epictetus, indeed, has given us what was good of the Stoics . . . Epictetus [the Stoic] & Epicurus [the Hedonist] give laws for governing ourselves, Jesus a supplement of the duties & charities we owe to others" (Thomas Jefferson to William Short, October 31, 1819).

It was only in the late 19th century that Epictetus and the Stoics were temporarily edged off the table. They went from being actively studied to being "reshelved" as German Idealists shifted away from Hellenistic thinkers towards Plato and Aristotle and Anglophone philosophers shifted away from ancient thinkers in general.

Such diminished status, however, did not last long. From the 1960s forward, Epictetus experienced a revival in scholarship and in popular culture more generally. Among academics, there has been a new recognition that Epictetus and the Stoics had produced philosophic work of greater sophistication and subtlety than previously thought. Scholars have come to recognize, for example, that the Stoics had been busy introducing innovations in logic and that their ethics was more nuanced than earlier portraits suggested. Among general readers, there has been a recognition that Epictetus and the Stoics still could speak to us across the ages about being human in an age of conflict. Perhaps the most striking example of this revival is the 1993 speech (and later monograph) by the decorated Vietnam war veteran and torture survivor James Stockdale. Vice-Admiral Stockdale titled his speech "Courage Under Fire: Testing Epictetus's Doctrines in a Laboratory of Human

Behavior," and that speech helped to make Epictetus a staple in U.S. military academies. Subsequently, Stockdale apparently inspired author Tom Wolfe to make one of his key characters adopt the philosophy of Epictetus in *A Man in Full*. And yet, even before these works, a modified version of Stoicism was already influencing popular culture through the original *Star Wars* movies. The Jedi Obi-Wan Kenobi willingly meets his own fate (as the Stoics recommend) and, invoking something much like the Stoic's cosmic fire, he insists that there is an "energy field" that "surrounds us and penetrates us . . . [and] binds the galaxy together."

My own interest in Epictetus and his role ethics arose from a fortuitous confluence of two events in graduate school. First, while trying out various time-management systems for tackling the unending "to do" lists that chase us all, I found myself especially helped by those authors who urged that we must first organize our activities around our basic values and then around our roles (or "hats"). I was struck by this idea of organizing my "to do" list around my roles because I implicitly conceptualized my life that way but, in practice, I was forcing all my tasks to fit on one master list. By organizing my activities around my roles, I found them easier to manage, to anticipate, *and* to prioritize. Second, while in a philosophy reading group at that time, I was assigned to present Epictetus's *Discourses* 1.2, titled "How may someone preserve what befits his role in every instance?" Epictetus there asserts that what is reasonable differs from person to person *and* that we judge what is reasonable, in part, according to our roles. On this basis, he uses roles to address questions of life or death and he connects such roles to our identity. In this discourse, then, Epictetus seemed to have put his hands on the deeper philosophic underpinnings of the commonsense idea I had just encountered, the idea that we organize our actions around our life roles.

I was thus hooked and I set about trying to make sense of what Epictetus had to say about roles. What are roles? How do we know when we have a role? Can we choose them or reject them? In researching these questions, I began with the assumption that my project would be a simple one. After all, Epictetus's point initially seemed very broad: in any ethical decision, we may refer to our roles in order to determine what is at stake. For example, the dominant Western ethical theories seem to agree that, barring extraordinary circumstances, parents should care for their children. A Kantian would account for this care-giving as the duty to regard one's child as an end-in-itself, an Aristotelian as the love and friendship necessary for happiness (or flourishing), and a utilitarian as activity likely to contribute to the general well-being. The parent-child roles, therefore, merely name the relevant circumstances to which a moral theory is applied, whether Kantian duty, Aristotelian happiness, or utilitarian goodness.

On that basis, I expected to write merely about how Epictetus highlights the relevance of roles to ethical reasoning. However, the more I searched out his account of roles, the more I came to see that Epictetus has a more original project in store. Epictetus has largely set aside the traditional Graeco-Roman talk of the virtues (justice, moderation, courage, wisdom) and replaced them with talk of roles. To a father who could not bear to be with his ill daughter, Epictetus does not speak of courage. Instead, he engages the father in a discussion about what is natural *for a father* to do. The discussion ends successfully with the father returning home to care for his daughter (*Discourses* 1.11). In much the same way, Epictetus even recasts the characteristically Stoic ethical obligations to be undisturbed about the fate of some external (like the death of a family member) as part of our role as human beings. Thus, he reframes his Stoic commitments into the language of roles and he shows how such a frame readily applies to the decisions we face in ordinary life as friends, family members, citizens, and professionals.

Moreover, in my research, I was surprised to learn that Epictetus makes these roles provide the bedrock justification for ethical action. As in the case of a parent caring for a child, Epictetus appears to hold that no other justification is necessary other than to say, "I do this care-giving because I am a parent." Being a parent not only justifies action, Epictetus thinks, it motivates action precisely because such roles are intimately connected with our own identity. Roles serve to answer the question, "Who am I?"; role fulfillment thus becomes about fulfilling who one truly is. Finally, Epictetus gives these roles such weight that they might even conflict with one another. This possibility for conflict became especially clear to me when I studied Epictetus's treatment of Socrates's roles because Epictetus implies that Socrates's role as public philosopher was in tension with his private role as a father. Between these two roles, Epictetus believes that Socrates rightly sided with his role as a philosopher, but Epictetus equally grants that Socrates's public philosopher role may not be right for the rest of us. In all these ways, then, Epictetus was offering his audience an ethics based on roles.

In the pages ahead, I aim to reconstruct the role ethics of Epictetus as sympathetically as possible. While I certainly would not claim to be a Stoic (I would, for example, be willingly and enormously grieved at the loss of a loved one), I hope that a charitable presentation of Epictetus's role ethics will best illuminate his project for skeptics and devotees alike.

Acknowledgments

My biggest fear in writing these acknowledgments is that I will forget one of my many debts built up across the many years it has taken me to write this book. I will take my cue from Epictetus and examine my roles in order to help organize where credit is due.

As a graduate student at the University of Chicago, my research on Epictetus benefited enormously from the special dedication, care, and oversight of three individuals. Elizabeth Asmis, without whom this book would never have been realized, was exceptionally generous with her time and her insights. She was the first to suggest the issue of role conflict and to point out that my account of Epictetus's educational program makes agents ethically good before they achieve perfect knowledge. Gabriel Lear was a continual source of enthusiasm and fresh ideas. She went far beyond the call of duty. The late, and dearly missed, Ian Mueller was tireless in his integrity, and I learned, not only from the content of his remarks, but from the careful honesty that produced them.

I am also grateful to several scholars who assisted me at important junctures. Richard Kraut was responsible for introducing me to Epictetus and for thoughtfully overseeing my initial studies of Hellenistic philosophy. Martha Nussbaum sparked my interest in Musonius (Epictetus's teacher) and gave me very kind support. Rachel Barney offered incisive observations on chapter 2 and helped me to understand a puzzle within Stoicism. William O. Stephens gave terrific feedback and encouragement on chapter 5, and his translation of Bonhöffer has been a companion to me from the beginning of this research. (Subsequent to my days at Chicago, Bill has continued to be a source of encouragement, support, and helpful advice.)

My peers at the University of Chicago assisted me through their interest, feedback, criticism, and support. Thank you John Hannon, David Svolba,

Elisabeth Schreiber, Hulya Adak, Nathan Bauer, Jay Elliot, Chad Flanders, and Chris Starr. I also want to thank the participants of the Chicago Ancient Philosophy workshop. In addition, the Writing Program at the University of Chicago had been a second home to me because it is inhabited by such supportive people as Kathy Cochran, Tracy Weiner, Larry McEnerny, and the late Joe Williams.

As a member of the Fordham community, I have benefited from feedback and support from my ancient philosophy colleagues, Dana Miller and Daryl Tress. My project also benefited from cross-pollination arising from stimulating conversation with the members of the Lincoln Center "lunch crew" in Natural Science, Mathematics, Psychology, and beyond. A Fordham graduate student assistant, Matthew Carrella, cheerfully went over the manuscript with a magnifying glass. In preparing to send this manuscript to publishers, I received valuable comments from Brian Davies and Stephen Grimm. Lastly, my work at Fordham has been supported by the kind encouragement of Fr. Robert Grimes.

As a participant in the broader ancient philosophy community, I have benefited from a number of anonymous readers. Their challenging feedback has made my work stronger even though I surely have not been able to answer all of them. Brad Inwood gave generous and detailed feedback on key parts of my argument. Gretchen Reydams-Schils provided valuable feedback on what became chapter 6 when I originally presented it at the American Philosophical Association. I am grateful to the journal *Epochê* for letting me reprint my 2012 article, which has been expanded into chapters 1 and 2 with a small portion used in chapters 8 and 9; their comments on an earlier version were extremely helpful. I am also grateful to Ronald Polansky at *Ancient Philosophy* for permitting me to reprint my 2012 article, which appears mostly in chapter 5 with a small portion in chapters 1 and 6; Polansky gave the article version a thorough scrubbing. The editor, Jana Hodges-Kluck, and the review team at Lexington have been excellent.

As a friend, I owe thanks to JBF, NEC, Robert Garmong, Jason Greif, Evren Karpak, Colin Smith, Ben Thomas, all of the "Young Turks" (you know who you are!), and David Waldman.

As a coffee patron and wandering scholar, I have haunted many locations in the initial writing of this manuscript, but I would like to single out special thanks to the cafes owned by Parviz Rasti of Sunnyvale, California, and Eunkyong Choi of Chicago, Illinois. And, I would like to thank the libraries at Stanford University and the University of Chicago for letting me type at my computer with a cup of coffee among the books.

Finally, as a member of a family, I would like to thank my partner, Judy, and my kin. Judy has inspired me as a constant source of drive and ambition. My brothers, Eric and Kevin, and my sisters-in-law, Helen and Meredith, have been very sympathetic. My brother Karl has set a remarkable example for his unassuming acceptance of his handicapped role in life. Most importantly, I am profoundly grateful to my late parents for their unfailing support.

Introduction

Upon earning his freedom from slavery, the Greek Stoic philosopher Epictetus (*circa* 50 to 130 A.D.) decided to preach the doctrines of Stoicism on the streets of Rome. Wearing the white cap of a freedman, he lectured passersby on a favorite trope of Stoic ethics: self-mastery. Self-mastery is centrally important to Stoic ethics because, among other things, Stoic ethics insists that happiness or well-being (*eudaimonia*) should not be subject to the vagaries of fortune. The Stoics maintain that our *eudaimonia* is indestructible and it is up to us.

In order to ensure this indestructibility, the Stoics hold that our actions must be in accordance with nature.[1] Since Stoic physics treats the whirling machinations of nature as inexorable, this condition is inescapable. We must follow nature or be dragged along. To follow nature, we must make ourselves a knowledgeable mirror of nature and of nature's aims. As the Stoics see it, nature is not blind nor is it accidental. Nature is God and is the animating fire which orders all things, but nature (or God) does not order the world according to any wishes or whims. Instead, nature orders the world logically so that the world is exactly as it ought to be. Indeed, since the Stoics believe that the cosmos is locked in a perpetual cycle of destroying itself by fire and re-creating itself like a phoenix, the cosmos has played out God's logical plan an infinite number of times before and will do so an infinite number of times in the future. Just as Epictetus preached street-side in the Roman Empire, so he has exhorted us in countless worlds (or *kosmoi*) before us and will do so again into infinity.

To follow nature, we must align our actions with the divine and supreme ordering principle of the world, the divine fire. First, we must accept that the operations of the world are beyond our control. It is a part of the structure of the world that animals need sustenance to live, that our bodies are subject to disease, that the sun provides light, and so on. And yet, it is equally clear that nature has equipped us to seek food when we are hungry, to take medicine when we are ill, and to rely on sunlight for our crops and many other things. Accordingly, the Stoics believe, these various items are ones that we should prefer because they are natural, but I should not value them as necessary to my happiness because they are beyond my control. If an athlete should break his leg, he should prefer medical attention and seek to have the bone set so that it should heal. But, if the bone should not heal well and thereby end his athletic career, he should accept it with equanimity. In classic parlance, we should treat external things—the "goods" of fortune—as "preferred indifferents."

Second, in order to mirror nature, we must not only seek the right sorts of things at the right time, we must seek them in the right manner and with understanding. Because nature does not act at random, neither should we. In so far as nature logically aligns each moment with the next, so we should align our actions with all of our circumstances. In other words, our actions exhibit the virtue of wisdom because it is through wisdom that we order up our actions. Our actions must account for our fellow human beings (thus exhibiting the virtue of justice). We must rise above valuing what is external (thus exhibiting the virtue of courage). Our actions must be orderly and self-controlled (thus exhibiting the virtue of temperance). We must, for example, rush into the battlefield not because we dread the invasion of our homeland but because courageous action is the natural, virtuous action to take.

Indeed, it is not simply that nature orders each moment but that all the actions of nature are logically perfect because each given state of the cosmos necessarily yields the next; nature does not err. We, too, should aspire to that perfection and, should we reach it, we would become sages. Our actions must therefore arise from the unshakeable certainty of virtuous knowledge rather than the plasticity of belief. We should value only what is up to us (our own virtue and knowledge) and we should only treat external goods (which are subject to fortune) as matters of mere preference. The only genuine value is virtue; all else is preference. In this way, our *eudaimonia* will be secured by an imperturbable and virtuous inner state because we will never want what fails to happen and what happens will always be what we wish. We will be the perfect mirror of nature.

And yet, despite the exalted and inspirational themes of Stoic ethics in its appeal to self-mastery and in following nature, Epictetus's street-side exhortations failed to hit the mark. Some listeners punched this "arrogant" freedman. Others insulted him, telling this preacher of self-mastery to go find his own master. Epictetus confides that he found such ripostes demoralizing, and he ruefully confesses that he gave up on street-side preaching (*Discourses* 2.12.23–25). Subsequently, Epictetus founded a school for young boys in Nicopolis (in Northern Greece) and he there found his stride. By the end of his life, Epictetus was sought for ethical guidance by men of eminent rank (e.g., 1.11). Not long after his death, the reports of his discourses were studied by none other than the emperor Marcus Aurelius. And, even well beyond his life, Epictetus's *Handbook* has continued to be a source of solace and wisdom for individuals high and low.

Between the time of his street-side harangues and the end of his life, Epictetus discovered how to reach an audience successfully. In this book, I operate on the hypothesis that Epictetus's successful transformation arose from his inventive (and sometimes unorthodox) reformulation of Stoic ethics. In Stoicism (and in ancient ethics more generally), ethical goodness is understood as the expression of character virtues such as justice or courage, but Epictetus holds that ethical goodness is the proper expression of one's roles, such as mother or teacher. I am a parent, so I must make lunch for my children. I am a teacher, so I must plan my lessons. Through the concept of ethical roles, Epictetus reformulates the abstract and forbidding virtues of Stoicism (such as justice or wisdom) into the concrete obligations that ordinary individuals recognize and associate with their roles. Epictetus could bridge the gap between the virtue ethics of Stoicism and the role-bound ethics common among non-philosophers.

Moreover, in his transformation, Epictetus also reformulated Stoic ethics by downplaying its elusive ethical ideal, the so-called Stoic sage. In orthodox Stoicism, only sages are able to achieve perfect knowledge and ethical goodness. Not surprisingly, given the near impossibility of becoming a sage in Stoic theory, ordinary Roman citizens were disinterested in (if not hostile to) Epictetus's early street-side preaching. But, the mature Epictetus does not limit ethical goodness to the sage. For Epictetus, ordinary individuals are ethically good if they perform those actions which can be reasonably defended as issuing from their roles in life.

The aim of this book, therefore, is to elucidate and systematize the ethics of the Stoic Epictetus around his account of roles. At the same time, it aims to provide a sustained argument against the standard interpretation of Epictetus as lacking an original ethical viewpoint distinct from that of orthodox Stoicism.

To begin to make my case, chapters 1 and 2 detail Epictetus's general account of ethical roles. In chapter 1, I argue that he connects the concept of an ethical role with its use in drama to mean a mask or a part. For Epictetus, we are all actors with roles on the cosmic stage: we have the role we play as human beings and we have many local roles that we play (such as friend, teacher, or sibling). In this way, Epictetus understands us to have two kinds of roles (cosmic and local). Our cosmic role is our universal, human role, which requires that we admire God (i.e., Nature) and preserve God's gift to us—our *prohairesis* (volition). Our local roles entail that we duly fulfill our manifold obligations: that we act well as a stranger, a guest, a friend, a counselor, an employee, a citizen, and so on.

Chapter 1 explores Epictetus's account of our most fundamental role as human beings. The subject is challenging because Epictetus provides no systematic account of our human role, so I spend time threading together Epictetus's disparate remarks about what it means to behave as a human being rather than as an animal. In Epictetus's view, such behavior requires rationality, trustworthiness, cosmopolitanism, sociability, piety, and the elimination of the passions. This role likewise rules out the possibility of an evil role (e.g., the "role" of a thief) for all such roles contradict our human role. By the end of chapter 1, we come to the surprising realization that Epictetus has downplayed the canonical Greek virtues of wisdom, courage, justice, and self-control. Instead, the universal role focuses on the more concrete obligations of a good human citizen, from acting in a civilized fashion to being trustworthy.

In chapter 2, I argue that Epictetus does not attempt to list or categorize our specific roles exhaustively; indeed, the type and quantity of roles may vary from person to person. Rather, Epictetus offers us four criteria by which we may locate our many roles: (1) Particular nature: our abilities both limit and prescribe specific roles. For example, strong legs suggest an athletic career. Aside from our abilities, Epictetus also holds that our entrenched sense of self-worth is an aspect of our nature that helps determine our roles. (2) Social relations: this criterion includes our natural relations (e.g., parent, child, or sibling) and our acquired relations (e.g., spouse, senator, neighbor). (3) Chosen roles: choice only obtains when our capacities permit us to pursue several possible careers. (4) Divine signs: Epictetus believes that our roles can be indicated by divination (such as Socrates's reception of the oracle at Delphi).

Through the discussion of these four criteria, we are positioned to appreciate some of the main themes of Epictetus's ethics. At the forefront of Epictetus's account is the importance of self-analysis to discover our own roles. Epictetus repeatedly asks his audience to consider, "Who *are* you?" To answer, we must examine our talents, our relations, our wishes, and, in special cases, even consult with an oracle. As we clarify ourselves and our roles, Epictetus believes, we will see that our roles situate us in overlapping communities where we have parts to play. We will see that every role represents a relation within some community (e.g., family, school, the workplace) and every role has meaningful obligations.

Since Epictetus believes that roles determine what is good and evil, chapter 3 proceeds to analyze how he connects roles to ethical action. Under orthodox Stoicism, human beings must do what is appropriate (or do their "duty" as in older translations) and, of course, virtuous action is always appropriate. But, how do we determine what is appropriate? The Stoics rather unhelpfully say that an appropriate action must have "consequentiality in life" (an ill-defined expression) and it must admit of a "reasonable defense." And yet, they caution that only a Stoic sage can truly know what that defense is; and, since they believe that the ethical quality of our action is determined by whether we know its rightness or not, only a sage can perform a virtuous action.

Epictetus shares with other Stoic philosophers the formal criteria by which appropriate action is measured (consequentiality and reasonableness); however, he uses his account of roles to give substance to the criteria in a way that ordinary individuals can understand and achieve in action. For consequentiality, he says that it is a term from logic in which we lay down a premise and infer a consequent. So, with roles, we lay down a role and infer an appropriate action. In the same way, we construct a reasonable defense on the basis of our roles. For example, that I am a father implies that I should defend my children, but, similarly, because I am a father, it is reasonable for me to defend my children. Thus, Epictetus again sets aside the canonical virtues and offers roles as an ethical theory which does the work of those canonical virtues.

Chapter 4 takes up Epictetus's program for educating his students, the significance of which is often missed. Epictetus divides the training of his students into three successive stages (*topoi*). *Topos* 1 studies desire and aversion; it teaches students to control their desire and prepares them to fulfill their human role. *Topos* 2 studies roles and appropriate action; it focuses on ethical training rather than professional training. *Topos* 3 seeks the mastery of judgment in all conditions through the study of logic. In Epictetus's account, these three topics are meant to be studied *successively* and it is within such ordering that he indicates the ethical significance of role-bound action. As Epictetus presents it, the third topic aims at making students into the so-called sage (whom orthodox Stoics treat as the only true instance of ethical action), and yet Epictetus insists that we become good in the *second* topic of study. Epictetus thereby implies that ordinary roles are sufficient for becoming ethically good; he resists the older Stoic claim that only sages are good. Hence, Epictetus offers a viable ethics for non-sages.

More broadly, I argue that his pedagogical theory emphasizes that ethical development is a process of mastering our desires and taking up our roles. His theory still accounts for the effort to become a Stoic sage but it treats that effort as a kind of post-graduate study, one that is inappropriate for most individuals and unnecessary for becoming fine and good persons. Accordingly, Epictetus downplays the orthodox ideal of the Stoic sage and replaces that figure with role-bound individuals (such as great athletes) who are supposed to inspire each of us to meet the challenges of our own roles. Instead of looking to Stoic sages, who have perfect knowledge and actions, Epictetus's new ethical hero is someone we need not imitate in knowledge or action.

Rather, we simply try to meet the challenges of our own roles as do our heroes.

Given that roles determine what is proper and improper, it is necessary to consider what happens in the instance of role conflict. Chapter 5 asks if the demands of my role as spouse might conflict with the demands of my role as a professional. Epictetus's recognition of conflict is another feature of his thought that is missed or downplayed in the scholarly literature (which may be a result of imposing orthodox Stoicism upon Epictetus). And yet, Epictetus's acceptance of conflict is another way in which he reaches ordinary individuals; as real people plan their day, they must confront the fact that it is often impossible to meet all of the obligations presented by their roles.

Chapter 5 is concerned solely to argue that Epictetus grants the possibility of role conflict. I analyze Epictetus's treatment of role conflict by drawing out how he recognized conflicting roles in the life of Socrates. As Epictetus sees it, Socrates's public and demanding role as philosophic "gadfly" to Athens was often in tension with the private demands of his roles as husband and father. I also analyze Epictetus's account of the heroic exploits of Heracles and demonstrate that Epictetus treats Heracles's role as hero as a sufficient reason for action, regardless of what is demanded by his role as a human being. My aim in both case studies is to demonstrate that particular roles are fixed points in the ethical reasoning of agents and thus I argue against what I term the "deflationary" reading, a reading according to which particular roles are nothing more than applications of one universal, human role to some set of circumstances.

Chapter 6 seeks to move the discussion forward by applying the insights from chapter 5 to Epictetus's most extended treatment of roles: *Discourse* 1.2. Epictetus commences *Discourse* 1.2 by announcing that rational agents cannot tolerate what is unreasonable but they can tolerate what is reasonable. Epictetus illustrates his point with seemingly paradoxical examples in which we can endure a whipping or even endure being hanged—if we feel that it is reasonable. He adds that we determine what is reasonable or not by reference to our roles. The difficulty of understanding what Epictetus means here is made frustratingly worse when he tries to illuminate these claims by means of a perplexing series of binary examples concerning the slave who resists versus the slave who obeys, the senator who speaks out against Caesar versus the senator who sits in silence, and so on. As Epictetus proceeds through these examples, he does not tell us precisely what roles he has in mind or how many are at stake in each case. Is he contrasting the right and wrong way to fulfill a role, is he contrasting better and worse courses of action, or is he contrasting equally valid but different roles?

To address that confusion, chapter 6 examines three interpretations of the roles presented in *Discourse* 1.2—a deflationary interpretation, a concessionary interpretation, and an egalitarian interpretation. The chapter begins by analyzing the problem posed by *Discourse* 1.2 in greater detail and then analyzes the strength of each interpretation by means of successive readings of *Discourse* 1.2. Throughout my analysis, I harness the work done in the previous chapters to fill out the detail in this highly compressed discourse. On the basis of that work, I conclude chapter 6 in favor of the egalitarian reading as the best interpretation.

In chapter 7, we approach the limits of Epictetus's account of roles and address the difficult issue of resolving conflict among specific roles, between my role as a brother and my role as, say, a teacher. We are at the very limits of Epictetus's account because he seems to have positioned us to recognize role conflicts but he provides no explicit resolution of them. Although Epictetus declares that "you cannot act the part of Thersites and that of Agamemnon too" (*Disc*. 4.2.10), what would happen if an individual were forced to play both parts, like the ailing Philoctetes who was built to be an aristocrat like Agamemnon but suffered a mangled body like Thersites?

Although I take the view that Epictetus fails to provide any clear-cut solution to role conflict, he has not left us without resources to think through role conflict. In this chapter, I argue that Epictetus supplies us with three cases that shed light on how we may resolve role conflict. The first two cases can reasonably be read as instances of conflict between specific roles, and I examine how Epictetus manages them. The third case concerns the possibility that even a single role could entail conflicting obligations, and I argue that such conflicts must be resolved from "outside" the role. In sum, Epictetus provides no pat answer to this problem; he solves these role conflicts (as real people often do) on a case-by-case basis.

Because Epictetus's remarks on roles appear so fragmentary, some scholars have looked to Cicero's earlier and more organized account of ethical roles in order to provide a framework for analyzing Epictetus. However, while Cicero is certainly working with a historically antecedent theory of roles (stemming from the Greek philosopher Panaetius), Epictetus employs roles in ways that are quite different from Cicero's (and Panaetius's) approach. Cicero's framework is therefore ill-suited for Epictetus. Chapter 8 thus serves to clear away the improper reliance by some scholars on Cicero's framework in their discussions of Epictetus's ethics. Chapter 8 also utilizes Cicero's account as a counterpoint to underscore Epictetus's originality. When we read Epictetus freed of Cicero's framework, when Epictetus is given his own soliloquy (as it were), we can come to see important features of Epictetus's philosophy that have been under-appreciated in the literature: in particular, that Epictetus supplies a robust account of roles and a complete ethics based on it.

For Cicero, roles (*personae*) are a tool in the service of the virtue of decorum where decorum is one of the four canonical virtues—justice, courage, wisdom, and decorum (also known as seemliness or self-control). In his view, we have exactly four roles, each of which offers a specific criterion for determining whether certain actions exhibit the virtue of decorum: (i) humanity; (ii) personality, (iii) social standing, and (iv) career. Cicero provides no detail concerning our role as human beings, but he provides detailed advice about the latter three roles. This gap is significant because it makes his *personae* an extension of one of the four canonical virtues and because *personae* turn out to be only one of many tools for determining what is seemly (albeit the most important of such tools). At the end of this account, I argue that Epictetus and Cicero understand the "role" metaphor in fundamentally different ways. For Cicero, a role is one we play as an actor before an audience and so it concerns how we present ourselves in front of others. For Epictetus, a role is a part with a function (whether anyone sees it or not).

This book concludes in chapter 9 with a reflection on what Epictetus has accomplished. The upshot of the previous chapters is that Epictetus's role theory has things to say about practical philosophical questions that are of great interest. When we consider Epictetus's theory next to Cicero's, it becomes apparent that Cicero's theory of the four *personae* (roles) is almost wholly concerned with public image. Although Cicero tries to stretch his theory to address such grave issues as suicide, his primary concern is our public personality. By contrast, it is apparent that Epictetus removes roles from the constraints of *decorum* and instead makes them the basis of an entire theory of ethics. Naturally, then, Epictetus's role theory is much broader in scope and ambition.

What is compelling about Epictetus's role ethics is how he has broken the mold of Stoic ethics (and ancient ethics in general) in a way that seems surprisingly modern. Epictetus moves beyond the canonical argument in classical ethics which seeks to infer our virtues from universal features of our humanity. If the function of a human being is to reason, so the classical argument goes, then reasoning well is a virtue. Epictetus remains interested in such an argument, but his role ethics exhibits a keen awareness of how our more particular identities (whether as friend or soldier) adds specialized, unique, and ethically worthy obligations. If the function of a parent is to care for children, then the virtue of a parent is to parent well. To be virtuous, we must realize our potential, not just as human beings, but as individualized role-bound human beings.

NOTE

1. The next several paragraphs are intended as a highly motivated primer on Stoicism, and my account is especially tailored to capture the appeal to cosmic nature as found in Epictetus. In framing Stoic ethics this way, I have benefited from the debate between John Cooper and Julia Annas regarding the role of cosmic nature in Stoic ethics (J. M. Cooper 1995 and Julia Annas 1995). Cooper takes the view that Stoic ethics relies on metaphysical claims about cosmic nature, whereas Annas takes the view that Stoic ethics can begin with considerations

about our own ultimate *telos* and need not make appeals to cosmic nature. Annas, of course, grants that Epictetus and Marcus Aurelius "choose to make use of cosmic nature directly" (605), but she maintains that "Stoics could at any time have chosen to present ethics in the relatively independent way, or as a part of Stoic theory as a whole" (604–605). In the work ahead, I hope to show that Epictetus's role ethics does allow us to begin independently by appealing to the preconceptions that agents have of their roles; in turn, reflection on their roles naturally leads them back to the consideration of their role in cosmic nature and the proper place of nature in their ethical reflections.

Chapter One

Epictetus's Role for Human Beings

Who am I? This difficult question is the foundation of Epictetus's role ethics. In framing his ethics with this question, Epictetus appears to have been inspired by Socrates's life and philosophic mission. The Socrates of Plato's *Apology* rather famously defends his life by arguing that he was stationed to be a kind of philosophical gadfly by the god at Delphi (Pl. *Ap.* 28d–29e, 30e, and 37e–38a). His special station in life was to cross-examine others because "the unexamined life is not worth living" (*Ap.* 38a). However, while Socrates expects others to engage in the same self-examination that he practiced, he appears to treat his own station of gadfly as nearly *sui generis* for he suggests that a man like him is hard to replace (Pl. *Ap.* 31a). In addition, he provides no hint about how others might interpret their *own* lives as a station with special obligations.

To the issue of how we might universalize the Socratic position in the *Apology*, Epictetus adopts the Socratic idea of a station (*taxis*) and asserts that the life of each person represents a post that is assigned by the divine general (*Discourses* 3.24.34 and 95–99; cf. 1.16.20–21). In turn, Epictetus appears to equate this military analogy with a stage-metaphor according to which *every* person should be understood as inhabiting a divinely given role (*prosôpon*):

> Remember that you are an actor in a drama, which is as the playwright wishes; if the playwright wishes it short, it will be short; if long, then long; if the playwright wishes you to play a beggar, [it is assigned] in order that you good-naturedly play even that role; [and similarly] if [you are assigned to play] a disabled person, an archon, or a lay person. For this is what is yours: to finely play the role [*prosôpon*] that is given; but to select [that role] itself is another's [i.e., the divine playwright]. (*Ench.* 17)

Just as Socrates insists that he must steadfastly remain in his military-like station or be disgraced (Pl. *Ap.* 28d), so Epictetus insists that each of us must fulfill our assigned role or else be disgraced (*Ench.* 37). Thus, when Epictetus discusses roles and self-knowledge, the example of Socrates's role often lurks in the background. In discussing the role of Socrates, Epictetus imagines the reaction of an anonymous interlocutor who is prompted to ask, "Am I *that kind* of person?" (3.1.24; cf. 1.2.33–34). Similarly, in discussing the life of a Cynic, who must live very much like Socrates, Epictetus advises a potential Cynic to "know yourself" (3.22.53).

But, how do each of us answer the summons to know thyself? Socrates—as Epictetus is well aware—had benefit of an oracle to guide him in identifying his role; so did Diogenes the Cynic and Zeno the founder of Stoicism (3.21.17–20). In a suggestive fragment, Epictetus helpfully explains that the Delphic injunction amounts to a more basic summons to know one's ability and position relative to others and to act accordingly: "If someone ordered a singer in a chorus to 'know himself,' would he not attend to the order by paying attention both to his fellow chorus members and to harmonizing with them? —Yes—And so for a sailor? or a soldier?" (fr. 1).[1] More broadly, self-knowledge includes the recognition of our humanity (*Discourses* 2.10.1–6) as well as knowledge of our own nature (3.15.9–10) and its implications about our own places in the world (4.12.16). In this way, "who am I?" amounts to the question "what are my roles?"[2]

Although Epictetus would certainly wish that we could each receive a divine sign about our roles (3.24.34–35), he does not set the bar for self-knowledge that high. Rather, Epictetus offers a series of heuristics for identifying our roles and for understanding their practical meaning. He helpfully appears to have worked out a simple classification scheme for the roles that we must play. He implies that our roles divide into two sorts (3.23.3–5), one sort is common to us as rational human beings (2.9.1–10), and another sort is more specific to us as individuals: "son, father, brother, citizen, husband, wife, neighbor, fellow-traveler, ruler, and subject" (2.14.8) and so on. Applied to Socrates, Epictetus's account means that Socrates had the common role of a human being, which includes the obligation to practice the canonical Greek virtues and treat externals as a matter of indifference. In addition, Socrates had the more specific role of philosophic teacher, which included such obligations as playing the gadfly and inflaming the jurors at his defense,[3] a role potentially shared by only a small sector of humanity. Applied to each of us, we each have the role of a human being and we have many specific roles, from friend to sibling.

In this chapter and the next, we shall explore what Epictetus has to say about each set of roles. This chapter will examine Epictetus's concept of a role, his division between the two sorts of roles, and the obligations that he attaches to our role as human beings. The next chapter will examine how

Epictetus believes that we should locate the roles that differ from person to person. Throughout, we will survey Epictetus's reflections and advice about how we should locate and act upon our roles.

FROM DRAMATIC ROLES TO ETHICAL ROLES

Epictetus's term *prosôpon* (Greek for "role") is best understood in the context of drama where it means "mask," a use which anchors the other meanings of the term. Since a mask is worn to show the appearance of a character, it can mean simply "face" or "countenance." By extension, since different characters wear different masks, role (*prosôpon*) can mean the "dramatic role" or "character" played by an actor. As both "mask" and "role," role (*prosôpon*) is associated with costumes, spoken lines, and conduct which signify and realize any given role. The "mask" of an aristocrat is associated with clever speech, a noble gait, and a proud disposition. Conversely, the "mask" of a victim is associated with lamentations, tattered clothes, and bitterness.[4] These theatrical uses and associations of role (*prosôpon*) as "role" are exploited by Epictetus to import the term into a Stoic context. As quoted earlier, Epictetus regards us as actors in a cosmic drama in which we each have a part to play (*Ench.* 17). His concept of role (*prosôpon*) therefore provides a metaphorical elaboration of the traditional Stoic doctrine that human beings should follow God's arrangement of the world.[5]

However, Epictetus also distinguishes dramatic roles from our roles in real life. First, he assumes that stage actors know their roles before the play begins because they are assigned their role by the play's manager, but living persons must sometimes work to discern their roles. The proper identification of our roles is critical because our roles determine what is good for each of us (1.2.5–7; *Ench.* 30) and we cannot play our part well if we select the wrong role. "If you take on some role that is beyond your powers, you disgrace yourself in that role, and you neglect the role that you were capable of fulfilling" (*Ench.* 37). Although Epictetus will take the view that some roles are obvious (see, e.g., 1.2.30–32),[6] he will disavow telling individuals what their role is if they do not know. To a slave or servant who is wondering about whether or not to obey a demeaning order, Epictetus refuses to say what role must be adopted because "you are the one who knows yourself" (1.2.11).

Moreover, theatrical roles differ from living roles by the kinds of roles that actors and real people can have as well as by the ways in which actors and persons can bear many roles. In drama, it seems, performers may play the role of a villain on stage, but real-life people should never take on evil roles.[7] In addition, living roles cannot be interchanged like dramatic roles. Actors can cycle through many different masks and hence play several competing roles within one play, from Thersites to Agamemnon, so long as these roles do not appear on stage at the same time. By contrast, real-life people bear many roles at once; as I shall argue below, Epictetus formalizes the fact that real-life people bear more than one role when he suggests that we bear the role of a human being as well as many specific roles. And yet, unlike actors, real people cannot play competing roles. We can play either Thersites *or* Agamemnon (4.2.10); of course, we should play well whichever role we have (*Ench.* 17), but we cannot play both at once.[8] In this way, actors can play many opposing roles but they can only play one role at a time; real-life people bear many roles at once but they cannot play contradictory roles.

Finally, Epictetus differentiates dramatic roles from living roles simply by the fact that he does not limit himself to the theatrical term *prosôpon* (role) to refer to real-life roles. When Epictetus invokes our universal role, he tends to speak of the "profession [*epangelian*] of a human being" (2.9.1) or our place (*chôra*) or position (*taxis*) as rational animals (1.10.10, 1.16.20–21 and 2.4.5). He also speaks in terms of the station (*stasis*) of a philosopher in contexts where he clearly means our universal role as ethical persons.[9] But, he is equally willing to refer to the role of a soldier, teacher, citizen, among others, as a place (*chôra*) or position (*taxis*), much as Socrates referred to his divine station as a *taxis*.[10] In this way, God might be described as a playwright that assigns a role (*Ench.* 17) or as a general that assigns a station (3.24.34, 95, and 99).[11] Similarly, the role of an athlete is once termed a *hupothesis* from which the athlete must infer what should to be done (1.29.38–41).[12] By contrast, the term *prosôpon* as "role" is used almost exclusively in contexts where he is discussing the specific role.[13] Although *prosôpon* is clearly not his only term for a specific role, it is by far the leading term used by Epictetus.

TWO SORTS OF ROLES: UNIVERSAL AND SPECIFIC

In order to discuss our role as human beings and our local roles (such as counselor or wife), we must properly distinguish them. Briefly stated, Epictetus identifies our universal role with our humanity and our specific role with professions such as carpenter or philosopher, personal relations such as brother or friend, and political roles such as Athenian citizen or Roman senator.[14] It is generally recognized that these non-universal roles are not individual in the sense of being *sui generis* or filled by numerically one person for all time.[15] Instead, Epictetus talks about non-universal roles as though they are tokens of a specific type (e.g., Antigone as a "sister," Diogenes as a "Cynic"), a type that is shared by some, but not all, human beings. In this way, even a monarch counts as a class-type of role since, over time, the role may be filled by more than one individual. Accordingly, I use the term "specific roles" for Epictetus because that term supplies the relevant contrast to the term "universal role," and it plausibly leaves open that these roles may apply to a class of individuals.

Epictetus implies the distinction between universal and specific roles in his discussion of roles in *Discourses* 2.10 when he tells us that we are first a human being (2.10.1–6) and then we are a son, a brother, a councilor or an elder, etc. (2.10.7–14).[16] However, Epictetus comes quite close to making this distinction explicit in a highly suggestive passage that is worth exploring in order to spell out the two types of roles:

> For, if we do not refer each of our actions to some standard, we shall be acting at random. . . . There is, besides, a common [*koinê*] and a specific [*idia*] standard.[17] First of all, in order that I [act] as a human being. What is included in this? Not [to act] as a sheep, gently but at random; nor destructively, like a wild beast. The specific [standard] applies to each person's pursuit [*epitêdeuma*] and volition [*prohairesis*].[18] The cithara-player is to act as a cithara-player, the carpenter as a carpenter, the philosopher as a philosopher, the rhetor as a rhetor. (3.23.3–5)[19]

Although this passage does not explicitly use the term "role" (*prosôpon*), it offers clues to suggest that roles are being invoked. The strongest clue arises from the fact that Epictetus links the "specific standard" to the fulfillment of professions like that of a harpist, carpenter, philosopher, or rhetor. Elsewhere, Epictetus explicitly identifies similar professions with the term "role" (*prosôpon*). He treats the profession of a servant or slave (1.2.8–11), an athlete (1.2.25–28), and a Cynic[20] (3.22.69) as roles.[21] In fact, in the lines before the passage quoted above, Epictetus discusses the case of an athlete who must choose who he wishes to be (3.23.1–2), suggesting that he would plausibly include being an athlete as a pursuit (*epitêdeuma*).[22] Moreover, the 3.23 passage uses language which conjures up the idea of playing a part or fulfilling a role: an *x* should act as an *x*. Given these parallels, it is reasonable to conclude that Epictetus understands "each person's pursuit [*epitêdeuma*]" as some sort of role (*prosôpon*).

The most puzzling feature of this passage is its claim that the specific standard also applies to our volition (*prohairesis*). Epictetus does not explicitly invoke volition (*prohairesis*) again in this chapter, so his meaning is not entirely clear, but the context suggests that he wishes to use volition in relation to the manner in which individuals approach their professional pursuits, particularly to the goals that they have. Does the lyre player aim towards being a lyre player or at being a crowd pleaser? After the 3.23.3–5 passage, Epictetus immediately goes on to criticize those who pursue professions for the sake of adulation (e.g., 3.23.6–8). Instead of praise, he says, we should aim at the fulfillment of a profession according to its own demands; that is, if we are a philosopher, we should not act as a crowd pleaser but simply as a philosopher (3.23.27–29). Since *prohairesis* refers to our volition, it is likely that Epictetus here wishes to use the term to identify the aims we choose for our professional roles. If we aim our volition at praise in our profession, we act badly; if we aim our volition at the requirements of our profession, we act well.

As a result, we can reformulate Epictetus's initial claim as follows: the specific standard applies to our professional roles and the aims we set for them. Naturally, if the standard here is "specific" (*idios*), the role in question must be "specific." That is, by transitivity, the professional role can be taken to be (a) the specific role or (b) a component of the specific role. In chapter 2, we will see that Epictetus identifies other roles besides the professional one (e.g., family roles), roles that are not universal and therefore qualify as specific roles. Accordingly, the 3.23 passage seems to imply that the specific standard refers to non-universal roles, such as a professional role, and that these roles can be understood as specific roles.

Now that the specific role has been located in the specific standard, it is possible to identify the common standard with the universal role. To begin with, 3.23.3–5 treats the common standard as though it is a post to be fulfilled. We should behave "as human beings" not as "sheep" or "beasts" (3.23.4). In addition, 3.23 contrasts that post with specific professions, such as acting like a rhetor or a philosopher. Finally, as we saw earlier, Epictetus uses role-type language to identify precisely this summons to behave as human beings: I should occupy "the place [*chôran*] of a human being" (2.4.5) and it is my station (*taxis*) to behave as a rational being (1.16.21). Taken together, this evidence suggests that the "common standard" refers to our universal role as human beings.

THE UNIVERSAL ROLE OF A HUMAN BEING

With both roles in hand, we are positioned to address Epictetus's treatment of our human role. When Epictetus discusses the human role, he frequently introduces it by instructing his audience to consider who they are. We should know ourselves because self-knowledge is requisite for goodness; for "who is a good man who does not know who he is?" (3.24.20).[23] To the question of who and what we are, Epictetus repeatedly answers, "A human being."[24] For Epictetus, this answer is significant because our humanity is partly up to us; those who fail to act as human beings destroy their humanity and are classified as beasts (2.9.1–10).[25] It is not enough to have the shape and appearance of a human being in order to qualify as a human being, any more than an apple-shaped piece of wax counts as an apple (4.5.19–20). Although it is not possible to undo completely our nature as human beings (2.20.18–20), it is possible to brutalize our own human rationality so that our "sense of shame and modesty have been chopped off" (1.5.9). We can therefore destroy what might be deemed parts of ourselves. If you act badly, "you will destroy the man of fidelity, the man with a sense of shame, the man of modesty" (3.7.36).[26]

Above all, for Epictetus, to say that we are human beings means that we are rational beings (as opposed to irrational animals) *and* that we should act rationally (2.9.1–2, 2.10.2, and 4.5.12–14).[27] To be rational means that we should follow nature (3.1.25–26) and that we should not act in a violent, careless, gluttonous, or passive manner (2.9.1–6 and 3.23.3–4). More particularly, Epictetus endorses the standard Stoic claim that rationality is exhibited in the operation of the mind on one's impressions of the external world. Epictetus succinctly connects the use of impressions to the universal role: "Know first who you are, and then adorn yourself accordingly. You are a human being; that is, a mortal animal who knows how to use impressions rationally. And what is 'rationally'? In agreement with nature and perfectly" (3.1.25–26).[28]

While Epictetus naturally frames the human role as the expression of rationality, it is curious that he does not also treat the human role as the expression of the canonical virtues of justice, courage, wisdom, and moderation; indeed, these traditional virtues make only isolated appearances in his *Discourses*.[29] Although it is fairly safe to assume that Epictetus would not deny the canonical virtues and it is quite possible that he would account for them as expressions of our rational faculty via the proper use of our impressions, Epictetus nonetheless seems to have pushed the traditional virtues into the background. Instead, Epictetus defends a wide variety of specialized appropriate acts as constitutive of the human role, from acting with modesty to acting with fidelity.[30] Each of these appropriate acts, he says, is grounded in our ability to use impressions rationally (1.20, 4.3.7–8, and fr. 4).[31] Similarly, when Epictetus discusses the virtues of being a human being, the canonical four virtues rarely appear in his account of roles.[32] Rather, he singles out the following connected set of appropriate acts: to act as a citizen of the world (2.10.1–4), to treat externals as a matter of indifference (cf. 4.3.1–11), to prefer volition (*prohairesis*) above all else (3.3.5–10 and 4.4.23–26), to eliminate the passions (3.2.2–3), to have fidelity (2.4.1–3 and 4.5.14), and to have a sense of shame (3.7.27–28). Epictetus does not explain why he associates humanity with a special set of appropriate acts as opposed to the canonical virtues, but I shall argue that his treatment of humane behavior elaborates on what it means to fill the role of a rational being in the cosmos. His treatment also appears to seek out those actions that support the proper fulfillment of our specific roles (such as sibling or friend) and satisfy what is prerequisite or essential for Stoic virtue more generally.

As above, Epictetus takes human beings to have the faculty for rational thought. In his view, our capacity to reason gives humans a higher station in the cosmos and the ability to understand that station:

> . . . you are a citizen of the cosmos, and a part of it, and not a subordinate part, but a principal part of it. For you are capable of understanding the divine administration, and of reasoning on what follows from that. What then is the profession [*epangelia*] of a citizen [of the world]? To have no private gain, never to deliberate as though detached [from the whole], but to be like the hand or the foot, which, if they had reason and understood the constitution of nature, would never exercise impulse or desire, except by reference to the whole. (2.10.3–4)

In practice, Epictetus takes this holistic approach to mean that the interests of the whole and the commands of God must take priority over our more local interests or commands. As he exemplifies it elsewhere, a foot by itself would seek to be clean but, if it could consider itself as a part of the whole body, it would actively seek to walk through the mud where necessary (2.6.9–10; cf. 2.10.5–6).[33]

Applied to roles, this obligation to think holistically indicates that our human role supersedes our specific roles so that we must fulfill our universal role before we fulfill our roles such as friend or brother. "I have one whom I should please, to whom [I should] submit, to obey: God, and after him, myself. God has entrusted me to myself . . ." (4.12.11–12; cf. 15–16). In other words, the role of cosmic citizenship must come before the role of our civic citizenship. Although we are citizens of two states, "the great [i.e., the cosmos] and the small" (2.15.10), we should give precedence to the greater state because it is "the greatest, the most authoritative and most comprehensive" (1.9.4). Moreover, it is this cosmic state which is "sufficient to enable us to live securely . . . and free us from grief and terrors" (1.9.7). Like his hero, Socrates, Epictetus therefore thinks that we should identify ourselves by saying "I am a citizen of the cosmos" (1.9.2). On this basis, we cannot prioritize our specific roles over our human role nor can we choose to do evil by appealing to a role because our human role should never go against cosmic nature and divine will.

Beyond stipulating that we benefit the whole, the maxim to "have no private gain" (2.10.4) entails the Stoic dictum to treat externals as matters of "preferred indifference."[34] According to this dictum, it is appropriate to prefer wealth by seeking it, but we should be indifferent about whether or not we become wealthy. Epictetus warns that when we fail to be indifferent about preferred externals, we act like "a stranger [in the cosmos] who is fighting against God" (3.24.21). In addition, Epictetus sees this Stoic principle about externals as flowing from the idea of a role itself. When he utilizes the dramatic connotations of role (*prosôpon*) within ethics, Epictetus chastises actors and people for confusing their roles with the costumes and mask that they wear on stage (1.29.41–43). He argues that the bare essence of a role is the lines that one speaks because only the lines truly distinguish one (masked) character from another. An actor can play Oedipus in either rags or in a purple robe (fr. 11). Accordingly, Epictetus wishes to divorce the activity of our real-life roles from the external trappings often associated with any given role (4.8.15–16). Similarly, Epictetus advises that we should not "make a tragedy" of our roles (4.7.15). We should therefore not grieve over our role nor invest its costumes and props with any importance; to do so would make us both bad actors and bad guests in the cosmos.[35]

Not surprisingly, because our human role entails treating externals as indifferent, Epictetus also connects our role with the counterpart claim that we preserve our own volition (*prohairesis*). The two obligations belong together because we are able to preserve our volition when we have the right attitude about preferred externals.[36] As Epictetus sees it, Zeus has commanded us, his cosmopolitan citizens, to concern ourselves with what is under our own control, namely, our own volition; and, like obedient soldiers, we should not concern ourselves with what lies beyond our power, namely, preferred externals (3.24.112–114).

Moreover, this approach to externals and our own volition (*prohairesis*) lays the groundwork for the proper fulfillment of our specific roles. In particular, Epictetus claims that social relations (*scheseis*) should be subordinate to the good *and* that such subordination is what makes social relations possible (3.3.5–10);[37] "the good is to be preferred above every form of relationship. My father is nothing to me, only the good [is something to me]" (3.3.5). To prefer the good is the rule of God (ibid.; cf. 4.12.9–12). In addition, we should not compromise on our own capacity for goodness for the sake of others (3.3.6–7) because we should never exchange our inner freedom for some preferred external (4.3.1–3).

In turn, this uncompromising stance is beneficial to social relations. First, he notes that social relations would not exist "if the good were something different than the noble and just" (3.3.6). Although Epictetus does not elaborate further on this remark, he seems to be thinking that social relations could not exist if vices really were to our benefit. As he explains elsewhere, the grounds for friendly feelings arise directly from the virtues. "For where else is there friendship than where there is fidelity, where there is modesty, where there is a gift of goodness and of nothing else besides?" (2.22.30). "If, therefore, I am where my volition [*prohairesis*] is, only then will I be a friend, a son, and a father such as I should be" (2.22.20).[38] Second, Epictetus argues that a proper relationship to preferred externals makes possible a proper relationship to others: "the one who gives up some externals is the one who achieves the good" (3.3.8). It appears that conflicts in social relations arise when we fight over preferred externals—for example, two sons fighting over an inheritance (3.3.8–9; cf. 1.22.14–16 and 4.5.33–37). But, the fight would be resolved if each son let go of his slavish desire for preferred externals and stood by his one inalienable possession, his own volition (3.3.10). In this way, our universal role makes our specific roles possible. Finally, if "we define the good as consisting in a correct volition [*prohairesis*], then the preservation itself of relations becomes a good . . ." (3.3.8). By focusing on the preservation of a relation, Epictetus focuses not on the individual who is the *object* of our relation, a father or a brother, but on the *subject* of the relation, we ourselves who are the other half of the relation. That is, Epictetus emphasizes not an external action, but the attitude behind our actions, not a preferred external, but our role in respect to the preferred external. This reorientation has the remarkable effect of transferring a relation from the unreliable world of externals to the stable (and internal) world of our own volition.[39] In this way, he says, "If you remember this, you will everywhere maintain your role [*prosôpon*] as it should be" (4.3.3).

Aside from preserving our own volition, Epictetus also links our human role to civilized behavior in general because he believes that being reasonable means being civilized rather than bestial (2.9.1–6, 2.10.2, 3.23.4, and 4.5.12–14). Naturally, the Stoic Epictetus connects this humane behavior to the elimination of the passions (3.2.2–3) because the passions make us "unable to listen to reason" (3.2.3). However, Epictetus also connects civility with the particular summons to be cooperative and faithful. As he says, "What is human nature? To bite and kick, to throw people into prison and to behead them? No, but to do well, to cooperate, and to give thanks" (4.1.122). Epictetus expands on this spirit of reasonable cooperation when he discusses the virtue of fidelity or trustworthiness. This virtue is identified with the universal role because Epictetus directly links fidelity to our humanity: "a human is born for fidelity and the one who subverts this subverts the characteristic quality of a human being" (2.4.1). Epictetus analyses this virtue of fidelity (and correlate vice) in the case of an adulterer (2.4.1–10). This adulterer has not only failed to fulfill his role as a human being, he has destroyed his community, his *philia*, and he has even subverted the *polis* itself (2.4.3). As a result, we cannot treat the adulterer as a neighbor, a friend, or even a citizen because we cannot trust him to fulfill any such position (2.4.5). Should the adulterer insist upon his right to continue in his vice, Epictetus replies, "Very well then, . . . be an adulterer and be faithless; and, instead of a human being, be a wolf or an ape" (2.4.11).

Finally, Epictetus seems to connect our human role to the exercise of our faculty for critical self-reflection. As human beings using impressions, we are able to make judgments about what is appropriate and inappropriate including those judgments that Epictetus thinks constitute shame (*aidôs*, 4.3.7–8; cf. 3.7.27–28 and 4.9).[40] As R. Kamtekar explains, shame is a "a type of judgment of appropriateness" that arises from our "capacity for self-evaluation" ("ΑΙΔΩΣ in Epictetus," 136), a judgment that must be "in accordance with one's nature, particularly one's human or rational nature" (ibid., 152).[41] It appears that these judgments are the product of our rationality because he believes that, when we destroy rationality, we will destroy our capacity for shame (1.5.9–10). And, since the role of a human being is to act rationally (2.10.1–3 and 3.1.25–26), Epictetus therefore identifies shame with our human nature and, by implication, with our universal, human role:

> And what is our nature? To be free, noble-spirited, modest. For what other animal blushes, what other comprehends the impression of shame? But pleasure must be subordinated to these as a servant, as an attendant, in order to excite our willingness to keep acting in accordance with nature. (3.7.27–28)[42]

For Epictetus, our capacity for shame supports our ability to obey nature. To play our human part we must therefore uphold our sense of shame.

In light of this account, we can reformulate the universal role as a set of appropriate acts and virtues which arise from our station as human beings, a divinely crafted station of which we must be self-aware. In the first instance, this role entails the virtue of rationality: we should use our impressions properly, we should eliminate the passions and be trustworthy, we should critically reflect on our actions, and we should embrace our citizenship in the cosmos. Accordingly, our universal role encompasses both sociability and piety. In the second instance, our human role requires that we should preserve our own volition (*prohairesis*): we should cultivate our virtue while treating preferred externals as a matter of indifference. As a result, our universal role encompasses our own capacity for goodness and for Stoic progress (cf. 1.4.18–21). In this way, the universal role is not merely a collection of Stoic virtues, it is a description of what is required for playing our role in the cosmos and our roles in our specific communities. Epictetus truly fashions our human role (*prosôpon*) into a cosmic role.

NOTES

1. Translations are primarily based, with modifications, on Hard and Gill 1995 which is often close to Oldfather 1928. The Hard and Gill translation tends to be more consistent and concise although there are some instances where it has introduced unnecessary changes to Oldfather's translation. In so far as I have further modified both of these translations, I have sought for an even more literal and consistent rendering. I have also benefited from consulting Dobbin 1998 as well as Dobbin 2008.

2. Interestingly, while the Delphic invocation is most often associated with moderation, Epictetus chooses to associate it more broadly with knowing our place. Nonetheless, Epictetus's use fits with the general idea of self-knowledge and staying within certain limits (i.e., moderation). In Plato's *Charmides*, Critias associates the Delphic inscription with moderation (164d–165b), a virtue which Plato identifies with keeping one's place in the *Republic* 430e. An anonymous reviewer at Lexington helpfully pointed me to Xenophon's *Memorabilia* 4.2 where—as the reviewer tightly summarizes it—Xenophon "talks about self-knowledge in

terms of examining one's qualifications with regard to human relationships, like states knowing their own strengths and weaknesses before going to war."

3. This is how Epictetus interprets Socrates. See 1.9.23–26 and 3.1.19–23; cf. the echoes in 1.16.21 and 3.24.99. Socrates's role is discussed at greater length in chapter 5.

4. These definitions are drawn from Liddell, Scott, and Jones (hereafter referred to as LSJ). See also De Lacy 1977, 163–164.

5. Cf. Long 2002, 242–244.

6. See also 2.10.1–11 and Stephens 2007, 134–141.

7. I owe this last point to Brunt 1975, 13. Although Epictetus does not say so, I suspect that he would argue that there is no such thing as an evil role because evil plays no part in the *kosmos*. Evil roles exist only in literature where they play a part in creating tension for a story.

8. Cf. 3.15.9–13 [= *Ench.* 29.7], 3.22.67–76 and *Ench.* 37. In 1.29.44–49, Epictetus considers the scenario in which a senator becomes a pauper, a scenario which appears to involve changing from an Agamemnon figure to a Thersites figure. However, his analysis implies that he considers this a change in fortune, not a change in role. Thus, the individual in question is still an Agamemnon (cf. 3.22.34 and fragment 11). In chapter 5, I consider the rare but interesting possibility of role conflict and what such conflicts mean for his role ethics.

9. 3.15.13 (*stasis* in 3.15.13 = *taxis* in *Ench.* 29.7), 3.19, and *Ench.* 48.1. For Epictetus, the role of the philosopher can also be a non-universal role (cf. 3.21).

10. For *chôra*, see 3.21.19 and 4.1.109; for *chôra* and *taxis*, see 3.24.99; cf. Plato *Apology* 28d7.

11. Schofield 2007, 73, also notices that Epictetus uses more terms than simply *prosôpon* and he correctly connects these terms to the discussion of roles in *Discourses* 1.2. However, his list is missing *stasis* and *hupothesis*.

12. 1.29.38–41 is further discussed in chapter 3.

13. Possible exceptions include 4.3.3 and 1.2.14. The former passage is the likeliest case; there, Epictetus says that you will preserve your *prosôpon* if you do not give precedence to preferred externals. In the latter passage, Epictetus makes what appears to be a general claim about one's role and preferred externals. However, since the claim is put in the mouth of an exceptional figure and it uses the expression *idiou prosôpou*, it probably refers to the "special character" of that illustrious figure (as Oldfather, Dobbin, and Hard and Gill translate it) or even his "individual role" (as in Kamtekar 1998, 150). Brunt 1975, 34 note 6, believes a "universal role" is also cited in 1.29.57 and 3.22.69, but I take 1.29.57 to identify a student's role and 3.22.69 to identify a Cynic's role (as with De Lacy 1977, 167). Thus, these passages still pick out the specific role.

14. This distinction in Epictetus has been detected by other scholars, sometimes with the language of universal versus individual roles; see Gill 1988, 189; Kamtekar 1998, 149; Long 2002, 233–234 and 240; and Annas 2007, 140–141.

15. *Pace* Sorabji 2006, 162–163. Sorabji holds that there are unique roles in Epictetus, but Sorabji rather curiously lists the roles of male and female as examples when these roles are surely class-type roles. Sorabji also points to the role of Helvidius (1.2.19–24) as a unique role, but Epictetus treats Helvidius's role as the role of the "purple stripe"—the same type of role held by Agrippinus (1.2.12–18).

16. Cf. 2.5.26, 3.1.25–27 and 4.12.15–16.

17. This term is difficult to translate in this context. While English translators often rely on the dependable translation of "private," that term does not work well to characterize public roles such as a rhetor, roles that Epictetus implicitly classifies as *idios*. In this latter instance, Epictetus contrasts what is *idios* with what is *koinos*, so he apparently intends to contrast what is not common to all (*idios*) with what is common to all (*koinos*). Cf. to his use of *idiôtikos* in 3.22.69 and 3.22.74 to separate our private familial obligations from the specialized and public obligations of the Cynic. I therefore translate *idios* with the term "specific" on the understanding that it preserves Epictetus's intended contrast with what is common or universal.

18. I will follow Long 2002, 28 and 210–222 in translating *prohairesis* as "volition." Long reasons: "I favour volition as the translation of *prohairesis*. This term comes as close as we can get to Epictetus's claim that the essence of the self is our decision-making, purposive, and evaluative disposition. Volition suits the fact that *prohairesis* is what persons can be held fully

responsible for and what is up to them. . . . When we characterize persons in terms of their volitions, we do not thereby adopt a view concerning the undetermined freedom of their will; for we take people to have volitions irrespective of whether these are predetermined or independent of antecedent causation" (220). Sorabji 2006 also helpfully suggests translating *prohairesis* as "decision" so long as we understand that it refers to decisions about appropriate acts (194–195). For more discussion of *prohairesis* in Epictetus, see Dobbin 1991; Bobzien 1998, 331–339; Asmis 2001; Sorabji 2007, 87–98; and Stephens 2007, 16–25.

19. Cf. also 4.12.11–12. The significance of 3.23.3–5 is often missed in the discussion of Epictetus's account of roles. The best discussion is Kamtekar 1998, 149, who correctly notes that the passage classifies roles into two sorts; but, her analysis focuses primarily on whether the opening line at 3.23.1 endorses chosen roles or not (see my discussion below). Long 2002, 240, briefly quotes this passage to show that our humanity must win out over our individual pursuits. My discussion here aims to establish firmly the connection between 3.23.3–5 and Epictetus's account of roles

20. For Epictetus, Cynics are almost a priestly class who follow a more stringent code. My aim here is merely to show that Epictetus incorporates Cynicism by treating the life of a Cynic as a specific role. Schofield 2007, 73, appears to have the same view. *Pace* Reydams-Schils 2005, 146, who seems to equate Epictetus's Cynic with the Stoic sage.

21. Cf. De Lacy 1977, 166.

22. On *epitêdeuma*, see Long and Sedley (hereafter L&S), 26H = Stobaeus 2.67, 5–12 (*SVF* 3.294).

23. Besides knowing your role, Epictetus believes that self-knowledge features in ethical development through self-censure. See 4.4.7; cf. the citation of the *Golden Verses* in 3.10.2–3 and 4.6.32–35. I owe the latter passages to Hijmans 1959, 87. For some discussion (and more passages) on self-examination in Epictetus, see Hijmans 1959, 87–91. In this way, Epictetus seems to treat self-analysis as rationality applied to the self (cf. *Discourses* 1.20).

24. 2.9.1–6, 2.10.1–6, 3.1.24–25, 4.5.11–14, and 4.6.18. See also Kamtekar 1998, 153.

25. See also 4.5.19–21. By not doing what is appropriate (*kathêkon*) for a human being (2.10.1–6), we become beasts (2.10.14–23). "See to it, then, that you do not act like a wild beast; if you do, you will have destroyed your humanity since you have not fulfilled your profession [*epangelian*] [as a human]" (2.9.3; cf. 8–12). In the same fashion, Epictetus says to a philosopher who has wrongly chosen what is indifferent over what is appropriate (*kathêkon*) (4.1.134–143), "Why, when you are a worm, do you say that you are a human?" (4.1.142; cf. 1.28.9 and 4.1.120–122). Cf. Long 1983, 188.

26. See also 2.3 and 3.18.6. Cf. 2.9.10: "But he becomes accustomed to writing ungrammatically, it is necessary that his art [of grammar] be destroyed and perish."

27. This issue is discussed by Long 1983, 185–186 and 190–191.

28. Cf. 1.1.12, 1.20, 3.3.1–2 and 4.3.4–7.

29. For justice (*dikê* and cognates), see 2.7.5, 2.22.30 and 3.1.8); for courage (*andreia*), see 1.6.28,1.6.43 and 4.1.109 (paired with *megalopsuchia*); for moderation (*sophrôsunê* and cognates), see 3.1.8 and 4.9.17; for wisdom (*phronêsis*), see 1.20.6. Cf. Bonhöffer 1996, 16–17 and Kamtekar 1998, 136. As Long 2002, points out, the "early Stoics made elaborate classifications of 'virtues' and other 'values.' Epictetus takes no interest in such technicalities" (33; see also 223–224). However, Bonhöffer makes a valiant attempt to classify Epictetus's virtues into "physical, ethical, and logical virtue" (Bonhöffer 1996, 17); see part II of Bonhöffer 1996.

30. Note that Epictetus even incorporates popular Roman virtues into his account: *pietas* and *fides* become *aidôs* and *pistis*. This syncretic approach is characteristic of Epictetus; it allows him to proceed from virtues accepted by his Roman students to considerations about what underlies all virtues.

31. I agree with Long 2002, 34, who suggests that Epictetus "was probably original in specifying the ethical project as 'making correct use of mental impressions.'"

32. Interestingly, Epictetus does speak of courage (and *megalopsuchia*) in connection with roles at 4.1.109 where he talks about needing courage to take up one's station. However, courage appears there only as a kind of "support" virtue, something needed to take up the demands of a role but not constitutive of the role itself.

33. Long 2002, 234, writes that "Epictetus . . . co-opts the concept [of cosmopolitanism] for his favourite theme of moral and psychological readiness for anything" (Cf. Long 1983, 187–188 and 189). While I agree with Long that readiness is a feature of Epictetus's cosmopolitanism, it is important to see that Epictetus is also adding the theme of holism. As in the example of a muddy foot, cosmopolitanism requires a new perspective from which to evaluate the appropriateness of an action.

34. On the basis of this claim, Bonhöffer 1996, 201–202 and 205, tries to locate the Christian obligation to "love one's enemy" as a (universal) appropriate act. However, 2.10.4 clearly concerns the doctrine of preferred externals as matters of indifference, a doctrine rather unlike that of Christian love.

35. Epictetus also implies that it is part of our station simply to admire the cosmic order as an aesthete would admire a work of art (1.6.23–27).

36. 4.4.23–26. Epictetus stresses precisely this point when he treats the station (*stasis*) of a philosopher as equivalent to the role of a human being.

37. Cf. 1.21.1, 1.22.9–16 and 2.22.20.

38. I owe the 2.22.30 passage to Long 2002, 237.

39. Long 2002, 236–238, and Hijmans 1959, 27, both independently arrive at the same solution about relations as preferred externals, namely, that external relations amount to something internal. As Long sums it, "The relevant relationship is entirely one-sided: us in relation to them, not them in relation to us" (237).

40. Shame is a robust concept in Epictetus which I can only treat in outline. For an excellent and detailed discussion, see Kamtekar 1998.

41. As opposed to Cicero's emphasis on social approval (see *De Off.* 1.98, "arouses the approval of one's fellows"), Epictetus's conception of shame appeals to a more cosmic criterion.

42. Cf. Marcus Aurelius *Meditations* 4.49, a passage which Oldfather 1928 believes is quoted from Epictetus; Oldfather labels the passage as fragment 28b.

Chapter Two

Bearing Many Roles: Specific Roles in an Individual's Life

As we have seen in the previous chapter, when we are confronted with the question "Who am I?" Epictetus believes that our immediate answer should be "A human being." Yet, such an answer is surely incomplete because each of us is different from the other and we frequently assign different obligations according to our differences. Some of us have children which need our care, others hold office or positions of authority that require special duties, and so on. To answer the call to "know oneself" as a particular person, Epictetus offers a set of criteria that one must consider in order to identify one's many specific roles (of which there is no set number). Of the criteria to identify our specific role as individual persons, Epictetus offers two fundamental criteria, (i) our particular capacities and (ii) our social relations (*scheseis*). In many cases, these two are sufficient to determine our specific roles. However, if we find ourselves qualified for several types of careers, for example, we may need to opt for one career over another; accordingly, Epictetus grants that we may sometimes locate our role on the basis of (iii) choice. Additionally, Epictetus makes it clear that our role may be indicated by a (iv) divine sign; our roles will not always be so openly indicated, he thinks, but we should accept it if we receive a sign and we should look for one especially in cases where the role in question entails a drastic lifestyle (such as that of a Cynic).[1]

I. PARTICULAR CAPACITIES

"Hey there," he says, "consider first what the matter is, and then your own nature, what you can endure" (3.15.9) for you must act "in conformity with your own nature and constitution" (1.6.15). Although such advice is rather broad, it appears to involve a consideration of our capacities as individual persons. As we shall see below, Epictetus regards each of us as having certain natural aptitudes which lay the basis for many kinds of roles from athlete to philosopher. These capacities both proscribe and prescribe certain specific roles. Epictetus will take these capacities to be our physical (and perhaps cognitive) ability to perform certain actions or not, and he will emphasize the need to train such abilities so that they function at their best. In addition, Epictetus's conception of our capacities appears to incorporate our very ability to bear doing certain difficult actions or not. Epictetus will surprisingly imply that such an ability remains relatively fixed even though it may require some training in order to be as strong as possible.

For Epictetus, our capacities (*dunameis*) both limit and determine our specific roles. Our capacities limit our roles because they limit how much we can do (cf. 1.26.16–17 and 4.5.12–13).[2] Thus, we cannot (and should not) take on roles which stretch beyond our powers (*Ench.* 37; cf. *Disc.* 3.13.20 and 3.22.8). For example, the role of a wrestler is limited to those with a certain kind of bodily strength (3.15.9). Similarly, the role of a philosopher requires not only wisdom but "a certain readiness and fitness" (3.21.18). In this way, when you consider your function in the city, he says, you should choose "whatever place you are able to have" (*Ench.* 24.4). And yet, our capacities can also prescribe our roles in a positive way, for "one person is naturally made for one thing, another for another" (3.15.10). This prescriptive use arises particularly in the case of extraordinary abilities. Those who have extraordinary abilities should take up the role that employs their special talents. "You are able to lead the army against Ilium, be Agamemnon. And you are able to fight Hector one on one, be Achilles" (3.22.7).[3] This point is also made when Epictetus considers the case of a great athlete who faces the prospect of medical castration to save his own life, a prospect that apparently amounts to losing his own role as an athlete.[4] Epictetus approvingly notes that this athlete chooses to die.[5] Such an athlete died "as a man, Epictetus said, and as a man who had contended in the Olympic games and who had been proclaimed victor, who dwelled in such a place, and had not merely been rubbed with oil in Bato's wrestling school" (1.2.26).[6] Here, Epictetus suggests that that athlete knew he had to be an athlete (and die as one) because he had the power to compete in the Olympics.

In this prescriptive use, Epictetus treats our capacities as both decisive about one's role and as self-evident to the bearer of such powers.[7] Epictetus draws out this use of the term *dunamis* (capacity) with his analogy of the bull and his analogy of an upper-class toga (marked by the purple stripe), analogies to which he often returns as a way of clarifying the position of an extraordinary individual.[8] In his analogy of the bull, the bull stands alone away from a herd of oxen because he knows that he can withstand the assault of an oncoming lion. "How is it," asks Epictetus, "that when the lion charges, the bull alone is aware of his own equipment and puts himself forward in defense of the whole herd? Or is it not clear that, together with the possession of the equipment [*paraskeuês*], the awareness of it immediately comes also? And with us now, whoever has such equipment will not be ignorant of it" (1.2.30–31).[9] Although this passage uses the term *paraskeuê*, the thrust of the passage clearly fits with the notion of a *dunamis* (capacity).[10] Similarly, in the analogy of the toga, Epictetus emphasizes that it is obvious to talented individuals what their position is. As he has an imagined paragon of virtue confidently declare: "*I* am such as the purple [stripe] in a robe; do not expect me to be the same as the rest or fault me for my nature which made me different from the others" (3.1.23; cf. 1.2.17–18).

It seems, then, that only in cases of extraordinary ability can our capacities single out one kind of role that is suitable for us to adopt given that Epictetus's examples of these kinds of capacities focus almost exclusively on the special roles of the philosopher, the Cynic, or some other heroic paragon. Even when the roles of Agamemnon and Thersites are contrasted by Epictetus, he does so in the context of his discourse on the Cynic (3.22.7–8), thus making the contrast act as a substitute for the opposition between the Cynic and ordinary individuals.[11] The one exception, which I have just discussed, is his example of a great athlete (1.2.25–28). However, it is important to bear in mind that Epictetus's lectures (as recorded by Arrian) are directed most often to his philosophically oriented students. Presumably, such an audience would motivate him to single out the role of a Cynic and philosopher for extended analysis.[12] Moreover, Epictetus can still hold that some other sorts of abilities are prescriptive (cf. 3.15.10 and perhaps *Ench.* 24.4). Thus, even if our abilities do not make us a bull among oxen, our abilities can (borrowing from Archilochus) make us hedgehogs or foxes (Diehl fr. 103).[13]

Beyond his general use of the term *dunamis* (capacity), Epictetus seems to believe that individuals differ in what they have the power to endure. This specialized ability appears in 1.2.5–11, a passage in which Epictetus considers the case of a slave or servant who must hold a chamber pot for his master. He suggests that one person may reasonably refuse to hold the chamber pot and another may not. In the case of the resistant slave, the individual in question finds it unendurable (*aphorêton*) to hold a chamber pot or even to have it held by someone else (1.2.9; cf. 3.15.9).[14] This phrasing is important because Epictetus does not explain the resistance on the grounds that it is right or wrong but on the grounds that one individual *cannot* bear to do it. The case of the obedient slave is more opaque, but the same principle seems to be involved such that the slave in question seems to find punishment itself unbearable. Epictetus therefore implies that this slave should hold the chamber pot because it is preferable to obey one's master and therefore avoid beatings and so on. Thus, Epictetus says to the latter individual, "if you measure your interest by these standards, go and hold the pot" (1.2.10). The logic here is quite compressed, but it appears to amount to the following: for one individual, it is so unbearable to hold the chamber pot that beatings, starvation, and so forth, become irrelevant; but, for other individuals, such a task is bearable enough, whereas a beating and starvation are unbearable (1.2.8–10 and 16–17).[15]

Accordingly, this specialized capacity to bear an activity or not is probably best understood as an entrenched estimate of one's self-worth.[16] As R. Kamtekar puts it, "one's self-evaluative judgments themselves partly constitute who one is."[17] Moreover, the term "self-worth" captures the pecuniary overtones that Epictetus uses when he describes the calculations of what is consistent with one's own role: you must consider "how much you are worth to yourself and for how much you are selling yourself. Different people sell themselves at different prices" (1.2.11).[18] The position of a "chamber pot holder" includes a different "price" set to oneself than the "price" of those who cannot bear such an action. Of course, we should never sell ourselves short because that sort of "exchange" amounts to selling our volition; nonetheless, Epictetus accepts that the "price" differs from person to person and urges none to sell themselves cheaply if they must sell at all (1.2.33). In this way, some individuals will be able to bear less than others, but they are still urged to place a premium on their own self-worth.

Epictetus is regrettably brief about how individuals can act in accordance with their self-worth, perhaps because self-worth is a matter which it "is necessary for you to 'add to the bill' in your inquiry, not I. For it is you who knows yourself . . ." (1.2.11).[19] Nonetheless, we can see traces of Epictetus's conception of self-worth in action when he praises the behavior of Odysseus:

> And when Odysseus was shipwrecked and cast ashore, did his difficulty humble him, or break him? No. But how did he advance upon the attendants [of Nausicaa] and ask for the necessities of life, when it seems shameful to beg from another? "As a mountain lion" [*Odyssey*, 6.130]. (3.26.33)

In other words, Odysseus was "no less distinguished in rags than in his thick purple robe" (fragment 11).[20] Of course, although Odysseus is much more of an extraordinary man (cf. 3.22.3–8), he nonetheless found that he was able to play the role of beggar and old man with a measure of dignity consistent with his noble role. If we apply the logic of this example to the slave who cannot bear to be punished and thus must obey his master's order, it would seem that the slave should preserve his self-worth by performing the demeaning task as deftly as possible while acting as if he does not notice the ugliness of his circumstances (cf. saluting a patron while the door is being slammed in one's face at 2.6.6–8 and 3.24.44–49).[21]

And yet, Epictetus's reliance on self-worth still raises questions about how ordinary people can use this special capacity to identify their roles. To what extent is self-worth under our control? If it is under our control, to what extent is Epictetus's discussion of extraordinary individuals normative rather than descriptive? If it is normative, why allow anyone to settle for less, why allow anyone to hold the chamber pot? Epictetus aims to answer these questions at the end of *Discourses* 1.2. There, he explicitly asserts that not all individuals can be extraordinary because, as Epictetus colorfully puts it, "not all horses can become swift" (1.2.34). Most individuals are not expected to perform the great deeds of a man like Socrates, but rather they are expected to do what is sufficient for their own role (1.2.33–35 and *Ench.* 24.4).[22] However, this maxim does not mean that they are free to stagnate in their roles, even though they are less than exceptional. "Because I am naturally untalented, shall I give up my diligence on that account? Heaven forbid!" he says, nor should we neglect "some other pursuit merely because we despair of arriving at the highest" (1.2.35 and 37). As Epictetus elsewhere urges: "don't let sheer habit make you give in readily and end up like the bad athlete going around beaten in the whole circuit like quails that run away" (3.25.5; A. A. Long translation).[23] While our ordinary self-worth is relatively fixed, we still need to train it in order to acclimatize to the special demands of our specific roles: "neither a bull nor a noble man comes to be all at once, but it is necessary to undertake a hard winter training, to prepare oneself, and not to leap rashly into what is inappropriate" (1.2.32). Accordingly, even if our ordinary self-worth dooms us to fall short of remarkable achievements, we should make sure that we "do not sell it cheap" (1.2.33). For extraordinary individuals, this apparently means taking the high ground in response to some challenge, even at the cost of one's life. For ordinary individuals, it seems to mean doing what is bearable within one's role (1.2.8–10 and 23) but doing so with as much dignity as possible.[24]

II. RELATIONS (*SCHESEIS*)

After one's inner capacities, Epictetus advises that we determine our specific roles by looking to our external relations (*scheseis*). While Epictetus clearly establishes nature as the most fundamental criterion, he devotes more attention to our external relations. Our capacities are established as more fundamental to our roles in the discourse on the role of a Cynic. Cynics are relieved of the obligations associated with their external relations because their extraordinary natural gifts override any obligation to assume any social roles, including the role of sibling or child (cf. 3.22 on the Cynic, esp. 3.22.69–81). Nonetheless, our own capacities do not determine all of our roles; in fact, they mostly appear responsible for indicating certain key roles such as a special profession. Accordingly, Epictetus implies that our relations are central instances of specific roles (*Ench.* 30). In the section ahead, I will outline the scope of this term and I will demonstrate how Epictetus looks to our circumstances and our designations to locate our relational roles. I will also suggest that Epictetus's treatment of relations as roles remains fairly conventional but that he resists conventional norms where he believes that they contradict nature.

As social beings, we have and acquire a wide variety of relations (*scheseis*) with others: "son, father, brother, citizen, husband, wife, neighbor, fellow-traveler, ruler, and subject" (2.14.8; cf. 3.2.4, and 4.6.26); *scheseis* even include the relation between a local or host and a stranger or guest (2.17.31).[25] Epictetus does not define the term *schesis*, but Bonhöffer helpfully suggests that *schesis* is a "technical term for the name of the intellectual and moral relationships of rational beings to one another . . . "[26] In other words, the term *schesis* seems to pick out any sort of social relation between rational beings that come into contact with each other, whether husbands and wives or strangers who meet on the road.[27] Epictetus himself divides relations into two sorts, "natural and acquired" (2.14.8, 3.2.4 and 4.8.20). While Epictetus explains that distinction no further, his meaning seems relatively clear. By "natural," Epictetus likely means those relations which we have from birth or which are naturally permanent, like that of child to parent (cf. *Ench.* 30). No matter the circumstances, we are always, by nature, someone's child. In much the same way, siblings always remain brothers or sisters. If this is so, natural relations must include our enduring relationship to God (cf. 2.14.26–28, 3.2.4 and 3.13.8).[28] By contrast, "acquired relations" seem to be those that we do not have from birth and which may admit of some flexibility. These relations are ones that arise for us at one time and may cease at another time. Accordingly, acquired relations appear to be those that we obtain because of changing circumstances, relations like that of friend, neighbor, or even guest-friend. If we move from one side of Rome to the other, our neighborly relations change.[29]

In calling some social roles "acquired," however, Epictetus does not mean that these roles can be taken up or put down at will.[30] Instead, he seems to hold that acquired roles are those roles which we receive as we grow up where we are stationed. Such roles, then, should neither be avoided nor necessarily sought. We should simply go about the business of living while responsibly taking up those roles that happen to come our way. "In everything guard your own goodness; and as for the rest, [guard them also] as they are given and in so far as you can act reasonably in them" (4.3.11). Epictetus stresses the obligation to be open to these roles when he chastises the traveler who is intoxicated on the pleasures of travel away from home:

> This is what is prescribed: to return to your country, to relieve the fear of your family, to do the acts of a citizen, to marry, to have children, to hold the customary offices. For you did not come into the world to select some nicer place, but to conduct yourself there where you were born and where you were appointed a citizen. (2.23.38–39; cf. 3.7.21 and 3.21.5)

Although Epictetus is so firm in his exhortation here that he appears to be ordering individuals to get married (cf. 3.7.25–26), he elsewhere makes clear that we should not force these roles. We should let our acquired roles happen as they may: "For this is what is always prescribed for the fine and good man: to be a praetor? No; but if it is given to him, to maintain his own ruling faculty in that matter. To marry? No; but if a marriage is given to him, to maintain himself in that matter as one who is in accordance with nature" (4.5.6–7).

In this way, it seems that our relations are suggested to us by our circumstances and so, to discover all our relations, we need to examine our circumstances. This point is indicated in one of Epictetus's conversations with God about one's role:

> But while I spend time in your [*viz.*, God's] service, what do you wish me to be? An official or a private citizen, a senator or a commoner, a soldier or a general, a teacher or the master of a household? . . . And where do you wish me to be? In Rome, or in Athens, or in Thebes, or in Gyara [a prison colony]? . . . If you send me to a place where it is not possible for humans to live in accordance with nature, I shall depart this life [by suicide], not out of disobedience to you but as though you were sounding for me the recall. I do not abandon you; heaven forbid! But I perceive that you have no need of me. But if living in accordance with nature be granted, I will seek no other place than that in which I am, nor any other people than those with whom I am. (3.24.98–102)

According to this passage, we should accept whatever social roles we find ourselves in, so long as we are able to live virtuously, that is, so long as we can fulfill our role as human beings.[31] If we find ourselves citizens in Rome, then we should be citizens of Rome.[32] Indeed, Epictetus's reference to suicide suggests that circumstances can go so far as to compel us to adopt a specific action.[33] As Epictetus elsewhere represents the command of circumstances: "'Take a governorship.' I take it; and having taken it, I show how an educated human being behaves. 'Lay aside your senatorial tunic, put on rags, and come forward in that role'" (1.29.44–45; cf. 1.24.12–14). We are urged to act well in all circumstances because circumstances are the divinely given material (*hulê*) through which ethical action is realized;[34] moreover, in order to act well, we must first *recognize* our circumstances and how they translate into our specific social roles (cf. *Ench.* 37).

Beyond our circumstances, Epictetus also suggests that we look to our titles or designations to infer our relational roles and their appropriate acts. "How is it possible to discover one's appropriate acts from one's designations [*onomatôn*]?" asks the chapter title of *Discourses* 2.10.[35] In that discussion, Epictetus considers the appropriate acts which arise from traditionally accepted relations such as son or brother, citizen or elder (2.10.7–14; cf. 4.6.26). Although the chapter focuses on how we may infer appropriate acts from such designations,[36] it implicitly treats these designations as markers of roles.

> Furthermore, if you are a councilor of some city, [remember] that you are a councilor; if a youth, [remember] that you are a youth; if a senior, that you are a senior; if a father, that you are a father. For each of these designations, upon reflection, always suggest the proper deeds. But if you go and censure your brother, I tell you, 'You have forgotten who you are and what your designation is.' (2.10.10–13; cf. 4.12.15–17 and *Ench.* 30)

Thus, conventional designations appear to operate as tools not only to identify our appropriate acts but even to infer our relations, and hence, our roles.

Unsurprisingly, then, when Epictetus does identify the acts appropriate to a given social role, he assigns appropriate acts that are both fairly general and rather conventional. To sons, Epictetus advises complete obedience to and unwavering support for their fathers (*Ench.* 30). Sons should take care of their fathers and treat their own possessions as though they belong to their father (ibid., 3.7.26, and 2.10.7). To brothers, he similarly advises "deference, obedience, [and] restrained speech" (2.10.8; cf. 2.10.12–13 and 3.21.5–6). To fathers, he urges that they must support and care for their family as well as render services to their in-laws (3.22.70–74). To citizens, Epictetus declares: "You live in an imperial *polis*; you should hold office, judge justly, keep your hands off the things of other people; no woman should appear beautiful to you other than your wife, no boy beautiful, no silver plate beautiful, no gold plate" (3.7.21–23). Citizens should be subordinate to the law (1.12.7), engage in public affairs (3.7.26), and assist their country by being good and playing their part (3.21.5; cf. *Ench.* 24.4).

Epictetus's logic here exposes him to the charge that his practical ethics merely adopts conventional Roman opinions about appropriate acts and roles.[37] There is certainly merit to that charge; however, although Epictetus is often not revolutionary about the content of our appropriate acts, he nonetheless believes that these conventional relations must be aligned with our nature or else be denied. For example, Epictetus frequently criticizes conventional figures because they misapply the name "philosopher" to individuals unable to live up to that designation. Similarly, "if we hear someone singing badly, we do not say, 'See how the musicians sing!' but rather, 'This one here is no musician'" (4.8.8).[38] Our designations must therefore obey the possibilities of our respective natures (cf. 1.22.10). When our conventional designations fail to match our nature, Epictetus implies that we should disobey convention in order to follow our nature. Thus, he insists that Cynics should be free of the conventional family roles that bind ordinary individuals because those conventional roles inhibit the Cynics' talent for the itinerant life of ethical reform (cf. 3.22.67–82). Similarly, Epictetus advises the individuals in *Discourses* 1.2 to obey or be insubordinate based on whether they have the ability to endure the consequences or not; he does not advise them purely on the basis of convention.

Moreover, Epictetus evidently resists what he takes to be the conventional approach to our relations, an approach which treats them as genuine goods rather than as preferred (in the Stoic sense of the term). Not only does Epictetus enjoin us not to covet other people's spouses or material goods, he also holds that nature commands us to treat externals as preferred indifferents (1.30). Aside from the deference and obedience expected of brothers, one of the jobs of a brother is "never to claim against your brother any of the things outside the sphere of volition but cheerfully to give these up, so that you may have more of the things that are subject to volition" (2.10.8; cf. 4.9.1–5). This maxim is important because Epictetus thinks that we sometimes resist the appropriate acts of our roles when they infringe on our preference for some preferred external; but, as he exhorts us, preferred externals are insignificant compared to preserving our volition and they are irrelevant to the fulfillment of our specific roles (ibid. and 1.29.41–45). Brothers should not allow the preferables (such as an inheritance) to be a source of division between themselves and their own kin (3.3.8–9).[39]

III. CHOICE

The subject of chosen roles in Epictetus is somewhat difficult because Epictetus is not precise on the matter, nor does he explicitly discuss roles in connection with choice.[40] However, Epictetus indirectly addresses the question of chosen roles without labeling them as such (perhaps owing to the unsystematic nature of his thought).[41] He examines career choice in a tantalizing passage at the beginning of *Discourses* 3.23. "Who do you wish to be? First tell yourself that. Then act accordingly in what you are doing. For in almost every other thing, we see that this is how it comes about. Athletes first decide what they want to be, and then they act accordingly in what follows" (3.23.1–2). Different types of athletes, he says, must pursue different regimens of diet and exercise (3.23.2). The same applies to the crafts. "If [you want to be] a carpenter, you have such and such [preparations]; if a coppersmith, such and such other" (3.23.3; cf. 5–6). Through the rest of 3.23, Epictetus argues that we should be concerned with the requirements of the career we have chosen rather than with the approval of others (cf. 3.21, 3.23, and 4.4.42–44). He makes this point with special emphasis on the career of a philosopher.[42]

The opening of 3.23 suggests limited choice in the following way: "Who do you wish to be? First tell yourself that. Then act accordingly in what you are doing" (3.23.1). Certainly, 3.23 soon restricts the breadth of this choice by an implicit appeal to the prescriptions of nature, but it appeals to nature only to show the ways in which nature limits or validates our choices rather than obliterates them. In the case of athletes (3.23.2), 3.23 implies that they are limited by nature because they are only shown choosing among various types of gymnastic pursuits; it does not discuss how athletes may choose between boxing *or* politics, wrestling *or* philosophy.[43] Yet, even though athletes seem confined by nature to vocations in the palaestra, they can choose from a multitude of athletic careers. Thus, when Epictetus says that "one person is naturally made for one thing, another for another" (3.15.10), he only seems committed to the claim that each person is naturally suited to some sort of activity. Similarly, when he says, "If [you wish to be] a wrestler, look to your shoulders . . ." (3.15.9), he only seems to be saying that we should restrict our wishes by reference to our natural limitations.[44] Finally, where 3.23 discusses the training of particular sports and crafts (3.23.2–3), it depicts such prescriptions as the consequence of some *initial* career choice.

On this basis, when Epictetus asks "who do you wish to be?" his question should be taken as offering a limited career choice. Granted, Epictetus constrains that choice by our own capacities, but our own capacities may be suited for more than one specific career role. A person may find, for example, that she is particularly good with her hands, but such a skill can lend itself to many different careers, from sculpture to surgery. For such a person, it would be necessary to choose between the possible career roles. At the same time, Epictetus suggests that we look to the needs of our community to help decide our career. In *Ench.* 24.4, Epictetus talks with a young man who is debating about what career path to take and Epictetus urges him to examine what role he is able to take up as well as what roles his city needs. And yet, cities have many needs so the young interlocutor may find himself able to take up many different roles. Here again, choice would be necessary to take up one role out of the many that are possible. For cases where our own capacities and our own relations signal several possible roles, we should choose from among them the ones that we wish for.

IV. DIVINE SIGNS

Beyond nature, social relations, and what job we wish for, Epictetus believes that—under special circumstances—our roles may be indicated or confirmed by a divine sign. In this way, his commitment to self-knowledge converges with his piety. He asserts this most explicitly in 3.21 during his discussion of the stringent prerequisites for taking on the role of a teacher of wisdom:

> Such things are to be approached in another way. This is a great matter, a solemn mystery,[45] not granted at random to all who come. Indeed, it may well be that not even wisdom suffices for the care of the young; one should also have a certain readiness, by Zeus, and fitness for this, and such a body, and above all, the recommendation from God that one should occupy this station, as he recommended to Socrates that he should hold the *elenchic* station, and to Diogenes of rebuking people in a kingly manner, and to Zeno that of instructing people and establishing doctrines. (3.21.17–20)

The examples here are highly suggestive because, according to classical tradition, each of these figures was said to have received his path in life by means of an oracle. Socrates began his mission upon hearing a perplexing oracle from Delphi about his wisdom (Pl. *Ap.* 20e–21a; Xen. *Ap.* 14–17). Similarly, Diogenes (the Cynic) supposedly took up his unconventional lifestyle when he was told by the oracle of Apollo to adulterate the coinage (Diogenes Laertius 6.20). Finally, Zeno of Citium, the founder of Stoicism, also consulted the oracle and, through its advice, eventually became a teacher of philosophy (ibid. 7.2–3).

Although these examples show that roles can be indicated by divine sign, they also suggest that divine signs are most important for extraordinary roles. In fact, each of the foregoing figures seem to be not just teachers but Cynics or philosophers. Socrates is clearly treated as extraordinary throughout the *Discourses* (see esp. 1.2.36 and 2.16.35–36) and receives honorable notice in Epictetus's 3.22 paean to Cynicism (3.22.26). Similarly, Diogenes the Cynic receives special attention in 3.22 as a shining example of Cynicism (3.22.24–25, 57–66, and 88–89).[46] Finally, Zeno is treated as an exceptional figure in conjunction with Socrates (3.24.38–39 and 4.9.6) and he is cited as an ethical exemplar (again comparable to Socrates; *Ench.* 33.12–13). Thus, Epictetus reasons, because such individuals have great roles (3.21.17), they must be especially certain about their own fitness; they must summon divine aid (3.21.11–16) and receive divine sanction (3.21.18–19). As he stresses in the 3.22 discourse on the role of the Cynic, Cynics must know that they have been "sent as a messenger from Zeus" (3.22.23). Similarly, to those considering the role of a Cynic, he advises: "Consider the matter more carefully, know yourself, consult the divinity, attempt nothing without God. For if God advises you, know that he wishes you to be great or to receive many blows" (3.22.53).

And yet, Epictetus leaves open the possibility that any role may be indicated by divine sign. He suggests this in 3.24.31–36 when he discusses the idea that Socrates's role as a philosopher was a "post" assigned by the General, that is, by God (cf. 3.1.19 and Pl. *Ap.* 28d–29a). In accordance with this military analogy, Epictetus advises that we all obediently assume our different posts. "One man must keep guard, another go out on reconnaissance, and another to fight" (3.24.31). In this way, "the life of each person is a kind of campaign, a long and diversified one. You have to maintain the [position] of a soldier, and do each thing at the command of the General; and, if possible, divine what He wishes" (3.24.34–35). Here, Epictetus does not limit divination to the extraordinary individual; instead, he commends it for each role, each act. Although he does not require divination in this case as he did for the exceptional role (recommending it "if possible" rather than "above all"), he still grants that we may each divine the commands of our own position, and, it seems, that very role itself.[47]

THE MEANING AND PRACTICAL FUNCTION OF ROLES

Having surveyed the extant details of Epictetus's account of roles, we can see that Epictetus's treatment emphasizes the guidelines for identifying our roles. Once we have properly identified these roles, he says, it will be clear what is appropriate for each to do (2.10.11). Although Epictetus fails to define the term *prosôpon*, the guidelines that he offers for identifying our roles are strongly suggestive about what roles are: they are functional memberships in some community, whether cosmic or local. Epictetus emphasizes each role as being a part that fulfills a specific function within a larger story. One actor must be the protagonist by defending a cause, another must be the antagonist by opposing it, still others the chorus. Each part is understood not in terms of how it will please an audience but in terms of what it does for the whole, the story. "You are able [*dunasai*] to lead the army against Ilium, be Agamemnon. You are able to fight one-on-one with Hector, be Achilles" (3.22.7).[48] No role is unimportant or demeaning because each role has a job that benefits the whole. Epictetus's account encompasses our whole lives as narratives in a communal story. For Epictetus, what is critical is that we correctly identify our roles in that story (cf. *Ench.* 37); once we have determined our parts, we have determined what we should do. Thus, Epictetus deploys roles to pick out those features of the self that signal our communal functions—our humanity, our specific capacities, and our relations. Our roles act as our guide to ethical action because they locate the functions that we must fulfill in the communities around us.

In turn, Epictetus's story model for roles supplies us with a useful metaphor for interpreting our own lives and determining what to do. I am a parent, so I must prepare my children for school; I am a teacher, so I must grade these essays; and so on. Indeed, ordinary persons, I suggest, are much more likely to think in terms of the roles that they bear and the attendant obligations that each role brings. By tapping into that kind of role-bound reasoning, Epictetus has found a way to engage a broad audience into dialectic about how best to live.

NOTES

1. The discussion of what I term "specific roles" in the scholarly literature has been rather piecemeal. Although scholars uniformly agree that our humanity seems to count as a kind of role, they vary about what other, more specific sorts of considerations feature in Epictetus's account of roles. Bonhöffer 1996, 10–11 and cf. 90, holds that a role consists of one's external station and inner dignity, but he does not believe that these factors generate any substantively specific roles for Epictetus. By contrast, Frede 2007, 155, resists associating roles with personal dignity when he criticizes J. Souilhé's translation of *prosôpon* in the Budé edition of Epictetus as *dignité personnelle*; rather, Frede suggests that we ought to understand *prosôpon* as "the sort of person somebody is" and "the person somebody is" and he deploys that description to speculate about personhood (154). Similarly against Bonhöffer, Long 2002 appears to hold that our specific or "secondary roles" do have substance because they consist of our own endowments that mediate the norms laid down by our humanity in the same way that our own circumstances mediate Aristotle's mean relative to us (232 and 237–241). Annas 2007, 148, appears to follow Long by treating roles as "embedded perspectives" which offer a way of "aspiring to the Stoic ideal in our everyday life." Brunt 1975, 14–15 and 31, and Dobbin 1998, 78–83, claim that roles involve not just one's station or relations but one's particular nature and "personality." Hijmans 1959, 26 fn. 4, draws a similar connection but hedges that Epictetus is not offering "a full grown notion of personality." Kamtekar 1998, 148–151, lists examples of factors which may shape one's role, from masculine identity to bodily strength, from circumstance to profession. Correspondingly, De Lacy 1977, 166–168, considers a number of examples of what factors may shape roles, but his discussion remains open-ended. Given this rather disorganized picture, I hope that my treatment in this chapter will crystallize Epictetus's account.
2. See also how Epictetus discusses the example of Sarpedon at 1.27.7–10.
3. Cf. the lines just before this where Epictetus imagines God meting out the cosmic role of the sun based on what the sun is able to do (3.22.4–5).
4. A Greek athlete would probably associate castration with the destruction of his masculine prowess. He may also associate it with the destruction of his appearance, an important issue since Greek athletics were performed in the nude. I return to this unusual case in chapter 6.
5. Because of examples like these in *Discourses* 1.2, Rist 1969, 252, says that 1.2 is essentially a study of suicide. Although Rist is right to point out 1.2's obsession with death, the figures therein do not commit suicide. Instead, they are put to death or they let nature take its course. Moreover, Epictetus also considers decisions that are not necessarily life threatening, e.g., holding the chamber pot or not (1.2.8–11).
6. Dobbin 1998, 80, thinks that our humanity is invoked at 1.2.26 where a great athlete's fatal decision is justified on the grounds that he acted "as a man," but the Greek is *anêr* not *anthrôpos*. In addition, Epictetus further qualifies the athlete's role as that of an Olympic athlete who thus differs even from ordinary athletes or non-athletes. Cf. 84–85 where Dobbin seems to concede this point.
7. Note that Epictetus is *not* saying that the role of the athlete *is* the capacity to compete in the Olympics; rather, Epictetus is saying that if you have that particular *dunamis*, you should take up the *prosôpon* of the athlete.
8. Interestingly, while these exceptional individuals feature prominently in Epictetus's thought, he supplies no label for them beyond his various metaphors. For these figures, Dobbin employs the nice term "moral aristocrat" (Dobbin 1998, 83–84), but I shall generally call them "extraordinary individuals" in order to avoid the implication that they are "more ethical" than ordinary individuals.

9. Cf. 3.1.22–23, 3.22.6, 3.22.99, and 4.8.41–43. Epictetus appears not to have explicitly considered the case of the false positive, the individual who believes himself to be extraordinary when he, in fact, is not (the so-called Dunning-Kruger effect). And yet, in practice, Epictetus exhibits some awareness of the problem because he continually reminds some of his listeners that they were not born to be the philosophers that they seek to be (see 2.24, 3.21, and 4.8). On this score, I think that Cicero is better informed because he recognizes how difficult such introspection is, especially when we are young (*De Officiis* 1.117; see page 213).

10. Elsewhere, in a similar context, Epictetus uses *paraskeuê* as though it is a synonym with *dunamis* (3.22.107–109). However, *paraskeuê* and *dunamis* do differ because *paraskeuê* can refer particularly to those impulses acquired by practice whereas a *dunamis* is more likely to be an inborn capacity. On *paraskeuê*, see Inwood 1985, 233–234.

11. Epictetus also contrasts Agamemnon and Thersites at 4.2.10, but the contrast there appears to amount to the difference between a good and a bad person.

12. The subject of Epictetus's audience is discussed by Long 2002, 43–51. Long is certainly correct that Epictetus's primary audience is his young (male) philosophy students, but we should not miss the appearance of other guests: an official (1.11), a Roman (2.14), a student of rhetoric (3.1), a procurator (3.4), a commissioner (3.7), a litigant on his way to Rome (3.9), and (possibly) a would-be craftsman (*Ench.* 24.4). In addition, many of Epictetus's discussions are clearly concerned with ethical issues that we all must confront from a dispute with a sibling (1.15) to anxiousness (2.13), from illness (3.5) to friendships and associations (4.2).

13. Cf. Epictetus's line: "If, at any rate, I am a nightingale, I should act as the nightingale; if a swan, as a swan" (1.16.20).

14. The attitude of this resistant servant resembles the behavior of Diogenes the Cynic, who, as a slave, openly rebuked and quarreled with the pirates who captured him and the master who owned him (Diogenes Laertius 6.30; see Epictetus *Disc.* 2.13.23–26 and 4.1.29–32, 114–117, and 151–158). That said, the case of the proud servant raises the question of why any good individual would get upset over a matter of preference (such as holding the pot or not). As a short answer, Epictetus could hold that individuals properly vary in what they prefer according to their role: for some roles, not holding the pot is more preferred; for other roles, not being beaten is more preferred. See chapter 6.

15. Bonhöffer 1996, 10–11, takes this as a non-normative claim. He thinks that Epictetus is merely making the factual claim that ordinary individuals do indeed hold the chamber pot. Bonhöffer thinks that, for Epictetus, no one should hold the chamber pot, but Bonhöffer misses the fact that the first slave resists the order because he finds it unbearable and not because it is *kakon*. Moreover, Bonhöffer's interpretation runs counter to Epictetus's claim that we cannot all be a figure such as Socrates (1.2.33–37). I return to these cases in greater detail in chapter 6.

16. Cf. Long 2002, 239–240. Dobbin 1998, 81–83, also seems to understand it this way. Alternatively, it could be captured as emotional stamina, a characterization which shows that the vigor of extraordinary figures arises from a *dunamis*. However, this characterization does not capture the pecuniary timbre of Epictetus's analogy, nor does it address the origin of this stamina—an estimate of one's own worth.

17. Kamtekar 1998, 151. In a somewhat similar vein, Bonhöffer 1996, 34, fills out the expression *to kata prosôpon* in 1.2.5–11 as "the command of honor." My interpretation is consistent with their views, although I do differ by treating self-worth as a capacity rather than a mere judgment.

18. This pecuniary model of evaluation appears elsewhere: 1.2.33, 3.3, 3.24.48–49, 4.3, 4.5.16–18 and *Ench.* 25. Cf. De Lacy 1977, 118: "The analogy with coins occurs frequently in Epictetus, e.g., ii.3, iii.3, iv.5.16–17."

19. Cf. "no one is nearer to me than myself" (4.6.11).

20. On this basis, Epictetus appears to doubt the Homeric tale that Odysseus wept (3.24.18–19; see *Odyssey* 8.521–534). Epictetus is convinced that tears would make Odysseus a bad man because it would mean that he is failing to treat externals as a matter of indifference.

21. By contrast, I suspect that Epictetus intends to ridicule the ordinary counterpart to Helvidius Priscus. Helvidius swore to oppose Caesar in the senate, even against Caesar's expressed wishes. Helvidius's anonymous counterpart, however, would "either sit there [in the senate] like a jug, or, if he spoke, would say what he knew Caesar wished and would pile on

still more" (1.2.24). Epictetus's derision here may mean that he would have exhorted the ordinary senator to take the path of mere silence over the path of flattery. See chapter 6.

22. See also 3.22 where the exemplary role of a Cynic is clearly treated as a special role that is not shared by all. I shall return to the subject of our relationship to preeminent figures such as Socrates in chapters 6, 7, and 9. For my present discussion, I am treating Socrates as having a role alongside other individuals who have differing roles.

23. Long 2002, 112. I use Long's translation because he renders the line beautifully.

24. Apart from ability and self-worth, Epictetus treats a third aspect of our nature as indicative of our specific roles: sexual identity. He employs gender to lay down standards for personal beauty and, it seems, to divide household work between men and women. His comments on both subjects, however, are brief and not very illuminating. He addresses beauty in *Discourses* 3.1 where he fervently argues that men should have beards because they naturally have facial hair while women should preserve their natural daintiness, smoothness, and softness of voice. With regards to household work, Epictetus appears to endorse the traditional roles for men and women (3.22.70–71) even though he holds that the volition of a woman is not subject to a man's control (4.1.67, 4.5.7, and *Ench.* 14). In both cases, Epictetus apparently echoes the views of his teacher, Musonius Rufus. See Musonius's chapter III, "That Women Too Should Study Philosophy," and IV, "Should Daughters Receive the Same Education as Sons?" (contained in Lutz 1947). For a more positive reading of Musonius on women, see Nussbaum 2002 and Reydams-Schils 2005, 147–159.

25. Brunt 1975, 33 (note 3), tries to enumerate the examples of these *scheseis* exhaustively: males, sons, fathers, husbands, wives, brothers, old, young, rulers, subjects, magistrates, councilors, citizens, generals, soldiers, neighbors, fellow-travelers, strangers, friends, masters of the household, teachers, the handicapped, and beggars.

26. See the Greek index to Bonhöffer 1996.

27. In this use here, we probably do not have a *schesis* with individuals whom we neither meet nor affect.

28. See De Lacy 1977, 171, and see 2.19.27 where Epictetus speaks of seeking "fellowship with Zeus." Nonetheless, our relationship to God is probably best understood as a feature of our universal role. See Chapter 1.

29. Annas 2007, 152, says that "there is no suggestion that there is a large ethical difference" between natural and acquired roles. However, as I have been arguing, Epictetus summons us to examine our relations as a heuristic for locating our roles. Accordingly, it is likely that Epictetus distinguishes between natural and acquired roles in order to remind his audience that they are as much bound by natural relations (such as siblings) as they are by acquired relations (such as marriage). Both sorts of roles carry obligations and so agents should examine both in order to discover all of their appropriate acts.

30. Curiously, Simplicius takes "acquired relations" to be prohairetic so that Epictetus is distinguishing between chosen roles (such as friends) and natural or unchosen roles (such as brothers). See his discussion of *Ench.* 30 in his *Commentarius in Epicteti enchiridion* 82,47–91,23. However, Simplicius appears to have arrived at his interpretation by employing Plato's method of division (e.g., he goes on to propose further subdivisions of natural and acquired roles) rather than by relying on the text of Epictetus. Furthermore, his proposed reading is poorly suited to manage politically appointed roles such as a governorship (e.g., 1.29.44–45). Such a role is surely an acquired role but Epictetus does not present it as a prohairetic role; it is one assigned to an individual who then must fulfill the obligations that it entails. In so far as Epictetus recognizes roles that we may choose, he appears to permit them in a very limited context (see below). Alternatively, we can describe every role as prohairetic since Epictetus thinks that we must assent to every circumstance presented (cf. 1.6.30–37); but, on that interpretation, the distinction between natural and acquired is moot because every role is therefore natural and prohairetic. Simplicius's commentary has been translated by Brennan and Brittain 2002.

31. Cf. *Ench.* 24.4, and Bonhöffer 1996, 94–95.

32. Cf. 1.13.3–4, 3.5.9–10, 3.24.36, and *Ench.* 17.

33. Cf. 1.25.19–21 and 3.26.28–30. Epictetus's doctrine on suicide is discussed by Bonhöffer 1996, 29–39. Although Bonhöffer grants that Epictetus permits suicide under special

circumstances, he argues that such circumstances are unlikely to occur. For a contrasting view on suicide, see Sandbach 1989, 51. Sandbach holds that Epictetus sees suicide as an appropriate hastening of death if our end is imminent.

34. A frequent refrain: on *hulê*, 1.7.2, 1.29.41, 2.5.7 and 22, 2.19.31–32, 3.3.1, 3.7.24–25, 3.22.20; on acting well under any circumstance, 1.15.2, 3.24.114, 4.1.89–90, 4.7.12–14 and 19–21. Note also the use of *hulê* in 4.5.6–7 cited above. See Dobbin 1998, 76.

35. Although the chapter titles may be later additions, they often capture the main topic (such as there is) of each chapter; *pace* De Lacy 1943, 113–114.

36. Bonhöffer 1996, 201, says that our duties are self-evident from names—only to the *scholastikon*. However, as this 2.10 passage makes clear, Epictetus supplies no such limitation.

37. E.g., Brunt 1975, 13, 16, 22–23, and 33 fn. 3. However, *pace* Brunt, Epictetus signals some awareness of competing religious and cultural customs at 1.11.12–13, 1.22.1–5, 2.9.19–21, and 2.11.13–16.

38. For the charge of imposter against fraudulent individuals, see also 2.19.28, 3.24.41–43, and 3.26.13.

39. Indeed, we should even "put up with abuse, bear with a senseless brother, father, son, neighbor, fellow-traveler" (3.21.5).

40. Although Epictetus literally describes these as wished for (*thelein*) roles much as Cicero describes the fourth *persona* as the one that we wish (*velimus* at *De Off.* 1.115), I use the term "choice" on the understanding that the selection among alternative career roles is not an indeterminate choice (i.e., a "free choice"). I also do not use the term "choice" to imply that these roles are prohairetic. At 3.24.69, Epictetus does say that we can use our impressions (the object of *prohairesis*) as we wish (*thelein*), but this is not to say that all wishing is prohairetic. If the choice of career roles is prohairetic, it would mean that the choice is unconstrained. Yet, career choices are constrained by what we can do (e.g., the bull in the herd at 1.2.30–32). For Epictetus, this career choice is not "up to me" since, as Bobzien 1998 convincingly argues, Epictetus uses "up to me" (*eph'hêmin*) to pick out "only those types of things which are in our power under all possible circumstances and with absolute certainty" (332), i.e., our *prohairesis* (333). Rather, where career is concerned, Epictetus seems to be saying that our career is sometimes determined *by* our wish (within the confines of nature) rather than determined *for* our wish by some other constraint. In either case, our wish is neither indeterminate nor can it do otherwise. (Note that the impossibility of doing otherwise raises a conundrum about how *prohairesis*, as a special kind of wish, might act against itself; this worry is discussed by Sorabji 2006, 185–186; cf. 190.)

41. Not surprisingly, there is some inconsistency in the literature about whether or not Epictetus permits chosen roles. Brunt 1975, De Lacy 1977, and Dobbin 1998 do not discuss the issue. Gill 1988, 190–191, suggests that rational choice is relevant to those intellectual powers that are necessary to becoming a philosopher, but he uses this thesis to argue that Epictetus is genuinely interested only in our universal role. Gill's discussion does not try to generalize on how choice is involved in specific roles. Stephens 1998 goes further and interprets *Ench.* 37 to say that "some roles can be freely chosen" so long as they accord with nature. Similarly, Sorabji 2006, 161, holds that "Epictetus recognizes the same mixture of choice and nature [as Cicero] . . . but with the complication that he sees our roles, character, ability, occupation, and status, as to some extent assigned by God."

By contrast, Kamtekar 1998, 149–150, argues that Epictetus accepts choice only as a form of assent. In this way, we do not choose our roles; instead, we assent to those roles as assigned by our given nature. She writes: "Despite the voluntarist note on which this passage [3.23.1] begins, it quickly becomes clear that . . . there is a choice that accords with one's nature and one that goes contrary to it" (149). She also notes a tension here "between the treatment of one's specific role as voluntary but given by nature, as to be chosen and yet to be discovered . . ." (150). In this way, choice is relevant only as a form of assent; we do not choose our roles, instead we must assent to the ones given by nature. On behalf of Kamtekar's reading, it is true that Epictetus often talks as though we have no choice about our roles. "'I do not want such a thing,' you say. Is it in your power to take any station [*hupothesin*] you choose? Such a body is given to you, such parents, such brothers, such a country, such a position [*taxis*] in it. . . . Besides, have you not the abilities to make use of what has been given? [You should say,] 'It is yours to set [my station], it is mine to practice it well'" (1.29.39–40; cf. 1.6.30–36, 1.12.28–35, 2.5.27–29 and esp. *Ench.* 17). In addition, Epictetus indeed will use the expression "if you wish *x*, you should do *y*" in contexts where he does not imply a choice; rather he seeks only to outline the necessary consequences for a given course of action (see 1.15.7–8, 2.18.2–4, 3.1.7, 3.15 (=*Ench.* 29), and 4.2.7–10). That is, he merely stresses the consequences of following one path rather than another without asserting that we can choose between various paths. As he succinctly put it, "If [you wish to be] a wrestler, look to your shoulders, your thighs, your back. For one person is naturally made for one thing, another for another" (3.15.9–10). This passage does not offer a choice among various professions. Instead, it expects that we conform our wishes to nature. Hence, Epictetus warns in *Ench.* 37 that we should not take up a role beyond our abilities.

However, the opening of 3.23 suggests limited choice in a way which is hard to deny. I shall thus argue that Gill, Stephens, and Sorabji are on the right track when they attribute chosen roles to Epictetus.

42. Accordingly, Gill charges that Epictetus is genuinely interested only in the career of the philosopher and the teacher, whereas it is Cicero who shows many different kinds of careers (Gill 1988, 190; and Gill 1994, 4620). While Gill is right that Epictetus's brief account places emphasis on the philosopher, his account admits of other career choices such as shoemaker (*Ench.* 24.4), carpenter, and blacksmith (3.23.3), and his account of *scheseis* reveals an interest in many different sorts of roles.

43. In this way, 3.23.2 might have been translated "the athletes first determine what sort [of athletes] they wish to be [*tines einai thelousin*]." This translation makes clear that the individuals in question do not choose *any* kind of career; instead, they may choose any kind of *athletic* career.

44. This is a frequent claim in Epictetus about wishing (*thelein*), especially in the context of preferred externals: "wish [*thele*] only for that to come to be which has come to be" (*Ench.* 33.10). See also 1.6.40, 1.27.10–11, 2.2, 2.13.1–15, 2.17.17–26, 3.4.6–12, 3.24.17–24, 3.26.10, 4.1.89, 4.7.20–21, *Ench.* 8, 14, and 31.2.

45. *Mustikon*, that is, connected to the Mysteries. The Mysteries are here invoked to echo the previous passage (3.21.12–16) in which Epictetus asserts that becoming a teacher of wisdom is akin to participating in the Mysteries of Eleusis. To participate in the Mysteries, one must perform all the appropriate rituals, adopt a special way of life, and have a pure frame of mind. One cannot imitate the cult merely by adopting a few superficial forms of cultic ritual, just as one cannot be a teacher of philosophy merely by spouting aphorisms. To do either is to "profane the Mysteries" (3.21.13).

46. See also 2.13.24–25 and 2.16.35–36 where he is praised alongside Socrates.

47. Epictetus would welcome divination of every role because, as Stephens 2007 points out, Epictetus holds that we each came into being because the universe had need of us (131–132; Stephens cites and discusses 3.24.94–95 and 3.26.30).

48. Cf. 3.22.5–6 on the role and function of the sun as well as the roles of calves versus bulls. The sun is weighed relative to what it can do for the *kosmos*; calves and bulls are weighed relative to what they can do for the herd when the herd is being attacked by a lion.

Chapter Three

Roles in Action: Appropriate Acts (or "Duties")

In the preceding chapters, we examined cases where roles, both universal and specific, indicate what is appropriate (*kathêkon*) for agents to do; for example, a great athlete confronts his choice between death versus medical castration on the basis of his roles as a man and an Olympic competitor (1.2.25–27). Given such cases, it seems clear that roles delineate appropriate actions (*kathêkonta*). Moreover, the reciprocal claim is also true: appropriate acts support roles because a role is destroyed if an agent fails to do what is appropriate for that role. Epictetus makes this point most clearly when he considers how the appropriate acts of a Cynic conflict with the appropriate acts of an ordinary, private individual (3.22.68–72). As we saw in the last chapter, Epictetus holds that a Cynic must be free of the familial appropriate acts that are incumbent on ordinary individuals. The Cynic, he says, "ought not be tied down by private appropriate acts [*kathêkousin idiôtikois*] nor involved in social relations which he cannot violate and still maintain his role [*prosôpon*] . . . , whereas, on the other hand, if he observes them, he will destroy the messenger, the scout, the herald of the gods" (3.22.69), that is, he will have "destroyed the Cynic" (3.22.16). To fulfill the role of a Cynic, Cynics must do what is appropriate for Cynics.[1]

Granted this reciprocal correlation between roles and appropriate actions, I want to examine in this chapter what Epictetus means by an appropriate act and—beyond the assertions cited above—how he connects that idea to roles. Interestingly, however, while there has been much written on the subject of appropriate actions (*kathêkonta*) in Stoicism, there has been little discussion of them in Epictetus.[2] Recent work on Epictetus has improved the situation considerably because a connection between roles and *kathêkonta* is now standardly recognized, but the consensus seems to be that Epictetus does not provide much explanation beyond a handful of examples of roles and their associated appropriate acts; a son ought to obey his father (2.10.7), a brother ought to be deferential to his elder siblings (2.10.8), and so on.[3]

The subject of Epictetus's roles and appropriate actions is certainly challenging because Epictetus does not define appropriate action and he appears largely silent about what an appropriate action is. However, while it remains true that Epictetus does not discuss appropriate action at length, it turns out that his remarks on how appropriate acts connect to roles provides us with a path of investigation. When his statements about appropriate acts are examined through the lens of roles, his *Discourses* yield more material than he has been given credit for. Indeed, we can answer the question "What is appropriate for Epictetus?" by answering the question "How does Epictetus expressly connect appropriate acts and roles?" This intersection between roles and appropriate acts sheds new light on the standard Stoic definition of appropriate action, on Epictetus's system for educating students in their appropriate acts, and on the thorny question of perfect versus intermediate appropriate acts.

THE STANDARD STOIC CONCEPTION OF APPROPRIATE ACTION (*TO KATHÊKON*)

For the Stoics, an appropriate act (*to kathêkon*) is an action which, simply enough, is appropriate for an agent to perform. As a normative term, it has understandably been translated as "duty," but, because "duty" communicates a kind of categorical obligation,[4] *kathêkon* is now customarily translated as "appropriate act" or sometimes as "proper function." It has also been translated as an "incumbent act" and what is "called for."[5] It is defined, according to Stobaeus's report, as "consequentiality [*to akolouthon*] in life, something which, when it has been done, admits of a reasonable [*eulogon*] justification [*apologian*]."[6] Stobaeus's definition is helpfully unpacked by Diogenes Laertius's claim that "Zeno was the first to use this term *kathêkon*, the name being derived from *kata tinas hêkein*, 'befits a particular person.'"[7] Although Diogenes's etymology may be incorrect, it is useful because it captures the idea of *x* befitting *y* or *x* being appropriate for *y*, namely, that *x* is *kata y*.

As Stobaeus's definition indicates, the appropriateness of an act is measured by two criteria: "consequentiality" and a "reasonable justification." "Consequentiality" is not well elaborated in the Stoic sources on ethics and it is even omitted from Cicero's own definition,[8] but it appears to pick out the standard Stoic idea of acting according to nature (cf. Long and Sedley, 365) because both Diogenes and Cicero report that *kathêkonta* are actions that accord with nature.[9] The idea of a "reasonable justification" appears to draw on both logical and legal roots. In logic, the Stoics defined an *eulogos* statement as "one that has to start with more chances of being true than not,"[10] that is, as a proposition which is probably true. As an example, Diogenes gives the claim "I will be alive tomorrow."[11] Thus, an *eulogos* justification of an act is one which shows that the action is probably right or appropriate; the justification is not infallible or necessary but reasonable.[12] In law, an *apologia* is a speech in one's defense. As Brad Inwood puts it, an *eulogos apologia* is "an adequate, though not certain, defense [which] could be given in some idealized court of 'law,' where one need not demonstrate the ultimate moral rightness of the act in order to win one's case."[13] In fact, this reasonable defense need not be provided by the agent performing the act. So long as a rational agent could provide the defense, an action counts as appropriate. Accordingly, plants and animals are not precluded from performing appropriate actions because, as Stobaeus says, they can act in a way that is "consequential upon their nature" (L&S 59B; cf. 59C) and reasonable observers can explain an animal's actions by reference to its nature and, in that way, justify it.

At its most basic, the grounds for these reasonable justifications rest in appeals to our rational nature as individuals or to cosmic nature itself.[14] Such a grounding requires robustness in the Stoic conception of the reasonable and of nature. Sedley stresses that the Stoic conception of the reasonable does not mean "what is reasonable in the light of prevailing social conventions," but it appears that the move from what is reasonable to what is conventional can be a short one for the Stoics.[15] As Diogenes Laertius explains, "Appropriate acts are ones which reason dictates our doing, such as honoring parents, brothers and country, spending time with friends . . ." (7.108–109).[16] Nonetheless, Sedley is right that the Stoics saw their appeals to nature as rational appeals; they did so because they conceived of nature in a teleological sense, as a kind of universal reason which ordered the world.[17] Nature, therefore, is both factual and normative. Thus, as Inwood's work has shown, a *eulogon* justification can appeal to broad facts about the world, facts that are "epistemological and justificatory, not prescriptive."[18] Such facts include our relationship to the gods and our relation to other individuals which the Stoics compare to the relation among parts of a body.[19] By themselves, these facts are not directly prescriptive, but for the Stoics, they should feature prominently in our ethical reasoning.

According to the Stoics, appropriate actions (*kathêkonta*) are divided into two sorts, intermediate and perfect (or "middle" and "complete" as Cicero terms them [*De Off.* 1.8]). Intermediate appropriate acts are simply called *kathêkonta* whereas perfect appropriate acts are called *katorthômata*.[20] While perfect and intermediate appropriate acts can be the same in their outward expression (like aiding a friend),[21] the two are distinguished by the mindset of the agent. It is only as performed by agents with a particular mindset that appropriate acts become either good or bad.[22] Intermediate appropriate acts are recognized, as we saw above, by the presence of a reasonable justification. They include any sort of act which is sometimes right but may not always be right, like getting married or having a conversation (L&S 59B). Perfect appropriate acts are described by the Stoics in a variety of ways (such as "to do X virtuously"),[23] but they agree that, at root, *katorthômata* are done on the basis of a correct reason (*orthos logos*).[24] In this way, says Cicero, intermediate *kathêkonta* are "available even for some who are not wise" (*De Fin.* 4.15),[25] whereas right action (*katorthôma*) can only be performed by the wise man (ibid.) because his wisdom is "complete" (*De Off.* 3.13). This crucial feature explains a variety of other features that the Stoics assign to perfect actions (*katorthômata*): they are always appropriate (Diogenes Laertius, 7.109), they "fulfill all the numbers" (Cicero, *De Off.* 3.14), and they harmonize with "the laws of life as a whole" (Seneca, *Letters*, 95.57).[26] They accord with virtue and therefore, by definition, are coextensive with virtuous actions (Stobaeus, L&S 59B).

In reference to this distinction, the Stoics emphasized that intermediate acts can become perfect while maintaining the ethical contrast between intermediate and perfect. Because the same acts can be either perfect (*katorthômata*) or ordinary (*kathêkonta*), the Stoics held that perfect appropriate acts arise out of the practice of intermediate ones. Intermediate *kathêkonta* can become perfect, Stobaeus says, when they "acquire the additional properties of firmness and tenor and their own particular fixity" (L&S, 59I), that is, when they take on the firmness of right reason (*orthos logos*) itself. Similarly, Cicero says that an appropriate act becomes "right" when the actor's "judgment is flawless" and the action is thus "duly" performed (*De Fin.* 3.59). So, for example, it is appropriate to care for our parents, but that act becomes perfect, as Sextus says, when we care for them "not . . . in other respects, but . . . on the basis of prudence."[27]

Nonetheless, the Stoics still held the distinction between intermediate and perfect acts to be a firm one: "it is still consistent to perform appropriate actions despite the fact that we regard them as neither good nor evil" (Cicero, *De Fin.*, 3.58).[28] As a result, this distinction between intermediate and perfect appropriate acts bifurcates the world of agents who concern themselves with the good.[29] On the one hand, there are agents who aim at the good but who have only a *eulogon* account of their actions. These individuals fall into the category of those who are making progress (*prokoptôn*) and their actions are not yet good. On the other hand, there are agents who have a right account (*orthos logos*) of their actions. These individuals count as wise men and their actions are good.[30]

EPICTETUS ON APPROPRIATE ACTION: "CONSEQUENTIALITY" AND "REASONABLENESS"

Epictetus nowhere sets out to define the term "appropriate action" (*kathêkon*).[31] The closest he comes to defining appropriate acts is in 3.2.2 where he summarizes the second stage of his educational program, a stage which deals with "appropriate action, so that he [*viz.*, the student of ethics] may act in an orderly fashion, reasonably [*eulogistôs*], and not carelessly."[32] While this is certainly not equivalent to the orthodox definition, it supplies no reason for thinking that Epictetus rejected the technical definition of an appropriate act as "consequentiality in life, something which, when it has been done, admits of a reasonable justification."[33] Instead, Epictetus's failure to give a definition fits with his general resistance to taxonomy and lexicography and he might very well have seen a rigid definition as unnecessary to the practice of virtue (cf. 2.17.29–38 and 4.4.16).

Moreover, Epictetus further complicates the matter because he supplies so few examples of appropriate actions arising from roles.[34] This paucity of examples, however, appears to arise not from any neglect on the part of Epictetus but rather from the kind of relationship he believes to hold between roles and the components of an appropriate act: consequentiality (*akolouthia*) and what is reasonable (*to eulogon*). I will argue that Epictetus understands one of the connections between a role and an appropriate act as a form of necessity (as marked by the term "consequentiality"). Accordingly, Epictetus probably thinks it redundant to provide us with many examples because, as he says, "[f]or each of these designations [*viz.*, the role of son and brother], upon consideration, always suggest the appropriate deeds" (2.10.11–12). Similarly, I shall argue that Epictetus treats an appropriate act as reasonable (*eulogon*) if agents are able to understand them in terms of their own roles (both universal and specific). If, as I argued in chapter 2, our specific roles are determined by examining our nature, our own circumstances, and our own choices, Epictetus cannot be expected to access those facts for us. As Epictetus tells a flustered student who wants merely to be told what befits his role: "That is an additional consideration, which it is necessary for you to 'add to the bill' in your inquiry, not I. For you are the one who knows yourself. . . ." (1.2.11).[35] What Epictetus *can* tell us about is his own role as a teacher of philosophy, a subject on which he has much to say (see 2.3, 2.9, and 4.8).

However, Epictetus makes distinctive contributions to our understanding of the key component terms in the Stoic definition: consequentiality (*akolouthia*) and what is reasonable (*eulogon*). Both of these terms are filled out by Epictetus's concept of a role, and, in turn, they elucidate the practical reasoning Epictetus thinks is involved in role-bound reasoning; thus, roles provide content where at first there appeared to be none. In the next two subsections, I shall analyze these components consecutively. The discussion, however, will not turn on the distinction between the universal and specific role; rather, the emphasis will fall on how the concept of a role *as such* connects to the elements of an appropriate act.

i. Consequentiality (*To Akolouthon*)

As we saw earlier, the expression "consequentiality [*to akolouthon*] in life" in the definition of an appropriate act appears to capture the idea that appropriate actions follow (*akolouthein*) upon nature. In this section, I will argue that Epictetus adds to that idea by drawing parallels between the use of the term "consequentiality" in logic and in ethics, suggesting that the consequent involved is from some antecedent whether that antecedent is a premise, nature itself, or a role. In turn, Epictetus applies that same description to the move from a role to its associated appropriate act, but he nonetheless leaves contextual leeway in that appropriate act. However, I shall also argue that Epictetus's elaboration of the notion of consequentiality remains incomplete because he does not specify *how* we are to understand the force of that necessity *nor* does he appear to justify it (instead he implicitly relies on Stoic teleology); but, I will suggest that we can make some sense of his remarks about consequentiality by considering what he wants to accomplish when he declares that appropriate acts (*kathêkonta*) are a consequent (*akolouthon*) of nature in general or roles in particular.

I will first review several places where Epictetus draws a parallel between the use of the term "consequent" in logic and in ethics. I shall refrain from an in-depth argument about consequentiality because the subject of Stoic logic is outside the scope of my study and it remains an extremely difficult topic in its own right. I will then examine two passages where Epictetus seems to apply the idea of consequentiality to the move from a role to its associated appropriate acts. Finally, I will argue that, although he thinks that the move from role to its appropriate act is necessary, Epictetus still thinks there is flexibility in the resulting appropriate act.

Epictetus explains the term "consequent" by drawing out its connection to its use in hypothetical arguments (*hupothetikous*):

> This also is the law governing hypotheses [*hupothetikos*]: to accept what follows [*to akolouthon*] from the hypothesis. But much more important is this law of life: to do what follows [*to akolouthon*] from nature. For if we wish in every matter and circumstance to observe what is in accordance with what is natural, it is clear that in everything we should make it our aim neither to avoid that which follows [*to akolouthon*] nor to accept that which contradicts. (1.26.1–2; cf. 1.7.10 and 1.25.11–13)

This passage lays out two sets of terms, one set is in the context of hypothetical arguments, a logical subject (see *Discourses* 1.7), the other set is in the context of life or living, a subject which fairly clearly means ethics.[36] In the logical use, Epictetus says that there are hypotheses and there are consequents of them; it seems safe to say that the movement from hypothesis to consequent is what is meant by consequentiality. He does not say what this consequent is, but he implies that its antithesis is what contradicts the hypothesis. In the ethical use, Epictetus says that there is nature and there is what follows from nature. By characterizing what is according to nature as doing what follows and avoiding what contradicts, he treats doing what follows (*to akolouthon*) as equivalent to doing what is according to nature. Epictetus draws two important parallels between the logical use and the ethical use.[37] First, he makes nature analogous to a hypothesis, which can yield a consequent which is a law for us to observe;[38] in neither case does he say what this consequent is, but he indicates that it is a kind of result (either of a hypothesis or of nature) that we must accept. Second, Epictetus parallels accepting the consequent in logic to doing the consequent in ethics. When he reformulates what it means to follow nature in 1.26.2, he says that we should accept the consequent, suggesting that accepting what follows from nature is equivalent to doing what follows from nature. To accept what is according to nature is to *do* what is according to nature.[39]

This transposition of consequentiality (*to akolouthon*) from logic to ethics appears to be confirmed by remarks Epictetus makes elsewhere. He says that "unless we decide that things are such-and-such, we do not perform the corresponding actions" (1.11.37), that is, unless we decide what the *nature* of each thing *is*, we will not do what is *consequent*. Similarly, Epictetus asks, what are "the principles" of a philosopher (i.e., an ethical person)?[40] They are, "as Zeno says, to understand the elements of reason, what each thing is like and how each fits together, and the consequences [*ta akoloutha*] of all these things" (4.8.12). And, he says, the fact that we have the power of understanding requires us to act following (*akolouthôs*) "our own nature and constitution" (1.6.15).[41]

By connecting the use of "consequentiality" (*to akolouthon*) in ethics with its use in logic, Epictetus implies that the expression "consequentiality in life" is not intended to invoke the more ordinary use of the term *akolouthon*.[42] However, in light of the above passages, what seems clear is that we are not being offered a well-defined theory of necessity when he asserts that a particular course of action is consequent upon life or nature. First, Epictetus seems to imagine an opponent who believes that nothing is consequent on being alive, upon being a human being, upon having a specific role.[43] Against these individuals, it is necessary to say that certain actions follow upon nature while other actions contradict it; the self-controlled individual is following nature but the profligate is denying nature (cf. 3.1.8–9). Epictetus appears to think he can do that, not because he has a developed theory of necessity, but because he accepts the Stoic model of the cosmos in which obligations follow as a consequence from nature because of God's providence over the world.[44]

Second, Epictetus wants to connect the result of what follows from nature with an action so that, if we accept what follows, we must do what follows, otherwise we have produced a contradiction. On Epictetus's view, the profligate cannot say "I accept that I must practice self-control, even though I have yet to try to be self-controlled" without producing a contradiction. Following the logic we saw in 1.26.1–2, we can either accept that an obligation follows from nature and we perform it, or we can deny that an obligation follows from nature and we do not perform it.

Given what Epictetus apparently wants to accomplish when he connects what is consequent in logic with what is consequent in ethics, it should be no surprise that he also applies the concept of consequentiality to our role-bound reasoning. He describes the move from a role to an action as the move from a hypothetical assertion (*hupothesis*) to a consequent (*to akolouthon*). That parallel is drawn by Epictetus in two distinct passages. In the first passage, the roles of a gladiator and of an athlete are treated as a kind of hypothesis (*hupothesis*; 1.29.35–43).[45] Epictetus begins by praising the gladiators who crave the challenge of combat and then he chastises his own students as if they were unwilling gladiators.

> I wanted . . . to see what my athlete is doing, how he was practicing his hypothesis [*hupothesin*].[46] "I do not want this," says he [the unwilling gladiator]. What, is it in your power to take any hypothesis you want? You have been given such a body, such parents, such brothers, such a country, such a position [*taxis*] in it; and then do you come to me and say, "Change the hypothesis [*hupothesin*] for me." . . . [You ought to say], "It is yours to set [the hypothesis], mine to practice it well." No, but [you *do* say], "Do not propose to me such-and-such a conditional but rather such-and-such a one; do not urge upon me such-and-such a conclusion but rather such-and-such a one." (1.29.38–41)

Roles are not explicitly named here, but *Discourses* 1.2 fairly clearly identifies being an athlete as a role (see 1.2.25–28).[47] Epictetus also affirms that he has roles in mind with the evidence he supplies to show that the athlete's role is that of a gladiator: the nature of his body (one of the criteria for determining one's role), parents and siblings (relation-type roles),[48] and a *taxis* (station).[49] Thus, the *hupothesis* here is the athlete's specific role. In addition, this passage shows that roles are being called hypotheses in a way related to hypotheses in logic. The *hupothesis* of the athlete is analogous to receiving a proposition from which he must reason out a conclusion. Although the term consequentiality (*akolouthia*) is not explicitly invoked, it is reasonable to suppose that the conclusion from the athlete's *hupothesis* is an instance of a consequence (*akolouthia*) because Epictetus uses a synonymous word, *epiphora* (conclusion). The emphasis falls on the fact that the athlete is responsible for treating his station as a starting point in his reasoning, a point from which he should reason out his training and performance. We cannot choose the hypotheses (roles) that we want; we have to take whatever is given.[50] In Stoic logic, we can derive consequents from any proposition;[51] in ethics, we can derive consequents from any role, whether we have chosen it or not.

A similar connection is drawn in the second passage, a passage which surrounds the one we saw above about hypothetical arguments:

> At the Saturnalia, a king is chosen by lot; for it has been decided to play this game. The king gives his commands: "You drink, you mix wine, you sing, you go, you come." I obey, so as not to be the one to break up the game. . . . Again, we have agreed to play the story of Agamemnon and Achilles. The one who has been appointed to play the part of Agamemnon says to me, "Go to Achilles, and drag away Briseis." I go. He says, "Come," and I come. For we ought to behave in life as we do in hypothetical arguments [*tôn hupothetikôn*]. "Let it be night."—Let it be.—"Well then, is it day?"—"No; for I assumed the hypothesis of its being night.—"Let it be that you believe that it is night."—Let it be.—"Then believe that it *is* night."—That does not follow [*akolouthei*] from the hypothesis.[52] "Let it be that you are unfortunate." Let it be. "Are you, then, without fortune?" Yes. "What then? Are you beset with bad fortune?" Yes. "But believe that your *are* in a bad state." That does not follow from the hypothesis. . . . How long, then, should we obey such things? As long as it is beneficial, and that means, as long as I preserve what is fitting[53] and consistent [*katallêlon*]. (1.25.8–14)[54]

In this passage, the connection to roles is metaphorical because the examples do not refer to real-life cases but to the pretend roles in a game. Nonetheless, the metaphorical examples do not disqualify this passage because Epictetus sometimes uses Agamemnon and Achilles as stand-ins for real-life roles[55] and because the idea invoked here, that of playing a part, is the common feature of both the stage use and the ethical use of roles. The passage also connects such roles with hypothetical arguments and with what follows (*akolouthei*) from a hypothesis. It makes an analogy between roles and their expected actions with hypotheses and what follows from them. In that vein, it reminds us that we should continue playing our roles so long as we can maintain what is fitting and consistent, and presumably this means that we should do what the Agamemnon character orders as long as it fits with our specific role; if we are playing Thersites, for example, we should not be a part of the ambassadors sent to placate Achilles, even if the "Saturnalia Agamemnon" ordered it.[56]

Both passages suggest therefore that we may understand roles as *hupotheseis* and that such *hupotheseis* generate obligatory actions as consequents;

naturally, such obligatory actions should be understood as appropriate actions (*kathêkonta*). Moreover, when we see that Epictetus treats roles as "antecedents" and appropriate acts as "consequents," we are positioned to see how Epictetus assumes that equation throughout his discussion of roles. "Bear in mind that you are a son," Epictetus says, and so the "profession of this role [*prosôpou*]" is "to treat everything that is one's own as belonging to his father . . ." (2.10.7). Likewise, "you are a brother," he adds, "to this role [*prosôpon*] belongs deference, obedience, kindly speech . . ." (2.10.8). Other roles are framed in much the same way (see 2.10.10–14). Although 2.10.7–14 does not call these inferences consequents (*akolouthia*), Epictetus is willing to set up the obligations of playing Agamemnon in apposition to the consequent (*to akolouthon*), and this apposition strongly suggests that the inferences in discourse 2.10 qualify as consequents (*ta akoloutha*) of their roles. Given the way 2.10 talks about roles, the claim of "Your role is X, therefore do Y" seems a good candidate for consequentiality (*to akolouthon*).

By connecting roles and appropriate acts to hypotheses and consequents, Epictetus adds another layer to the thought that began this chapter: if we fail to do what is *kathêkon* for a role, we will destroy that role (cf. 3.22.68–72). In the language of consequentiality, if we fail to do what follows from a role, we have produced a contradiction and therefore we have negated that role. If *p*, consequently *not-p*, then *p* must be false. If a role "necessitates" a course of action, but that action is not performed, then that role is "false."

Now that we have sketched the use of consequents in Epictetus's ethics, we must consider the generality of a role's consequent. In the above cases, I take it that Epictetus understands "if you are a son, you should obey" to mean "for all sons, if you are a son, you should obey"; but, Epictetus does not say whether obedience means "perform this particular action in this particular context" or "perform actions of such a sort." I shall argue that, from the few examples that Epictetus has given us of reasoning about roles and their appropriate acts, he seems to understand ethical consequents as types of actions even though he also seems to think that, once the context and circumstances have been specified for a particular agent, a more particular action may be required. For example, the role of an athlete requires that one train one's body, an appropriate act that does not apply to other sorts of roles, such as carpenter or father; but the requirement to train does not contain, in itself, the details of when, where, or how to train. Such details must wait until we work out the details of the athlete's body and circumstances.

Perhaps the best passage to make this clear is 3.24.31–36 where Epictetus considers the role of soldiers and sailors. Soldiers have an obligation to obey their general just as sailors have the obligation to obey their captain. In other words, if the role of soldier or sailor is a hypothesis, it generates obedience to a commanding officer as a consequent appropriate act.[57] But, in the case of soldiers, Epictetus notes how "it is necessary for one to mount guard, another go out on reconnaissance, and another out to fight" (3.24.31). Similarly, it seems that some sailors ought to row, others ought to secure the riggings, while others still ought to navigate (3.24.33). Epictetus emphasizes that they each ought to take up some particular task on the orders of their commander (3.24.33–34). In this way, it seems that this appropriate act to obey gets translated into more detailed actions only in a particular context. For one soldier, obedience requires that he build a palisade, for another, it requires that he take the night watch. Similarly, for a ship in a storm, obedience to the commander and activity for the ship's benefit may require a different set of actions than for a ship in a calm sea. Thus, even though obedience is a consequent of certain roles, the scope of that consequent remains to be determined by other factors.

Nonetheless, while Epictetus finds the move from the role of soldier or younger brother to the appropriate act of obedience an immediate inference from hypothesis to consequent (2.10.8), it is not clear that the application of obedience to the circumstances is equally immediate or easy. Soldiers, for example, know that obedience is a consequent of their role (3.24.31–35), but it is not always clear how that obedience ought to be applied. They could receive ambiguous, contradictory, or even impossible orders; or, in the breakdown of command, it may not even be clear whom to obey. As Epictetus says about the virtue of piety, all agree that piety is what should be prized above all, but each religion applies the virtue differently (1.22.1–10). Of course, Epictetus seems to imply that there is a right and wrong way of applying a virtue like piety, but he does not appear to think that the right way is an immediate inference of the form if *p*, then *q*. He tells us only that what is needed for correct application of a concept is that we be educated (1.22.9–10; cf. 1.2.6), an education that appears to consist of Stoic doctrine (cf. 1.22.10–21). Such a picture, therefore, does not relieve us of having to perform further reflections about their appropriate acts, even though appropriate acts are consequences of our roles.

ii. The Reasonable (*To Eulogon*)

In this section, we will examine how Epictetus generally appears to accept the orthodox interpretation of *to eulogon* (what is reasonable) in the definition of an appropriate act and that he sees roles as one key way of determining what the reasonable (*to eulogon*) act is. We shall briefly note how the orthodox picture of appropriate acts implicitly refers to roles. Moreover, we will see how, in *Discourses* 1.2, Epictetus goes further by connecting reasonableness explicitly to roles, suggesting that appropriate acts *simpliciter* (not just those concerning propriety) depend on roles. Like his view of consequentiality (*akolouthia*), Epictetus believes that we calculate what is reasonable on the basis of our roles (whether universal or specific). Finally, we shall consider how the terms "what is reasonable" (*to eulogon*) and "what is consequent" (*to akolouthon*) represent two different perspectives on the same appropriate action.

As is often the case with Epictetus, he offers no formal definition of what is reasonable (*to eulogon*), but he generally uses the term as the Stoics do. First, as with his predecessors, he understands *to eulogon* to pick out what is reasonable or justifiable. For example, Epictetus appeals to the term in order to justify his own candor with his students: "how could it be my part to pass by you while you're uninformed? If at some time in the future you come to your senses, you will reasonably [*eulogôs*] accuse me" (3.1.12).[58] Similarly, he says, "what is more reasonable [*eulogôteron*] than for those who have devoted themselves to something to have the advantage in that to which they have devoted themselves?" (4.6.25). Second, Epictetus expressly believes that it is reasonable to follow nature.[59] He says, for example, that family affection is according to nature and therefore it is reasonable (1.11.16–20). It is wrong, therefore, to ask if the course of nature is unreasonable (1.6.31; cf. 2.16.13).

Although Epictetus's Stoic predecessors primarily use the term *to eulogon* to pick out a reasonable defense, as Inwood terms it, "given in some idealized court of 'law'" (125), there is a hint of role theory in the Stoic picture of that reasonable defense. Earlier, when we reviewed the Stoic position, we saw that appropriate acts "are ones which reason dictates our doing, such as honoring parents, brothers and country, spending time with friends . . ." (Diogenes Laertius 7.108–109).[60] These examples are fairly typical,[61] and they are striking because they line up with the kinds of roles we have seen in the preceding chapters: son, brother, and citizen. The obligation to honor one's parents can be translated and expanded into the claim "you are a son or daughter, so you should honor your parents." The same would equally apply to other Stoic examples of the recognized appropriate acts for brothers, citizens, and friends.

For our discussion here, what I want to draw out is the fact that Epictetus makes explicit this move between a role (*prosôpon*) and an appropriate act such as honoring parents because he directly connects roles to what is reasonable (*to eulogon*—one of the key components of the definition of appropriate action). As Epictetus says in *Discourses* 1.2, we can determine what is reasonable (*eulogon*) by reference to our roles:

> It happens that the reasonable [*eulogon*] and the unreasonable[62] are different for different persons, just as good and evil, and the profitable and unprofitable, are different for different persons. It is for this reason especially that we need education, so as to learn how to apply to particular cases our preconception of what is reasonable [*eulogou*] and unreasonable in conformity with nature. But in respect to judging the reasonable and the unreasonable, we employ not only

> [our estimates of] the value of external things but also [the criterion] of that which is in accordance with one's own role [*kata to prosôpon*]. (1.2.5–7)

Epictetus exemplifies this very doctrine through the cases in *Discourses* 1.2. It is one man's role to be an outspoken senator and exemplar, so it is reasonable for him to speak out against the will of Caesar (1.2.19–24).[63]

Having briefly accounted for what is reasonable, it remains to say how the concepts of reasonableness and consequentiality are related. Since both terms are set up side by side in the definition ("consequentiality [*to akolouthon*] in life, something which, when it has been done, admits of a reasonable [*eulogon*] justification" [L&S 59B]), we would expect the terms to cover the same ground. And, in Epictetus's use, they do pick out the same sorts of actions, although he apparently uses the terms to highlight different aspects of those same actions. From the earlier discussion of consequentiality (*akolouthia*), we surmised that *to akolouthon* means a consequent and so the *akolouthon* relation between a role and its appropriate act is the same as a premise and a consequent. In this sense, it is a calculation that can be performed even by an outside observer of an agent's actions. By contrast, *to eulogon* concerns what is reasonable based on our roles and appears to pick out what is intelligible or what makes sense for an agent. Epictetus implies that reasonableness concerns what is acceptable and comprehensible to an agent when he connects reasonableness and unreasonableness to what is and is not endurable. For example, Epictetus says that

> Blows by nature are not unendurable. . . . Observe how Lacedaemonians take a whipping when they learn that it is reasonable [*eulogon*].[64]—But isn't it intolerable to be hanged?—At any rate, whenever someone feels that it is reasonable, he goes and hangs himself. [4] Put simply, if we observe, we shall find that a [rational] animal is distressed by nothing so much as by the unreasonable and again attracted to nothing so much as the reasonable [*eulogon*]. (1.2.2–4)

Indeed, throughout the *Discourses* 1.2 examples, Epictetus stresses that individuals are able to endure what is reasonable given their roles and unable to endure what is unreasonable. Moreover, when *Discourses* 1.2 analyzes what is reasonable (*to eulogon*) through the lens of roles (1.2.5–7), Epictetus does not convince individuals that their obligations make sense by telling them that they are a consequent of their role; rather, he spends his time convincing individuals to accept their roles, whatever those roles may be. It seems that Epictetus tends to invoke what is consequent (*to akolouthon*) to capture what follows from a role, but he invokes what is reasonable (*to eulogon*) to capture what we can accept and understand.

Epictetus's interpretation of reasonableness seems to leave open the possibility that two agents could arrive at reasonably different interpretations of the same role, but I suspect that what Epictetus wants us to conclude is that we ought, in all cases, to find *to akolouthon* (what follows) to be *to eulogon* (reasonable). In practice, we can say that a claim is intelligible even before we know it follows and, likewise, we can say that a claim follows even before we can fully make sense of it.[65] For example, it is often a matter of surprise to beginning students of mathematics that it is impossible, for a given circle, to construct a rectilinear figure with the same area. Even when students learn to prove that it is impossible to square the circle, it may still take time for them to accept this fact as credible. Similarly, it is credible to us that a square can always be divided into two equal triangles even before we can establish, in a rigorous fashion, that it is necessary for squares to be so divisible.

If we again return, then, to the definition of an appropriate action as "consequentiality [*to akolouthon*] in life, something which, when it has been done, admits of a reasonable [*eulogon*] justification [*apologian*]" (L&S 59B), we can see that, for Epictetus, this definition holds agents to a very high standard about how they connect their appropriate acts to their roles. In the case of consequentiality, Epictetus tells agents that their actions ought to follow from their roles just as a conclusion follows from a hypothesis. In the case of reasonableness, Epictetus tells agents that their actions ought to make sense in light of their roles. Their actions ought to both follow (*akolouthon*) and reasonably make sense (*eulogon*). In both ways, the idea of an appropriate action is intimately woven with the idea of a role (*prosôpon*).

PRACTICAL ADVICE BEFORE THEORY

In the preceding sections, we gathered evidence to determine what Epictetus has to say about the Stoic definition of appropriate action. Throughout our analysis, Epictetus proved elusive but he provided just enough clues to enable us to sketch his view. Compared to the previous two chapters, we can now say that we have examined Epictetus's role theory on its own terms (in chapters 1 and 2) and on canonical Stoic terms (in the present chapter). By juxtaposing the three chapters in this way, we arrive at the realization that Epictetus has underplayed the technical details in his own understanding of appropriate action in order to articulate a number of practical points about roles and how we recognize them. Relative to the Stoic definition, Epictetus extends our understanding of the neglected criterion of consequentiality and he supplies roles as a novel criterion for what is consequent *and* what is reasonable. And yet, Epictetus leaves that theoretical work under the surface; he references it only by implication. Instead, he forefronts his claims about roles, nature, and relations. For Epictetus, even path-breaking technical work should serve merely as a support for his more practical advice about how to live as a ethical human being laden with many roles.

NOTES

1. Less explicit (but no less convincing) variations of this theme appear throughout the *Discourses*, especially in application to our role as human beings. By not doing what is appropriate for a human being (2.10.1–6), we become beasts (2.10.14–23). "See to it, then, that you never act like a wild beast; if you do, you will have destroyed your humanity since you have not fulfilled your profession [as a human]" (2.9.3; cf. .8–12 and .17). In the same fashion, Epictetus says to a philosopher who has chosen what is indifferent over what is appropriate (4.1.134–143), "Why, when you are a worm, do you claim that you are a human?" (4.1.143; cf. 4.1.121–122). For similar cases of losing our humanity, see 1.5.9–10, 1.28.9, 2.9.1–10, 3.2.12, and 4.5.19–21. For examples of this language applied to "the man of fidelity," see 2.4.1–11, 3.7.36, and 3.18.6–7. Cf. Long 1983, 188.

2. In Bonhöffer's lengthy appendix on *kathêkonta* at the end of *The Ethics of the Stoic Epictetus* 1996, for example, there is no discussion of roles. Similarly, in his monograph on Epictetus's educational system, Hijmans 1959 briefly notes that Epictetus connects *kathêkonta* to names like "brother" or "son" (in 2.10.1–13), but he does not explore in any detail what Epictetus means by *kathêkonta* nor does he consider why Epictetus would connect *kathêkonta* to names like "brother" (i.e., to roles) (Hijmans 1959, 83). Rather, Hijmans's discussion of the topics of Epictetus's education focuses on issues of teaching method and the subjects of impulses (*hormai*), choice (*prohairesis*), and logic (ibid., 38–41 and 64–65).

3. A. A. Long 2002, 257, for instance, seems to hold that we cannot say very much about what is appropriate (*kathêkon*) because "Epictetus . . . hardly gives any exposition of the term *kathêkon* . . ." Thus, Long's chapter on "Appropriate Actions and Feelings" (231f.) concerns itself not with *kathêkonta* but with what a role is, with the kinds of roles we have (such as the role of a human being), and with the content of some of our ethical obligations to others (e.g., tolerance). His chapter does not discuss how roles and appropriate acts are connected.

4. See chapter 8.

5. Cooper 1999, 437. Graver 2007, 43.

6. 2.85, 13–86, 4 (*SVF* 3.494), cited and translated by Long and Sedley 1987 59B. Hereafter, Long and Sedley 1987 will be abbreviated as L&S.

7. 7.107 (*SVF* 3.493), L&S (59C). L&S translate *kata tinas hêkein* as "to have arrived in accordance with certain persons." Cooper 1999 adapts Sedley's translation to "comes down on a particular person," and I have further adapted it to "befits a particular person." Cooper, who follows LSJ, cites an instance of *kata* in Epictetus where we must wait at a feast for whatever "comes to you [*kata se*]" (*Ench.* 15). Using the feast image, Cooper's preferred translation puts an emphasis on, as he says, "what it is your turn or your place to do" (436).

8. Cicero, *De Officiis*, 1.101: no one should "do anything for which he cannot give a persuasive justification [*causam probabilem*]: that is practically a definition of duty [*officii*]."

9. Diogenes, ibid.; Cicero, *De Fin.* 3.17.20–2 (L&S 59D).

10. Diogenes Laertius, 6.76 (*SVF* 2.201). I owe this passage and translation to Engberg-Pedersen 1986, 179–180.

11. Ibid.

12. Cf. L&S 365. As evidence that what is *eulogos* is fallible, L&S point to D.L. 7.177 (*SVF* 1.625). See also Inwood 1999, 102. I am here following the traditional interpretation of *eulogos* as set forth by Long and Sedley. Their interpretation has been challenged by Brennan 1996. In Brennan's view, *eulogos* does not mean "reasonable" (where reasonable is more permissive than right reason) but means "something like 'in accordance with right reason'" (330). Although I cannot mount a complete reply to Brennan, I here set forth several reasons for resisting Brennan's interpretation: (1) Epictetus provides us with an indication of his own views about *eulogos* in *Discourses* 1.2 and he explains that we determine what is reasonable by reference to our roles and external goods—and yet it is precisely this latter measure that Brennan's position

requires him to deny (see 332). In addition, Epictetus begins *Discourses* 1.2 with what he apparently takes to be commonsense examples of how *eulogos* action is relative to the agent's perspective, e.g., Spartan boys accepting a ritual whipping or a man hanging himself. Their actions are *eulogos* because the agent is able to make sense of his own actions. On Brennan's view, we must say that their actions are *eulogos* because they have accidentally hit upon the same action and justification of a sage, an especially surprising claim to apply to Spartan youths and their Spartan-only custom! Instead, I note that Epictetus's emphasis falls wholly on the fact that the agent finds the action, as we would say in English, reasonable. At the very least, then, Epictetus seems to be following the view of *eulogos* that Long and Sedley ascribe to the Stoics at large. (2) Brennan focuses on the episode with Sphaerus in which he reaches for some wax pomegranates but justifies his "error" by claiming that he merely assented to the claim that it was reasonable that they were pomegranates (L&S 40F). Brennan reads the episode to say that *eulogos* cannot mean merely what is reasonable, but I think that Brennan only succeeds in showing that we can have impressions of impressions (meta-impressions?) that differ in their respective certainty. Sphaerus has the reasonable impression of seeing pomegranates; he could assent to the reasonable *axiôma* that "These are pomegranates" or he could assent to the kataleptic impression "It is reasonable that these are pomegranates." (3) If Brennan is right, we have no term to describe the *logos* of one who is making progress since their *kathêkon* actions will be identical to the Sage's *katorthôma* albeit "with a very different psychic state" (330). On the traditional interpretation, however, we can describe the *logos* of a *prokoptôn* as *eulogos* and the *logos* of the Sage as *orthos*. (4) Brenann rejects the claim that *eulogon* could mean "reasonable" because reasonable courses of action may conflict with each other but "There are no competing duties in Stoicism" (329; cf. 330). While Brennan may be right about standard Stoicism, his claim does not apply to Epictetus; as I argue in chapters 5 and 6, Epictetus recognizes that our various roles may indeed commit us to competing appropriate actions.

13. Inwood 1999, 123.

14. This suggests that *to akolouthon* and *to eulogon* capture two aspects of "following nature": *to akolouthon* identifies a feature of the action itself, namely, that it is consequent upon nature; *to eulogon* identifies the epistemic features of an action, namely, that it can be defended by appeal to nature.

15. Sedley 1999, 128.

16. *SVF* 3.495, 496; L&S 59E with slight revision.

17. Cf. Engberg-Pederson 1986, 147–150.

18. Inwood 1999, 117.

19. See also L&S, 365–366.

20. Because the term *kathêkôn* can refer to ordinary and perfect appropriate acts, Sedley wonders what territory was covered by the now lost Stoic handbooks *peri kathêkonta*. "Were these merely handbooks for the non-wise" (Sedley 1999, 132) or were they aimed at the wise, too? Based on the available evidence, Sedley argues that they were for both and that it was uncommon for the Stoics "to emphasize the difference between the proper conduct of the foolish and that of the wise man" (133).

21. On these grounds, Long and Sedley rightly note that intermediate appropriate acts should not be understood as a "second best" or alternative morality to perfect appropriate acts (L&S vol. I, 365–366).

22. Since the same actions can be either perfect or intermediate, or even neither good nor bad (see L&S 59M), it makes sense that the acts themselves which compose *kathêkonta* are neither good nor bad. These acts, from caring for one's health to returning property, can be done well or badly depending on the epistemic state of the agent. I owe this point to L&S, 366–367. See also Kidd 1978, 248.

23. E.g., "to walk prudently." As Inwood 1999 justly complains, these descriptions are "universal but vacuous" (102) and work simply by containing "a built-in reference to virtue or vice: 'prudent walking,' or more generally 'virtuous action'" (103; cf. 106).

24. L&S, 367; Long 1983, 191–192; Sandbach 1989, 45–47; Bonhöffer 1996, 213; Dyck 1996, 78. Dyck cites Tsekourakis 1974, 21 ff. See Cicero *De Fin.* 3.59.

25. Note that this possibility does not mean that all non-wise acts are intermediate; presumably, evil acts are neither perfect nor intermediate because they are never appropriate.

26. Cited in L&S vol. I, 367.

27. Sextus Empiricus, *Against the Professors*, 11.200 (*SVF* 3.516); L&S 59G.

28. L&S 59F. Cf. 59M. Technically speaking, ordinary *kathêkonta* are matters of indifference whereas only *katorthômata* are good. For a discussion of this puzzling claim, see Rachel Barney 2003. See also Brennan 2005, chapter 13.

29. Those who do not aim at the good at all are simply base individuals (*phauloi*).

30. See Stobaeus 2.65–68, Diogenes Laertius, 120–124, and Cicero, *De Fin.*, 3.70. I owe these citations to Bonhöffer 1996, 211. Interestingly, because perfect appropriate acts (*katorthômata*) count as a kind of appropriate act (*kathêkon*), the Stoics face a tension about the meaning of the term "reasonable" (*to eulogon*). If the definition of a *kathêkon* includes what is reasonable (*eulogon*) and if perfect appropriate acts count as a kind of appropriate act (*kathêkon*), then the term "reasonable" (*to eulogon*) must include correct reason (*orthos logos*). This tension has not been well addressed by the Stoics and it is rarely noticed by their modern commentators. (However, Ian Kidd notices a version the problem. See Kidd 1978, 249. He formulates the tension as follows: "at first sight there seems to be a horizontal division between *kathêkon* and *katorthôma*, although progression assumes a developed [i.e., non-horizontal] relationship between the two." Although Kidd does not directly discuss this tension in connection with *to eulogon*, his point applies equally to *to eulogon*. For a brief discussion of this definitional problem as applied to the use of the term *logos*, see Bonhöffer 1996, 224–226. Interestingly, as Bonhöffer 1996, 193, notes, the skeptic Arcesilaus connected *to eulogon*, not with *kathêkon* but with *katorthôma* (see Sextus 7.158). In order to remain consistent, the Stoics must make the concept of what is reasonable (*to eulogon*) perform double duty. In the context of an intermediate appropriate act, *to eulogon* must capture what is reasonable, but, in the context of a perfect appropriate act, the term must also accommodate a right reason (*orthos logos*). The Stoics could have made these two uses coherent if they held that the broadest use of what is reasonable (*to eulogon*) meant "justifiable" or "defendable" or the like and that such defenses could be either plausible or perfect. However, it appears that later Stoicism quietly solved this difficulty in a different manner by severing *katorthômata* from *kathêkonta*. According to Dyck 1996, 75, "As perfect appropriate actions, κατορθώματα form a subset of καθήκοντα (cf. introduction, § 1; L&S, 366–67). . . . By the time of Epictetus, however, this relation no longer obtained; rather the two terms appear side by side as objects of different kinds of impulse (cf. Inwood 1985, 117)."

31. This is not unusual because the *Discourses* certainly employ technical vocabulary without explanation (e.g., the logical vocabulary in 1.7 and 1.29.39–42; see Barnes 1997, 27–28, and Hijmans 1959, 41). What is unclear is whether Epictetus actually taught such technical topics himself (as Long 2002, 117, and Barnes 1997, 75, believe) or whether he counted on previous formal training, either by his own advanced students (as Hijmans 1959, 44–45, implies) or by training even prior to his school (as Hijmans 1959, 35, also implies).

32. Cf. also 3.12.13 and 4.12.17–18 which appear to invoke the idea of acting *eulogistôs* by emphasizing the need to act at the right time and under the right circumstances.

33. 2.85, 13–86, 4 (*SVF* 3.494) = L&S 59B.

34. Sedley 1999, too, has noticed this issue (138). Cf. Bonhöffer 1996, 89–90, who says that Epictetus is vague about non-universal duties and is so because specific roles have little substance; in the section ahead, I hope to show that Bonhöffer is wrong about Epictetus's vagueness. I will directly address Bonhöffer's assertion in chapter 5.

35. Cf. "no one is closer to me than I am" (4.6.11).

36. See, for example, Stobaeus's report that a *kathêkon* is "consequentiality in one's way of life [*en biôi*]" (L&S 59B).

37. For a similar transposition of logical terms to an ethical context, see his use of *thentes*, *labontes*, and *epagousi* at 4.8.9.

38. Cf. 1.29.4. See also Barnes 1997, 90–91, for a discussion of what it means to call a principle a *nomos* of logic.

39. Cf. Aristotle, *Nicomachean Ethics*, VI.2.

40. See chapters 1 and 2 for cases where Epictetus uses "the philosopher" as a stand-in for an ethical man.

41. The subject of what our nature comprises (in this context) was addressed in chapter 2.

42. In its more ordinary use in Epictetus and elsewhere, *akolouth-* generally means "to follow (behind)" someone or something (e.g., 2.13.23 and 3.26.29) or "to be obedient to" (e.g., *akolouthos* "servant" in 4.7.20), especially to be obedient to god (see 1.30.5, 4.10.14, and *Ench.* 31.1).

43. See, for example, 1.11 where Epictetus debates with a father who says that it was natural for him to run away from his sick daughter.

44. See Long 1970. In that article, Long goes so far as to suggest that the division between factual and normative breaks down in Stoic ethics because their teleological conception of nature makes it impossible for them to give a strictly "factual" account of nature. Thus, Long argues *contra* Hume that the Stoic arguments from nature have "no illegitimate transition here from facts to values" (147).

45. Barnes 1997, 29, notes that Marcus Aurelius also uses *hupothesis* "in the sense of 'role in life'" and he points to the *Meditations* 8.1.2, 10.31.5, and 11.7.

46. It is difficult in this context to find a good English translation for the word *hupothesis*. Clearly, the word here does not invoke its most concrete sense of a "standing under" nor does it invoke its most abstract sense which picks out a type of expression. Bonhöffer 1996, 23, translates it as "basic elements." Oldfather 1928, and Hard and Gill 1995, translate this term as "task" while Dobbin 1998 translates it as "material" and "circumstances." I think Long 2002, 242, is closer to the mark when he translates it as "plot" and thus connects it to the theater. As I argue here, Epictetus's use of *hupothesis* here is consistent with his use of *prosôpon* for he is describing a position with consequent obligations.

47. 1.2 is analyzed in chapter 6.

48. See chapter 2.

49. On *taxis* and roles, see chapter 1.

50. Cf. Epictetus's example of the good soldier (3.24.31–37). The soldier does not question his station but rather accepts whatever task he is assigned.

51. See Barnes 1997, 85–98, and Bobzien 1997.

52. Bobzien translation for sections 11–13. See Bobzien 1997, 305.

53. *To prepon* appears to be stand-in for what is appropriate (*kathêkei*). Compare 4.6.26 and *Ench*. 30, where the two terms do the same work in connection to relations (*scheseis*).

54. This translation is based on Oldfather 1928 excepting section 13, which is based on Bobzien 1997.

55. See chapter 2.

56. For a discussion of rules about accepting a *hupothesis*, including the stipulation that they be consistent, see Barnes 1997, 91–96.

57. Cf. the appropriate acts of a younger brother, 2.10.8; see above. Presumably, soldiers and sailors also have an obligation to benefit the army or ship so that, if cut free from a commander (as in Xenophon's *Anabasis*), they ought to select actions that assist the army or the ship.

58. See also 2.5.23 and 3.7.7 as well as his use of *eulogistein* and *eulogôs* at 2.23.35, 3.13.21, 4.3.11, and fragment 2.

59. 2.10.6, 4.7.19–20, and fragment 3.

60. *SVF* 3.495, 496; L&S 59E.

61. E.g., L&S 59G.

62. *Alogon*: I have translated *alogon* as "unreasonable" although it could simply be translated as "without reasons." In the latter case, it is difficult to see why Epictetus would merely want to contrast "with reasons" against "without reasons" because ethical action would hardly be robust if it merely required *a* reason for action as opposed to a reasonable reason. I have therefore drawn the stronger contrast between *to eulogon* and *to alogon*. However, if Epictetus intended a distinction between "reasonable" and "without reasons," I do not think it matters for my discussion since Epictetus is interested in the reasonable half of the alternative. Particularly, I take Epictetus to be picking up the Stoic requirement that an appropriate action ought to be

reasonable and so his claim acquires force when he adds that we determine what is reasonable by reference to our roles.

63. Cf. 3.22.6–7, where Epictetus puts these roles metaphorically: "You are a calf; when the lion appears, do what is expected of you, . . . *You* are a bull; come on and fight, for this is expected of you, it befits [*prepei*] you, and you are able to do it." In chapter 6, I analyze the role-bound examples of *Discourses* 1.2 at length.

64. Oldfather 1928: "Referring to the scourging of Spartan youths before the altar of Artemis" (vol. 1, 17).

65. Alternatively, I think Epictetus could fill out this distinction as one between "what appears" versus "what is" or between philosophical arguments versus rhetorical arguments, a distinction that has a long history in Greek thought (e.g., Plato's *Gorgias*). However, I have resisted those ways of distinguishing *to eulogon* and *to akolouthon* because they are usually made with the aim of downgrading perception or rhetoric, but I find no evidence that Epictetus downgrades what would be the sensible or rhetorical half, namely, *to eulogon*.

Chapter Four

Education and the Good of Epictetean Roles

We have thus far located Epictetus's account of appropriate action. Nonetheless, we have yet to discover whether Epictetus adopts the Stoic distinction between perfect and imperfect appropriate action, that is, between the virtuous action of sages and those who are not sages. Interestingly, the subject of perfect appropriate acts is one that has sparked some discussion in the literature on Epictetus. Based on the scholarly literature in the field, it would seem that the distinction between perfect and intermediate action is either not present in Epictetus or that Epictetus manages the distinction haphazarD.L.y.[1] The question is whether or not Epictetus believes that the appropriate acts of the non-wise are good.

In the chapter ahead, I shall argue that Epictetus does indeed accept that there are perfect appropriate acts; moreover, I shall argue for the radical claim that Epictetus does not deny goodness to intermediate appropriate acts. My case will rest on Epictetus's own three-part educational plan for teaching students to do what is appropriate, a plan that puts roles and appropriate acts together at its center. I shall examine what reasons Epictetus gives for why he has structured the topics of education as he has in order to show how each topic lays the foundation for the next topic. While scholarship has accurately pinpointed aspects of this process, the complete picture has not been given. As I will show, students of Epictetus's program begin with a study of desire and aversion in the first topic, then they move on to a study of roles and their appropriate acts in the second topic, and—if they are fortunate—solidify their correct beliefs with a study of logic in the third topic. Epictetus believes that, through the mastery of Stoic logic, trainees can achieve a state of unshakeable certainty (2.17.33), a state equivalent to the "right reason" (*orthos logos*; *SVF* 3.500) or complete wisdom (Cicero, *De Off.* 3.13) that signifies the Stoic sage.

While it initially appears that Epictetus either has no account or has an ambiguous account of perfect appropriate action (the kind of action performed by the Stoic sage), I shall argue that we find his account squarely in his treatment of the purpose of the third stage of study. And yet, Epictetus declares that we may study the third topic only after we have become fine and good (*kaloi k'agathoi*) at the end of the second topic. Because Epictetus has structured his topic sequentially, Epictetus thus implies that the mastery of logic is not a condition for being a good person; it is possible to be good on the basis of correct belief (*ortha dogmata*). In this way, I will be arguing that Epictetus's outline of topics for education is not merely a useful pedagogy; rather, when taken as a whole, they represent an unorthodox reengineering and reevaluation of progress towards virtue in Stoicism. His outline of topics both downplays Stoic sages—relegating them to a kind of appendix—while holding that mere correct beliefs are sufficient to make students fine and good (*kaloi k'agathoi*). Virtue is not the exclusive domain of the Stoic sage.[2]

THE *TOPOI* AS THREE SUCCESSIVE STAGES OF EDUCATION: *DISCOURSES* 2.17.29–34

At several places in the *Discourses* and the *Encheiridion*, Epictetus divides education into three topics (*topoi*): (1) desire and aversion; (2) appropriate action (*to kathêkon*) and roles; (3) logic and assent.[3] Epictetus best illustrates the threefold sequence of the topics in 2.17.29–34 where he wistfully imagines an encounter with an ideal student who has come to study with the right aims in mind. Upon entering the school, this young pupil says to Epictetus: "I for my part yield up all the rest: it suffices me, if I become able to pass my life free from hindrance and distress, and to hold up my head in the face of events like a free man, and to look up to heaven as the friend of god, fearing nothing that can happen" (2.17.29). Epictetus indicates his approval of this student by grandiloquently declaring that this young man is "destined to be an ornament to philosophy" (2.17.30). After an enthusiastic reception by Epictetus, the student is ushered into a three-part course of study, a course which is clearly Epictetus's own educational program (cf. 3.2.1–6).[4]

In the 2.17 account of the *topoi*, Epictetus hurries past the details of the first topic, telling us that his ideal student wanted to study it in order "to be free of passion and perturbation" (2.17.31; cf. 2.17.14 and 29). Nonetheless, this stated goal for the first topic helps to explain what is said elsewhere about the subject of the first topic. According to Epictetus, the first topic concerns "desires and aversions, so that that he [*viz.*, the student] may neither fail to get what he desires nor fall into what he would avoid" (3.2.2; cf. 1.4.11 and 3.12.13). The first field of study teaches us what to desire and what to cast away by teaching us what is under our control and what is not under our control. For Epictetus and the Stoics, desire and aversion is an important subject because "the origin of distress is wishing for something that does not come about" (1.27.10; cf. 1.17.23–28 and 3.2.3). This field is "the principal, and most urgent" topic (3.2.3) not only because it makes us untroubled but because fierce passions make us "incapable of listening to reason" (ibid.; cf. 1.4.12).

On the basis of this brief characterization of the first topic, it seems clear that it is not concerned with Stoic physics (as some have claimed).[5] Rather, it is concerned with a very traditional subject in Stoic ethics, namely, the ethics of desire and the indifference of external things. Moreover, we can see that Epictetus is preparing his students to perform appropriate acts (as studied in the second topic). According to Epictetus, we cannot perform appropriate acts unless we seek only what is under our control (1.22.9–16; cf. 2.22.20 and 3.3.5–10). If we fail to distinguish between what is and is not under our control, or if we assign goodness to what is not under our control, we will desire what is external; we will therefore sow the seeds of theft and war and no longer be able to perform "what is appropriate towards Zeus" (1.22.15; cf. 2.8.28–29, 2.17.23–26, and 3.22.42–44). In much the same way, he argues that if we spend our time lamenting or avoiding what is inevitable (e.g., death), we will neglect our appropriate acts (1.27.7–14 and 2.7.1–2). As he concisely puts it, "if . . . it is your appropriate action to go, [then] go, and put up with what happens. . . ." (*Ench.* 33.13). This basic connection between appropriate actions (*kathêkonta*) and what is under our control suggests that, for Epictetus, appropriate actions are the proper actualization of our capacity for volition (*prohairesis*) itself, the core of what is under our control. As a result, it seems that the subject of the first topic is therapeutic and clears the ground for us to do all our appropriate acts as studied in the second topic.

After Epictetus's imaginary student has "labored at this first area of study and thoroughly mastered it" (2.17.31), he is led on to the second field of study. The idealized student says that he aims in this study "to know what is appropriate [*kathêkon*] for me to the gods, to my parents, to my brothers, to my country, and to strangers" (2.17.31). Epictetus justifies the fact that the second topic concerns appropriate acts in the following way: "The second [topic] has to do with appropriate action; for I should not be unfeeling like a statue[6] but should preserve my natural and acquired relations as a man who honors the gods, as a son, as a brother, as a father, as a citizen" (3.2.4). While the first topic disengages us from preferred externals, the second topic re-engages us with the world by summoning us to our roles, that is, with "rendering to my relationships their due" (4.10.13).[7] As a result of the second topic, an agent acts "in an orderly manner, reasonably, and not carelessly" (3.2.2; cf. 1.4.11 and 3.12.13).[8]

What is striking about this second topic is the fact that Epictetus intertwines two subjects here, appropriate action and roles (including our relations [*scheseis*]) such as son or citizen. Epictetus's inclusion of roles is important because he is breaking new ground with his account of roles. As we have seen in earlier chapters, Epictetus holds that roles and good action are intimately connected because he believes that we perform appropriate actions by fulfilling our roles in life (see *Discourses* 1.2 and 2.10). Moreover, he goes so far as to say the we must even refer to our own roles in order to determine what is reasonable and unreasonable as well as what is good and bad (1.2.5–7). It is not simply that we must do what is appropriate; it is that we cannot even know what is appropriate without looking to our own roles. Thus, the second topic is not simply a reiteration of Stoic ethics; it is a special course of study that connects good action to the concept of a person as a role-bound agent.

In addition, when Epictetus connects roles and appropriate actions (*kathêkonta*), he clarifies another way in which the first topic paves the way for the appropriate actions studied in the second topic. Epictetus believes that we must have the right attitude towards preferred externals (an object of study in the first topic) in order to do what is appropriate to others (3.3.5–10).[9] In Epictetus's view, our relations are put in jeopardy when we value preferred externals because the origin of conflict between individuals is a battle over preferred externals.[10] To establish that point, Epictetus considers the case of a son who is in conflict with his father and with his brother. In this scenario, the son complains that his father is stealing his money and that his brother will receive a larger share of the family farm (3.3.9). Epictetus reminds the son that there is no injury in the theft because it cannot harm his capacity for good action (3.3.9–10). Epictetus admonishes the son that his dispute arises over a matter of preferred externals, over what is not under his control. To end the conflict, Epictetus urges the son to let go of preferred externals; let the father and brother take what they want (3.3.9). If we extrapolate from this episode, it seems apparent that, according to Epictetus, we fight with our associates over matters like wealth, space, and even the attention or approval of a third party—all matters that Epictetus would classify as preferred externals (3.3.5–10 and 1.27.7–14). On these grounds, when 3.3.5–10 stresses that the right attitude to preferables (the subject of the first topic) makes possible the right relation to others (the second topic), it makes the first topic a prologue to the second topic.[11]

After studying the second topic, Epictetus's imaginary student declares his intention to master his own judgments against error, even error in drunkenness. At this moment, Epictetus's tale of the ideal student reaches its penultimate moment and he replies with a measure of irony *and* approval:

"You are a god, man; how great are your designs!" (2.17.33).[12] To realize this ambitious plan, the student will have to be initiated into the third and final topic, which "falls to those who are already making progress and is concerned with the achievement of certainty [*asphaleian*] in the matters already covered [*viz.*, the second topic], so that even in dreams, or drunkenness, or melancholy no untested impression may catch us off guard" (3.2.5; cf. 2.17.33 and 4.10.13). We pursue this subject when we are already "fine and good [*kalon kai agathon*]" (3.2.7; cf. 4.10.13). The third topic "has to do with assent and what is plausible and attractive" (3.12.14; cf. 1.4.11, 2.17.15, and 3.2.2). In general, this field of study teaches us to examine our impressions (3.12.14–15); in particular, this field teaches Stoic logic, a subject which "derives conclusions by questioning, [which studies] hypothetical premises, [and which examines fallacies like] *The Liar*" (3.2.6; cf. 2.17.34). Study in the third topic helps trainees attain "freedom from deception and hasty judgment" (3.2.2) so that they "may not be liable to be deceived" (1.4.11).

Epictetus's third topic appears merely to duplicate the field of logic, especially as it is studied by the Stoics. However, while the substance of the third topic is logic, part of the function of the third topic is the perfection of the practical reasoning in the second topic (*kathêkonta*). Because Epictetus treats appropriate acts as one of the key applications of logic, he thus makes the second topic the subject matter of the third.[13] To this latter claim about the third topic, we now turn.

THE THIRD *TOPOS* AND THE ROLE OF LOGIC IN BECOMING A SAGE

To complete my analysis of Epictetus's educational plan in the *topoi*, I will defend my structural claim about the relationship between the second and third topic as well as my claim that the third topic is part of Epictetus's plan for ethical training. My claim about the function of logic in the third topic is best brought out by supplementing the preceding analysis of 2.17 with a brief analysis of *Discourses* 1.7. *Discourses* 1.7 purports to discuss "the use of arguments resting on equivocations, and hypothetical arguments, and the like" (1.7.title) and it is commonly studied for what it reveals about the technical details of Stoic logic.[14] I shall focus on the opening section of *Discourses* 1.7 which attempts to situate the technical subjects of logic in the curriculum and on how it bears on the setup and resolution of Epictetus's tale of the imaginary student's journey through the three *topoi* in 2.17.

Epictetus begins *Discourses* 1.7 by declaring that "it escapes most people" that the hanD.L.ing of many kinds of arguments "concerns appropriate action" (1.7.1–2; cf. 3.2.5). In turn, Epictetus justifies this controversial claim by forcefully reminding us that "what we seek in every matter is how the fine and good man [*kalos kai agathos*] may find the path he should follow and the appropriate [*kathêkousan*] way he should behave with regard to it" (1.7.2; cf. 1.17.13–19). The man who does what is appropriate either ought to avoid arguments altogether or he ought to be able to navigate the give and take of arguments (1.7.2-4; cf. 11–12).

Although Epictetus's initial claim that logic concerns appropriate action suggests that logic *applies* to appropriate acts, he is ambiguous in his follow-up claim that we ought to find the appropriate way concerning it. He could either mean that we ought to find the appropriate way in every action (by means of logic) or in every matter (including the subject of logic). Epictetus may be vague here because he is thinking of *both* options so that logic discovers the right course of action *and* our course through logic is itself a matter of right action.[15] The fact that both options are likely emerges from the defense he goes on to give of these opening claims. In support of his opening assertions, Epictetus engages his students in a debate and, while using a bit of Socratic-style *elenchus*, he forces his listeners to admit that logic is incomplete unless it can be applied to circumstances and action (1.7.5–10). Epictetus begins his *elenchus* with a question: what does logic claim it can do (1.7.5)? Without missing a beat, one of his nameless students supplies an answer, "to establish what is true, to reject what is false, and to suspend judgment in doubtful cases" (ibid.). But, demands Epictetus, "Is this enough . . . ?" (ibid.). The student assures his teacher that it is; Epictetus does not object. Instead, like Socrates, he turns to a craft-analogy to examine the consequences of the student's affirmation. Is it sufficient, asks Epictetus, for a money-changer to know that he must not accept any counterfeit coins (1.7.6)? Surely not, the student says; the money-changer must also be able to tell what is counterfeit and what is not (1.7.7).

Through the money-changer example, Epictetus implies that logic is not merely about truth in our claims. The money-changer needs to be able to do more than know what statements follow from the maxim to reject counterfeit coins; he must know the *facts* of the world relating to his maxim, namely, that an excessively light coin must have some impurities, that pure brass tarnishes quickly, and so forth. At the very least, this means that logic concerns claims and facts. In addition, as Epictetus states it, just as with the money-changer example so "in *logos* also, mere speech is not enough" (1.7.8). It is not sufficient to know what spoken claims are necessary, we must also more generally "learn how such a thing follows [*akolouthon*] from certain other things, and how sometimes it follows from one single thing, and sometimes from several together" (1.7.10). Students of logic must study what follows (*to akolouthon*) where "what follows" can be the conclusion that follows from a premise or it can be the action that follows from some circumstance (cf. 1.26.1–2).

Given that "what follows" in speech is not enough, it seems that the student of logic must also learn what facts relate to a claim as well as what actions follow upon a claim. For example, a doctor knows that light meats are good for sick patients.[16] If doctors employ logic as Epictetus prescribes, they easily infer that heavy meats are bad for patients but they must also learn what sorts of meat are light as well as what patients count as sick. They must likewise know that, as doctors, it follows that they must perform the action of prescribing light meats such as chicken to a patient suffering from a high fever. Students of logic must learn to infer every type of consequent. And, it seems, they study logic in order to derive claims and actions with perfection; while Epictetus seems to think that most of us can do that reasonably well without formal training in logic, he also seems to think that we must master logic in order to learn how to infer claims and actions with perfection and certainty.

Beyond its purely logical content, the remainder of *Discourses* 1.7 exemplifies how logic concerns appropriate acts. Epictetus proceeds to analyze two sorts of faulty arguments, showing how good people will need to see through false practical reasoning in each type. In the case of equivocal premises (1.7.13–21), he discusses an argument about debts (one reminiscent of Strepsiades's arguments in Aristophanes's *Clouds*) and reminds us that we need to see through the fallacy in order that "we may not behave inappropriately, or randomly, or confuseD.L.y" (1.7.21). In the case of hypothetical arguments (1.7.22–29), he outlines the sorts of difficult questions these arguments raise in order to demonstrate how carefully we must manage them if we want to avoid behaving "casually and randomly" (1.7.27). The discourse ends by explaining that mistakes in logic and in ethics are equivalent because both involve the manner in which we use "the impressions presented to our minds" (1.7.33).

Aside from *Discourses* 1.7, Epictetus elsewhere affirms the ethical purpose of logic when he criticizes those who treat logic as an end-in-itself that can be studied in isolation of other fields. He confirms that the third topic needs the second (and the first) topic with the very way he sets up and resolves his tale about the ideal student and the three *topoi* in the 2.17 account examined earlier. First, just before starting his tale of the ideal student, Epictetus criticizes some of his students for thinking that they are educated (2.17.26–28). As he contemptuously asks, "What kind of education, man? The fact that you have studied syllogisms and arguments with equivocal premises? Will you not consent to unlearn all this, if at all possible, and make a fresh start, in the realization that hitherto you have not even touched on the principal matter?" (2.17.27). Instead, he says, students must begin their education by studying what is and is not under their control (2.17.27–28), a subject that we identified as under the first topic.

Second, Epictetus begins his tale of the ideal student, as we saw, by having the student declare "I for my part yield up all the rest: it suffices me, if I become able to pass my life free from hindrance and distress" (2.17.29). This declaration signals the importance of practical (i.e., ethical) matters. By giving up "all the rest," it appears that the student not only lets go of externals, but he even lets go of knowing other subjects as ends-in-themselves. The meaning of this farewell becomes especially apparent in view of *Discourses* 4.4 which addresses those who seek tranquility (just as the ideal student here). In 4.4, Epictetus criticizes students who focus on reading treatises or listening to lectures instead of attending to the practice of virtue. "If we read a treatise *On Impulse*," he says, we should do so "not in order to see what is said about impulse but so that we can direct our own impulses well" (4.4.16; cf. 1.4.13–17 and 1.29.35–36). Applied to logic, Epictetus's claim means that students should be satisfied with logic in so far as it provides them with tranquility, that is, in so far as it serves the aims of ethics.

Finally, after excitedly narrating the ideal student's journey through the three fields of study, Epictetus's *Discourses* 2.17 tale ends with an indictment of his students and, indeed, of philosophy as it is often practiced. "But no," says Epictetus as he shatters the image of the ideal student, this is not how it goes, "instead someone [enters my school and] says, 'I want to know what Chrysippus means in his work on [the logical puzzle called] *The Liar*.' If that is your design, go hang yourself, you wretch!" (2.17.34). As Epictetus elsewhere complains, "present philosophers, while neglecting the first topic and the second, busy themselves with the third" (3.2.6; cf. 2.23.46 and *Ench.* 52).

This plot twist at the end of his tale affirms that we have good reasons for thinking that even the third topic has an ethical aim, thus forming the third part of what amounts to a plan for ethical education. Not only did Epictetus unfold his 2.17 account as a series of stages in a student's ethical training, but our above reconstruction shows that Epictetus has reasons for structuring the topics as he has. Before we can accomplish anything else, we must master our passions; hence, the first topic. Once we have silenced our passions enough that we can heed our own reason, we must immediately seek to become virtuous; that is, we should take up our roles in life and do what is appropriate; hence, the second topic. Finally, if we have made progress and we can afford the time to study, we should perfect our understanding (especially of ethical action) through the study of logic; hence the third topic.

PERFECT VERSUS INTERMEDIATE APPROPRIATE ACTS IN THE *TOPOI*

Having established a sequential structure to the *topoi*, we can now address the question of whether or not Epictetus distinguishes between the perfect ethical action of sages and the so-called intermediate appropriate action of those who are not sages; we can also consider whether or not he believes that the appropriate acts of the non-wise are good. In the previous chapter, we saw that, according to standard Stoic thinking, intermediate actions are performed on the basis of a "reasonable [*eulogon*] justification [*apologian*]" (L&S 59B). They are performed by those who are "making progress" but who are not sages and therefore who are not yet truly good (L&S 59F). By contrast, only the sage can perform perfect appropriate actions (*katorthômata*). Perfect appropriate acts are described by the Stoics in a variety of ways (such as "to do X virtuously"),[17] but they agree that, at root, perfect appropriate acts are done on the basis of correct reason (*orthos logos*).[18] In this way, says Cicero, intermediate appropriate acts can be performed by those who are not wise (*De Fin.* 4.15), whereas right action (*katorthôma*) can only be performed by the wise (ibid.) because their wisdom is complete (*De Off.* 3.13).

In the section ahead, I will argue that Epictetus's *topoi* contain his position about intermediate and perfect appropriate action. I shall argue that Epictetus discusses perfect appropriate acts (*katorthômata*) without directly naming them when he discusses the elements associated with the virtuous action of sages. At the same time, I will lay the groundwork for my radical claim that Epictetus implies that goodness can be attributed to non-sages, to those who are making progress. I will show that Epictetus identifies correct reason (*orthos logos*) with the perfection of God and with the aim of a philosopher's training. I will demonstrate that Epictetus uses the verb "to act correctly" (*katorthoun*, from whence we get *katorthômata* or perfect appropriate action) to describe virtuous action that accords with correct or true reason. In both cases, Epictetus will leave open the possibility that good action is possible even without correct reason; and, I will argue that Epictetus holds the heterodox claim that good action is possible on the basis of correct judgments (*ortha dogmata*), judgments that are proper but less firm than correct reason. Finally, I will establish that Epictetus intends the third *topos* as a course of training for producing the correct reason of the sage. Once we have located the sage in the third topic, we will be in a position to evaluate Epictetus's striking claim that students may not enter the third topic until they are "fine and good [*kalon kai agathon*]" (3.2.7). In this way, Epictetus will confirm our suspicion that he does not limit virtuous action to the correct reason of the sage.

Let us begin the evidence with the Stoic concept of "correct reason" (*orthos logos*). The expression *orthos logos* makes two brief and somewhat vague appearances in Epictetus, but the appearances are at least consistent with Stoic usage. In the beginning of *Discourses* 2.8, Epictetus considers what the being (*ousia*) of the good (*agathon*) is and he says that it must be found in the being of God (2.8.1–2). "What, then," he asks, "is the being [*ousia*] of God. . . . It is intelligence [*nous*], knowledge [*epistêmê*], right reason [*logos orthos*]" (2.8.2–3). Epictetus here sets up God as a model of goodness (*agathon*) and connects this goodness with correct reason (*orthos logos*). Throughout *Discourses* 2.8, Epictetus lectures his students on the fact that we share in God's nature even though so many of us fail to act as though we share in the divine. At the end of this discourse, Epictetus summarizes what it means to live and die in a god-like fashion, a summary that strikingly parallels the content of the three *topoi*: We must have "Desire that never fails in its achievement; aversion that never meets with what it would avoid [*topos* 1]; appropriate impulse; carefully considered volition [*topos* 2]; and an assent that is never precipitate [*topos* 3]" (2.8.29). Epictetus's summary tells us that we ourselves can emulate God's features (intelligence, knowledge, and correct reason) if we master the three *topoi*. Indeed, as we saw Epictetus declare to the student who wished to master the third and final subject of study: "You are a god, man!" (2.17.33). Although Epictetus's summary does not explicitly say that correct reason is what makes an appropriate act perfect, it does connect right reason with God (a perfect intellect) and it holds that emulation of God includes appropriate acts.

In the second instance of correct reason (*orthos logos*), Epictetus is again vague, but nothing in his use contradicts the Stoic use. He appears to invoke the term to explain the end (*telos*) of a philosopher: "to keep one's reason right [*to orthon echein ton logon*]" (4.8.12). Certainly, we would expect a philosopher to seek the Stoic ideal of an *orthos logos* and, not surprisingly, Epictetus is telling philosophers that their job is to make right (*orthos*) their own reason (*ton logon*). But, what is missing from the reference at 4.8.12 and its surrounding context is any account of what this would mean for the philosopher's appropriate acts. If philosophers succeeded in making their reason right, would perfect proper action follow? In other words, is "right reason" here invoked in a diluted sense or in the full-strength sense held by the Stoics? Epictetus does not answer here, but his discussion of correcting or perfecting our actions suggests that he would answer in the affirmative.

Beyond the concept of right reason, Epictetus signals an awareness and partial acceptance of perfect appropriate acts (*katorthôma*) through his use of the verb *katorthoun* (to act correctly), the root behind the technical term *katorthôma*.[19] Certainly, this verb can be used in a non-technical sense. But, among Epictetus's uses,[20] there are two cases where he speaks of a correct (*orthos*) or true (*alêthês*) cognitive state that entails correct action (*kator-*

thoun) and necessarily produces what is good. This claim is reflective of standard Stoic claims. Nonetheless, Epictetus also seems to alter the Stoic position because neither passage privileges correct reason (*orthos logos*) as the sole basis of good action.

In the first passage on correct action (*to katorthoun*), Epictetus is debating with a student who believes we merely need to master the words of Chrysippus without studying the substance of logic:

> What, then, is the admirable thing [in learning Chrysippus]? "To understand the will of nature." Well, then, do you understand it on your own account? In that case, what need have you for any one else? For, if it be true, that all men who err do so involuntarily, and you have learned the truth, you must of necessity be acting correctly [*katorthoun*] already. "But, by Zeus, I do not understand the will of nature." (1.17.14–15)

Epictetus concludes that we need to learn to discern things for ourselves (1.17.16–19). This passages connects truth (*alêtheia*) and correctness (*katorthoun*). Because "the truth" here picks out a true cognitive state, it appears to do the same work as right reason in the orthodox conception of perfect appropriate acts. That is, Epictetus is saying that a right epistemic state necessarily leads to right action.[21] Nonetheless, the passage does not say that *only* a knowledge of the truth will yield correct action nor does it limit knowledge of the truth to the sage. This omission tacitly permits reasonable (*eulogon*) opinions as a possible ground for correct action.[22] In sum, the 1.17 passage says that right reason perfects action, but it does not preclude reasonable account (*to eulogon*) from producing correct action.

In the second passage on correct action (*to katorthoun*), Epictetus is discoursing about various capacities like the power to speak and he considers which power is most important:

> But if you ask me what is the most excellent of things, what am I to say? The faculty of eloquence? I cannot. But rather that of volition, whenever it becomes right [*orthê*] volition. For it is volition that makes use of the faculty of eloquence and all the other faculties, both great and small. If this be set right [*katorthôthentos*], a man becomes good; if it goes wrong, a man becomes bad. It is through this that we are unfortunate or fortunate; that we disapprove or approve one another. In a word, it is this that produces unhappiness when neglected, and, when properly tended, happiness. (2.23.27–29)

This passage is more promising for locating perfect appropriate acts because it more clearly connects what is correct (*orthos*) with being good and such a use is consistent with the Stoic use. Moreover, Epictetus elsewhere connects the correction of *prohairesis* with the correction of opinions or beliefs (*dogmata*): "The essence [*ousia*] of the good [*agathou*] is a certain disposition of our volition [*prohairesis*], and the essence of evil likewise. . . . For its opinions [*dogmata*] about material things, if they are correct [*ortha*], make our volition [*prohairesin*] good [*agathon*], and if they are distorted and perverse, make it bad" (1.29.1 and 3; cf. 3.9.3–5 and 4.8.3). This passage says that correct belief or opinion, like correct reason (*orthos logos*), will generate good action.

Although the foregoing passages are not conclusive, they suggest that Epictetus would accept the claim that right reason (*orthos logos*) must yield virtuous action. However, Epictetus has not said that good action requires right reason (*orthos logos*). Because he seems to emphasize epistemic correctness generally rather than correct reason in particular, he appears to widen the sphere—beyond the narrow confines of orthodox Stoicism—of what states can produce good action.[23]

Interestingly, Epictetus seems to capture that wider epistemic state with the phrase "correct judgments" (*ortha dogmata*), as found in 1.29.1–3. While correct judgments would initially appear to be co-extensive with right reason (*orthos logos*), the two phrases are not identical. According to the Stoics, right reason (*orthos logos*) is held only by the wise and the wise hold their judgments "securely [*asphalôs*] and firmly [*bebaiôs*]" (L&S 41G); thus, right reason is unchangeable. By contrast, Epictetus treats correct judgments (*ortha dogmata*) as changeable and not necessarily firm. As he says, "These are the ways in which human beings are undone . . . when their correct judgments [*ta dogmata ta ortha*] are demolished, when these are destroyed" (1.28.25; cf. 4.6.24). Nonetheless, a correct judgment can produce good action (1.29.1–3; see above); in this sense it can act like right reason. And yet, it can be overturned by volition (*prohairesis*) itself.[24] Epictetus's use of the concept of a correct judgment (*orthon dogma*) appears flexible enough to accommodate both what is truly good in the Stoic sense and what is insecure.[25]

In addition, Epictetus seems to characterize correct judgments (*ortha dogmata*) not as much by an epistemic state but by a state of character, a condition created by the repeated use of one's volition (*prohairesis*). Hence, correct judgments are "the things that one ought to practice[26] all day long . . ." (2.16.27); we need to "exercise" ourselves like "the true athlete" (2.18.27; cf. 2.9.13–14 and fr. 16).[27] The need for practice makes sense when we consider what Epictetus thinks these judgments consist of: they do not concern a complicated body of knowledge; rather, they consist of basic doctrines about what is and is not under our control (as studied in the first topic).[28] Our relationship to such knowledge is much like the relation that young musicians have to music they have recently learned: they know the notes of a song, but they will perform it haltingly until practice makes it a habit (cf. 2.9.10f.).[29] At the same time, if they do not practice a song, they will forget it, just as students lose their school notes when their wax tablets melt in the sun (3.16.9–16). Hence, to arrive at these correct judgments, we do not need perfect knowledge, we need steadfast *exercise* (2.18.27–32).[30] Thus, when Epictetus speaks of correcting our volition (*prohairesis*) and our judgments (*dogmata*), he means our ongoing effort to choose to abide only by that which is under our control (2.23.40 and 3.5.2). As with the previous passage, Epictetus commits to a formal truism: when your volition is corrected, you will be good. But, he does not limit this correct state to right reason (*orthos logos*) or to the sage.

Since Epictetus apparently connects goodness to the wider concept of correct judgment (which can be held by ordinary individuals; 1.29.1–3) rather than to the narrow concept of right reason (possessed only by the sage), he thereby widens the scope of virtue to include the non-wise. Insofar as ordinary individuals have arrived at a correct judgment, their actions are good. In other words, it seems that individuals can arrive at a virtuous action either proceeding from the sage's right reason (*orthos logos*) or by means of a habituated appeal to correct judgment (*orthon dogma*).

If it is true, then, that Epictetus distinguishes between a correct judgment and correct reason, where is the latter, more perfect state to be realized? Here, we can now summon the work of the previous section on the *topoi*. Epictetus appears to account for a higher epistemic state in the third topic because he implies that the third topic is about correcting and perfecting our judgments. In the story of the imaginary, ideal student we saw earlier, the pupil states his lofty aim, an aim which Epictetus says would be fulfilled by the third topic: "I would like to be secure [*asphalôs*] and unshaken [*aseistôs*], not only while awake, but even when asleep, and drunk, and depressed" (2.17.33). Although the student's comments might appear exaggerated, Epictetus himself employs the very same language elsewhere, thus affirming that the third topic concerns the security of judgment under all conditions (3.2.5 and 4.10.13).[31] What is striking about this description is the fact that it is almost identical to Stobaeus's claim that the judgments of the Stoic sage (which arise from an *orthos logos*) are held "securely [*asphalôs*] and firmly [*bebaiôs*]" (L&S, 41G). Epictetus's claim differs only in that *bebaiôs* is replaced by the synonym *aseistôs*. Besides the terms shared by these two characterizations of unshakeable judgment (*viz*., *asphalôs*), it seems clear that the student is aiming for the perfect epistemic state of a sage because he wishes security even in altered states like drunkenness; that is, he seeks a security that cannot be torn down. So, while the content of the third topic is logic, its aim is the security or certainty (*asphaleia*) of the first two *topoi* (3.2.5). These are good grounds for concluding that the third topic aims at right reason (*orthos logos*) and that Epictetus's ideal student seeks to have the correct reason of a Stoic sage.

Moreover, Epictetus appears to follow the Stoic position in holding that the possession of correct reason is rare, even if he does not make it quite as rare as the phoenix (L&S 61N). This again emerges in his tale of the imaginary ideal student. Given Epictetus's excitement at the idea of a student who is ready for the final field of study, it would seem that not many do reach the third topic (2.17.33). As he says elsewhere, "I should like . . . to perfect [*epanorthoun*] the faculty that deals with impressions . . . and, if I am so fortunate, to advance to the third field of study, that which deals with the attainment of secure [*asphaleian*] judgments" (4.10.13). By calling the third topic a matter of good fortune, Epictetus underscores how rare it is for anyone to be fit for undertaking its study. Thus, when Epictetus's imaginary student announces that he intends to enter the third field of study and Epictetus replies "You are a god, man!" (2.17.33), Epictetus shows both his enthusiasm for the nobility of the quest and his understanding of how uniquely difficult it is.[32]

Notwithstanding the place made for correct reason, Epictetus downplays the importance of its status because, as we have seen, he seems to allow the non-wise to become good. While he follows the Stoic orthodoxy in saying that the "third topic falls to those who are already making progress" (3.2.5), he also subverts the orthodoxy when he says that we may enter the third topic only *after* we are "fine and good [*kalon kai agathon*]" (3.2.7). This epithet is significant because, as Stobaeus says, the Stoics say that "every fine and good [*kalon kai agathon*] man is complete [*teleion*] because he is lacking in no virtue."[33] Epictetus's *topoi* put the study of action before the study of logic and he criticizes those who would do otherwise. In standard Stoicism, progress belongs to those who strive for the good but have not yet undergone the transition into wisdom and goodness.[34] For Epictetus, it appears that "making progress" is relegated primarily to the mastery of desire and aversion (see 1.4) as in the first *topos*, but being fine and good can apply to those who fulfill their roles as in the second *topos*—even though they lack invincible perfection. Accordingly, while the third topic may indeed help to perfect our judgments, it is not clear that this perfection improves our ethical standing any further. Contrary to standard Stoicism, Epictetus seems to content himself with our ordinary understanding by counting on the second topic to make us good.[35] Given Epictetus's claim elsewhere that the good is in our volition (*prohairesis*, 1.19.1–3), he is telling us that the second *topos* makes us good because it teaches us to assent to the following maxim: "Therefore, the fine and good man—remembering who he is, where he came from, and by whom he was created—attends to this sole thing: how he may fulfill his place [*chôran*][36] in a manner that is orderly and obedient to God" (3.24.95).

THE STOIC WISE MAN IN EPICTETUS: *QUO VADIS*?

Given the preceding chapter, we can now globally assess what Epictetus has done in relation to the Stoic position. Epictetus tries both to accommodate standard Stoicism and to include the goodness of non-sages. Instead of an outright revision of Stoic ethics, Epictetus's approach has been to supplement it. He does not strike down the Stoic claim that perfect appropriate acts arise from correct reason. Rather, he retains their interest in perfection and places it in the third topic. But, he does not pin the struggle to become good exclusively on reaching that final field of study and its nearly impossible ideal of perfect knowledge. Instead, he pins goodness on correct judgment and on the challenging (but possible) aim of realizing our roles, the subject of the second—and central—topic.[37]

In addition, not only does Epictetus downplay the sage, he provides that elite figure with very little coverage.[38] Instead, as we saw in chapter 2, Epictetus gives repeated attention to the roles of extraordinary individuals: the elite senator, the philosopher, the Olympic athlete, and so on.[39] If Epictetus does not deny the sage, he has, in a sense, replaced that figure. Epictetus seems to change emphasis from the sage to the extraordinary individual, from emphasizing a perfect epistemic state to emphasizing how some individuals face challenging appropriate acts.

In this way, the Stoic sage does not, in fact, appear to be a role.[40] Indeed, sages *per se* are not suited to exemplify role-bound action. Instead, it turns out that extraordinary individuals, including even talented athletes, *are* well suited. As I argued in chapter 2, the "purple stripe in the white toga" is a specific role; and, while it applies only to select individuals, it is a much better counterpart to other specific roles because it exemplifies performing appropriate acts in accordance with a role. Extraordinary individuals take up their role as a kind of Archimedean point upon which there is no compromise and then they perform its difficult appropriate acts with expertise and finesse. Although extraordinary individuals perform appropriate acts different from those of ordinary individuals, this difference serves to motivate ordinary individuals with a kind of ethical ambition. Extraordinary individuals supply "stretch goals" for ordinary individuals and thus, as Epictetus says, they are "displayed as a fine example to the rest" (1.2.22).

Consider the case of an adult caring for an ailing parent, an action that Epictetus would surely regard as an appropriate act for an adult son. In the hard daily activities of care-giving, such a son may search for sources of inspiration. The more standard account of Stoicism provides the example of a sage, whose knowledge is perfect and who therefore perfectly exhibits justice, courage, wisdom, and moderation. Although such an example would apply, in form, to the son's activities, it is many logical steps removed from the specific role and appropriate act that he is performing. By contrast, the son may very well be comforted by the example of the athlete in Epictetus's *Discourses* 1.2 who chose death over medical castration in honor of his specific role as a kind of end-in-itself (1.2.25–28). As with many ordinary individuals, the son may believe that the example of extraordinary athletic excellence speaks to him.[41] While the son does not face the exact same alternative as the athlete, he does face unpleasant obligations (emptying bed pans) and it is realistic to think that he would be inspired by the case of an athlete whose role and circumstances demanded a painful death. It would be a quick leap from the athlete example to the conclusion "If he can do such a difficult act, then surely I can do something a bit easier such as care for my father" (cf. 1.24.1–2). Quite literally, then, the extraordinary individual is a role model.

In view of these results, I would like to end this chapter on a more speculative note and offer a hypothesis about what I think motivates Epictetus's ethical education as well as his innovations and his revisions of Stoicism. Although Epictetus's direct students appear to be philosophy students, it is clear that he addresses all manner of individuals, from the senator who could not bear his own grief at his daughter's sickness (1.11)[42] to a shoemaker debating about his career (*Ench.* 24.4), from the Olympic athlete and victor (1.2.26) to an apparently average Roman (2.14).[43] And, there is good reason within Stoicism for Epictetus to be interested in such individuals since Stoicism holds that, in principle, all human agents have a *logos* that qualifies them for being able to achieve genuine goodness.[44] However, because Stoicism asserts that only the sage has achieved ethical goodness, Stoicism does not have a good answer for why agents should bother performing non-sagely actions given that they lack goodness. When students come to the Stoics looking to become good, they are instead offered the mere hope of becoming good.

By contrast, Epictetus can tell students and visitors to his school that they will become good if they seek only that which they can control (the subject of the first topic) and if they perform the actions appropriate to their roles (the subject of the second topic). He does not require perfect knowledge for genuine goodness because he offers us a way to achieve that goodness which is immediately within our grasp: the study of our own roles. Unlike in Stoicism proper, it is not a matter of indifference for ordinary individuals to honor their parents, to care for their children, to aid their friends, and so on; it is a matter of goodness.[45] Epictetus appears to recognize that we cannot all be sages because, as he asks rhetorically, "do all horses become swift?" (1.2.34). And yet, Epictetus wishes to make sure that we are not defeated by the impossibility of being a sage. So, he says, "because I am not naturally gifted, shall I, on that account, put away my pursuit? Heaven forbid!" nor should we neglect "some other pursuit merely because we despair of arriving at the highest" (1.2.35 and 37). Epictetus has given us a reason not to give up our self-control because, even among the discipline of non-swift horses, we find goodness. Epictetus does not rely on the standard of the sage which amounts to an ideal that may never be made real. Instead, he relies on a standard of goodness that measures our ethical victories by what each person, whether slave or senator, can achieve.

NOTES

1. Long 2002, 112, appears to resist the idea that the *kathêkonta* of the non-wise constitute a secondary goodness; Long's resistance emerges in his opposition to Inwood, to whom he attributes the belief that the *kathêkonta* of the non-wise count as a kind of secondary goodness. Long also claims that "Epictetus never refers to this distinction [between perfect and intermediate *kathêkonta*], in keeping with his frequent reticence concerning ideal wisdom" (257). Kamtekar 1998 asserts that roles (which are studied in the second *topos*) can guide a Stoic trainee in how to act without having access to the perfect wisdom of a Stoic sage. She holds that we turn to roles when we cannot infer the will of nature and so she treats roles as a kind of second best way for calculating what is right (148–149). Bonhöffer 1996 addresses the issue at length, but he appears ambivalent. On the one hand, he accuses Epictetus of using the terms *kathêkon* (appropriate act) and *katorthôma* (perfect appropriate act) "indiscriminately" (199). He also says that the wise and the non-wise differ in the firmness of their judgment but not so much in "moral quality" (221), and so he rightly interprets Epictetus's doctrine as a softening of the rigid Stoic position. On the other hand, Bonhöffer wants Epictetus to preserve something of the standard position that only the Stoic sage can do good (212–216) by saying that the individual who is making progress (the *prokoptôn*) has "relative moral value" (227) or has "moral value only as a transitional stage" (220). Bonhöffer justifies the latter claim by comparing the *prokoptôn* to the converted sinner in Christianity who is saved and yet remains a sinner (218). Nonetheless, Bonhöffer seems to be aware that his reconstruction is problematic and he blames it on the sources (221–222). As will become evident in this chapter, I agree with the first half of Bonhöffer's view but not the second.

2. Long 2002, 32–33, and 37, agrees that Epictetus downplays the sage, but Long appears to regard that stance as mostly a matter of emphasis. I take my position to be pushing much further than Long because I am arguing that Epictetus downplays the sage by dethroning his exclusive goodness. Long notices that Epictetus makes references to the wise man with the term *phronimos* but he misses the sage's implicit yet critical presence in the final topic of education. Long also notes Epictetus's use of *kaloi k'agathoi* (fine and good) but misses its significance at the end of the second topic.

3. See *Discourses* 2.17.29–34, 3.2.1–6, 3.12.12–17, and *Encheiridion* 52. Partial but explicit references also occur at 17.7.4 and 21, 1.17.22–23, 2.17.15–18, 4.10.13, fragment 27 and possibly 4.2.1 and 4.12.14–18.

While these subjects are seemingly straightforward, scholarship has been divided on their meaning and significance. Concerning the topics, Oldfather 1928 dismisses them in his translation of Epictetus: "This triple division of philosophy . . . is the only original element which the minute studies of many investigators have found in Epictetus, and it is rather a pedagogical device for lucid presentation than an innovation in thought" (vol. 1, xxi). In much the same vein, Barnes 1997 more recently asserts that Epictetus's division of topics "seems little more than a convenient expository device. . . . And in general, he is ready enough—like other ancient philosophers—to use the word 'τόπος' for an area of thought without having any particular cartography in mind" (34–35).

Other scholars, see more substance in Epictetus's educational schema because they identify it with the Stoic division of philosophy into physics, ethics, and logic. Bonhöffer 1894 certainly takes this view (22–28 and 257–259). Hadot 1995, 191–195, argues that Epictetus's division of topics is a practical variation on the Stoic division of philosophy. Accordingly, Hadot connects Epictetus's second topic, which concerns appropriate action, with the practice of ethics while he connects Epictetus's third topic with the practice of Stoic logic. But, Hadot struggles on the first topic, which concerns desire and aversion, because it does not easily map onto Stoic physics. To effect that connection, Hadot suggests that we need a knowledge of physics in order to train our desires and our aversions. Thus, he says, "the discipline of desire does indeed seem to be a kind of applied physics, which one lives and experiences in the manner of a spiritual exercise" (194). Following Hadot, Long 2002 also holds that Epictetus's threefold division follows the Stoic division of philosophy (117–118). And, Long reaffirms that this division may very well be an original invention by Epictetus (112).

Because Bonhöffer, Hadot, and Long stress that Epictetus's division of education topics is a practical version of the divisions of philosophy, Hadot and Long answer the worry that Epictetus's education program is "little more than a convenient expository device" (Barnes 1997, 34). However, if we accept Bonhöffer, Hadot, and Long, we have answered the worry at several important costs: First, we seem to have forced a connection between Stoic physics and Epictetus's account of desire and aversion. This connection is less than ideal because the subject of Stoic physics covers a wide array of topics from cosmology to a theory of matter, topics that Epictetus rarely discusses, either by themselves or in connection to desire and aversion. Second, if we connect Epictetus's topics to the Stoic division of philosophy, we have undercut the very originality that has been attributed to Epictetus. On this view, Epictetus simply reiterates a standard Stoic division. For reservations similar to my first two, see Barnes 1997, 34; Dobbin 1998, 94; Asmis 2001, 393–394; Crivelli 2007, 21; Cooper 2007, 15. See also Inwood 1985, 290 note 46: "There is no reason to make Epictetus's topics match up with the traditional Stoic tripartite division of philosophy as a whole."

Third, we are forced to treat Epictetus's second topic as a mere reiteration of traditional Stoic ethics, namely, the study of appropriate action. By implication, this treatment inadvertently ascribes to Epictetus a concern for perfect ethical knowledge and it glosses over Epictetus's unique addition to the second topic: the study of roles. If Epictetus straightforwardly followed the Stoics, he would center his ethics on the Stoic sage, the individual with complete wisdom who also happens to be the only person who counts as truly good. And yet, the sage does not seem to be the center of Epictetus's *topoi* nor is the sage anywhere discussed in connection with the second topic.

Although the Bonhöffer, Hadot, and Long interpretation does not succeed in mapping Epictetus's division onto the canonical Stoic division, they are right to emphasize the practical dimensions of the division. Indeed, *pace* Oldfather and Barnes, it is this practical emphasis that has proved fruitful in the literature on Epictetus's *topoi*. One of the earliest advocates of this view is Hijmans 1959, 38–41 and 64–65. Hijmans takes the view that Epictetus's *topoi* represent the components of Epictetus's system for training. In turn, Hijmans's view has been developed by more recent scholars who highlight the *topoi* as a serial ordering of training subjects through which students make progress. Dobbin 1998 calls the *topoi* "three stages" (92) which appear to reflect Panaetius's "particular interest in training progressives" (94). This approach to the *topoi* has productively applied to specialized topics within Epictetus. Asmis 2001, 392–406, profitably uses the stages of the *topoi* to illuminate Epictetus's account of volition (*prohairesis*) by examining the successive stages through which agents train their *prohairesis*. Similarly, Cooper 2007 utilizes the *topoi* to elucidate Epictetus's account of the training of desire (15–19).

While I take this latter interpretation to be the right approach, it has some difficulty in making sense of the fact that Epictetus places logic last. For example, Barnes 1997, 62–70, holds that logic is the bedrock of all learning and therefore must be studied first. Dobbin defends Epictetus from any difficulty here by pleading that Epictetus's "three topics are structured for educational rather than theoretical ends, and in any case desire and avoidance, the first topic, serve rather a propaedeutic function in the whole programme" (93). In addition, the second topic contains its own oddity. The second *topos* is often treated as a reiteration of Stoic ethics, and Epictetus's inclusion of roles in the second topic is frequently glossed over (e.g., Hijmans 1959, 64–65, makes no reference to roles in his discussion of the second *topos*; similarly for Cooper 2007, 16–17). Nonetheless, the inclusion of roles is important because it signals that Epictetus sees the second *topos* as accomplishing something more or different than a canonical account of Stoic ethics. Finally, in another unorthodox move, Epictetus includes logic in the third topic. The ordering of the *topoi* thus inverts the teachings of Zeno of Citium and Chrysippus who put logic first and ethics last (D.L. 7.40; cf. L&S 26C). Just as the third *topos* is the closest analogue to the Stoic division of philosophy, so it is the piece that seems to belie the view that Epictetus is strictly proposing a serial division of ethical subjects. Not surprisingly, some scholars seem to share the intuition that the third *topos* does not quite fit. Hijmans 1959 says that the third topic "is to be treated as a *moralis philosophiae ancilla* only" (39). Dobbin 1998, 93–94, aptly suggests that the third *topos* is about securing belief but he still worries that Epictetus makes it the *last* subject as though logic is being demoted in importance.

4. In my discussion of the *topoi*, I am not addressing any question about precisely how Epictetus thinks the sequence of the *topoi* should be put into practice. In part, I do not think that question is pertinent to the point I am making, but, I also am not sure that the *Discourses* provide us with any answer. As far as anyone has been able to detect, the *Discourses* do not appear to have any structure at all. However, it is worth noting that my sequential reading is implicitly opposed by De Lacy 1977 and Barnes 1997, 62–70, who read Epictetus to say that logic is the bedrock of all learning and therefore must be studied first. Although I think the foregoing evidence is sufficient to support my sequential reading and I do not think that the *Discourses* provide us with a detailed teacher's manual, it nonetheless seems that the point made by De Lacy and Barnes is readily addressed. First, even if Epictetus requires some rudimentary understanding of logic, this requirement is no different than his practice in ethics where he counts on his students coming to his school with certain preconceptions that he can then dialectically sculpt to accord with Stoicism (1.2.6 and 1.22.9; cf. Hijmans 1959, 40–41). His goal, it seems, is to build on such ordinary preconceptions with Stoicism. Second, Epictetus may have treated the *topoi* as subjects of emphasis rather than rigid boundaries; thus, student training begins with a little discussion of logic (*topos* 3) and a great deal of discussion about desire (*topos* 1). Alternatively, Epictetus could hold that logic *is* indeed treated first because it is implicitly present in the manner in which he discusses *every* subject. He could hold that, just as children acquire some grammar from the way language is spoken to them, so students could acquire some principles of logic from the way subjects are analyzed for them. In this last alternative, the progression of Epictetus's *topoi* is circular—students successively circle back to analyze the same issues under the rubric of each of the *topoi*.

5. *Pace* Hadot 1995, 194.

6. For a discussion of this curious phrase, see Long 2002, 232. In brief, Long holds that Epictetus is advising us "not to be stony or impervious" in our relationships. Adding to Long's point, I would note that Epictetus may also intend the statue image to mock individuals who are inactive when it is important that, where our relations are concerned, we do not merely "stand there."

7. As Long 2002, 115, puts it, "these two fields draw distinctions between inner and outer, or oneself and other persons."

8. Epictetus also says that the second *topos* concerns "the impulse to act [*hormas*] and not to act [*aphormas*], and in general, appropriate acts [*kathêkon*]" (3.2.2; cf. 2.17.15). He appears to group impulses and appropriate acts together because, at root, impulses are inclinations to act (cf.1.18.1–2 and 3.22.43). The cycle of action begins with a conception of what is *kathêkon*, then an inclination arises in the soul, and finally we perform the appropriate act. For a study of inclinations (or impulse; *hormê*) in Stoicism, see Inwood 1985.

9. I owe this specific point to Long 2002, 114, but the reference to 3.3.5–10 is my own. Our reading (or emphasis) contrasts with Bonhöffer 1996, 200–201, who reads the second *topos* as about the perfection of the first *topos*.

10. Of course, when we value preferred externals, we also put our happiness in jeopardy (1.27.7–14).

11. In this way, I disagree with Long 2002, 113, that "the first field of study is at the heart of Epictetus's Stoicism." As I have been arguing throughout this book, roles are central to Epictetus's ethics and, in this chapter, I have been highlighting the centrality of the second topic. Thus, I take the second topic as the heart of his ethics.

12. Long 2002, 117, reads this exclamation as pure hyperbole because the student has indicated a desire to achieve secure judgments even in drunkenness and sleep, a state that Epictetus thinks (according to Long) could really only be achieved by a god. However, Epictetus straightforwardly ascribes just such an aim to the third *topos* at 3.2.5. This suggests that, even if Epictetus is being ironic in 2.17.33, he is only partly so and he is also genuinely pleased with the progress and plans of this imaginary student. In taking this position, Epictetus appears to be following Cleanthes, who thinks that virtue cannot be lost because cognitive impressions

are firm (*dia bebaious katalêpseis*); by contrast, Epictetus diverges from Chrysippus, who thinks that virtue can be overturned by drunkenness or melancholy (Diogenes Laertius, 7.127). For a helpful discussion of the Diogenes passage and related references, see Graver 2007, 115–116. I further discuss the significance of the student's declared aims below.

13. However, ethics is not the exclusive application of logic. Epictetus also employs logic to tackle the skeptic of logic (2.25) and to refute an Epicurean and an Academic skeptic (2.20). Moreover, Epictetus certainly shows an interest in logical puzzles; as Barnes says, Epictetus "collects them" like "fine porcelain" (Barnes 1997, 64). Nonetheless, even granted these passages, logic must be framed by Epictetus's larger ethical project (cf. Hijmans 1959, 39) and Epictetus stresses that logical puzzles are a pastime (3.9.19; Barnes 1997, ibid.).

14. For a discussion of the strictly logical content of 1.7, see Barnes 1997, 38–145, and Susanne Bobzien 1997.

15. On these grounds, I think Barnes 1997 is too restricted in his reading of Epictetus's claim that logic concerns appropriate acts. Barnes says that Epictetus "does not mean, in the utilitarian vein, that logic must be *applied to* moral matters. Rather, he means that logic *is itself* a moral matter. . . . For a mistake in logic is itself a moral error—every mistake is a moral error" (65).

16. I am drawing my example from Aristotle's *EN* 1141b15–23 where we are told that it is not enough to know that light meats are healthy; we must also know that bird meat counts as light meat.

17. E.g., "to walk prudently." See Inwood 1999, 95–127. As Inwood complains, these descriptions are "universal but vacuous" (102) and work simply by containing "a built-in reference to virtue or vice: 'prudent walking,' or more generally 'virtuous action'" (103; cf. 106).

18. L&S, 367; Bonhöffer 1996, 213. Cf. Cicero *De Fin.* 3.59. See also Long 1983, 189–192; Sandbach 1989, 45–47.

19. Epictetus uses the expression *katorthôma* as a substantive only once: to describe a man who acts with "the impression [*phantasian*] of rightness [*katorthômatos*]" (2.26.5) even though he is acting on a mistake (2.26.4–6); it seems clear that this does not necessarily invoke the technical use of the term (*pace* Bonhöffer 1996, 251).

20. Seven times: 1.17.15, 1.27.8,1.28.30, 2.3.5, 2.23.28, 2.26.1, and 3.9.2.

21. In effect, Epictetus has interpreted the Stoic orthodoxy as a kind of Socratic intellectualism. Cf. 2.26.1 and 2.22.4 which implies that only the *phronimos* has *epistêmê*; see also Long 2002, 253; Hijmans 1959, 36 and 67–68; and De Lacy 1977, 121 and 123.

22. Cf. the argument of the *Meno* at 96d–99c where right opinion can properly guide individuals even though it is "less stable" than knowledge. Indeed, Epictetus comes close to such a position when he says that "If one had to be taught by fictions that things external and outside the sphere of volition are nothing to us, I, for my part, should wish for such a fiction as would enable me to live henceforth in peace of mind and free from perturbation" (1.4.27). Certainly, if Epictetus intended such an explanation, it would have been heterodox Stoicism; see L&S vol. I, 258.

23. Again, in standard Stoicism, only the sage is good. Just as a we may drown even if we are one inch below the surface of the water (L&S 61T), so we, too, lack genuine goodness even if we are one step away from having an *orthos logos*.

24. See Epictetus's claim that "nothing can overcome volition [*prohairesis*] except itself. . . ." (1.29.12). Also, see Asmis 2001, 405–406.

25. Bonhöffer 1996, 272–273, recognizes that Epictetus thinks that the individual making progress (the *prokoptôn*) has *ortha dogmata*, and that this state puts them above the unlearned in virtue but beneath the perfection of the wise. By implication, Bonhöffer accepts that *ortha dogmata* are not firm because he argues, at the end of his essay, that what really separates those who are making progress from the wise is the firmness of their judgments (276–277). Nonetheless, while I agree with Bonhöffer, I do not think his own claims about *ortha dogmata* are textually grounded and, as argued earlier, I think that he fluctuates on the issue of whether or not Epictetus makes the *prokoptôn* count as ethically good.

26. *Meletônta*: this verb can also be translated as "to care for" or "attend to." This suggests that *ortha dogmata* are things that need to be looked after or shepherded. Such "day long" care

conveys something of the fragility of *ortha dogmata*. See 1.11.33 where *hupoleipseis* and *dogmata* are the cause of action and thus Epictetus insists that we must go to school in order to spend time examining these *dogmata* (1.11.39–40).

27. For discussion, see Asmis 2001, 391 and 405–406. See also the citations in Barnes 1997, 47. Barnes connects the emphasis on practice with Aristotle (*EN* 1103a30–b2) and with Galen's medical writings.

28. See 2.16.27–28; cf. 3.26.34–35 and 4.12.12. Cf. Kidd's claim that the "Greek equivalent for *decreta* is *dogmata*, and refers to the ultimate philosophical principles that the 'wise' man knows and operates in right action [Seneca *Ep.* 95.10]" (Kidd 1978, 251).

29. Cf. Kamtekar 1998 on habituation, 151–152. The Aristotelianism of Epictetus's position (especially in 2.9) has been widely noted. See Hijmans 1959, 63–64 and 102; and Dobbin 1998, 80.

30. On these grounds, it seems that Epictetus wishes to blend elements of Socratic intellectualism with Aristotelian *hexeis*. Compare Epictetus's claim that no one errs willingly (1.17.14–15; cf. 1.28.4–6) with the denial of *akrasia* in the *Protagoras*, an intellectualist aspect to Epictetus that has been widely noted (see above); likewise, compare the example of habituating grammar in *Discourses* 2.9.10f. with *Nicomachean Ethics* 1105a17–26. For Epictetus, an *orthos logos* is achieved both by correct learning *and* assiduous habituation. There is a tension for Epictetus in holding this position because intellectualism is only supposed to require knowledge (and not practice) to make certainty secure, but that paradoxical stance nonetheless appears to be Epictetus's position. I suspect that Epictetus would resolve the tension by claiming that a perfect intellectual state necessarily leads to good action (a modified intellectualism) but that such a state consists of both knowledge and habit (Aristotelianism). As far as I know, this tension between intellectualism and habituation is not discussed in the literature on Epictetus. Hijmans's lengthy 1959 monograph on training (*askêsis*), for example, does not discuss it, even though he appears aware that training results in *hexeis* (Hijmans 1959, 87). However, for a good general discussion of Aristotelianism and intellectualism, see Mitsis 1993, 286–291 and 299.

31. In the literature on the Epictetus's *topoi*, it is only Dobbin 1998, 93, and Crivelli 2007, 22, who seem to appreciate that 3.2.2–5 describe the epistemic state of a sage. I agree with their view but take my analysis here to offer much more evidence for the fact that Epictetus self-consciously connects the third *topos* with the Stoic sage.

32. As I have noted, Long 2002, 117, reads this exclamation differently. See note 12.

33. This translation is taken from Pomeroy 1999, 11g (= *SVF* 3.54).

34. L&S 59I, 61I, 61S, and vol. 1, 254–259.

35. In personal conversation, Brad Inwood ventured the following interesting objection: that "fine and good [*kalon k'agathon*]" merely means something like "upstanding" or "decent." If Inwood is right, of course, then Epictetus is making a much less radical claim than I am suggesting. However, there are good grounds for thinking that Epictetus would agree with Stobaeus's more strict description of what the Stoics mean by *kalon k'agathon*. Epictetus appears to use the phrase in order to pick out the virtuous agent; see 1.7.2, 1.12.7, 2.10.5, 3.24.18, 50 and 95, and 4.5.1. Long 2002, 33, agrees that Epictetus uses *kalos kai agathos* to refer to the Stoic sage; in his notes to chapter 1, Long also helpfully lists all appearances of the phrase (37).

36. As I argue in chapter 1, *chôran* is employed by Epictetus as a synonym for role (*prosôpon*).

37. In this way, I agree with Long 2002 and Kamtekar 1998 that Epictetus resists treating perfect knowledge as the sole basis of good acts, but I hold that Epictetus does imply a distinction between perfect and intermediate appropriate actions. My stance also differs from Bonhöffer 1996 because I do not hold that ordinary individuals who perform their appropriate acts have merely "relative moral value" (227) or are comparable to the converted sinner in Christianity; instead, I hold that, for Epictetus, individuals who fulfill their roles are fine and good (*kaloi k'agathoi*) and they are encouraged by Epictetus's *topoi* to seek perfection in order to ensure that they settle for nothing less than the complete fulfillment of their roles.

38. For Epictetus's passing references to the *phronimos*, see 2.21.9, 2.22.3, 3.22.37, and 4.1.92. For his passing references to the *sophos*, see 1.23.3, 2.21.11, 3.13.22, 3.21.18, 3.22.67, 4.11.24 and *Ench.* 53.2.

39. See chapter 2 for all the appearances of the extraordinary individual in the *Discourses*.

40. If sagehood were to be a role, it would have to serve as the aim of our human role and it would serve as an example for specific roles only in so far as sages perfectly and rationally execute all their appropriate acts since the wise man represents the ideal at which *all* human beings must aim. However, the human role as sage is a hypothetical suggestion on my part. As should be evident from chapter 1's discussion of the universal (human) role, sagehood is nowhere connected by Epictetus to our universal role.

41. Not surprisingly, athlete examples abound in Epictetus. See 1.2.25–29, 1.4.13–17, 1.24.1–5, 1.29.34–37, 3.15 [=*Ench.* 39], 2.17.30, 3.15.1–7, 3.20.9–10, 3.22.57–61, 3.23.1–3, 3.25.4–5, and 4.4.11–13. Nonetheless, Epictetus would prefer us to take inspiration from witnessing the struggle of a good man over that of the mere struggle of a good athlete (2.18.22–23 and 3.22.58). In other words, while Epictetus grants that we can and often do look to the athlete for inspiration, it is best to look to the extraordinary individual who achieves victory in personal virtue.

42. For a wonderful discussion of the father-daughter episode in 1.11, see Reydams-Schils 2005, 119–123. Indeed, it is precisely Epictetus's discussion of these sorts of roles that makes me skeptical of Reydams-Schils's later claim that Epictetus expects his pupils to "inhibit 'normal' social modes of behavior if they want to make moral progress in his sanatorium for the soul" (169). While I think that the first *topos* could be described as a kind of inhibition, I have argued that the second *topos* concerns reengaging the world.

43. See chapter 2, note 12.

44. See, for example, Seneca, *Letters* 76.9–10 and 90.1.

45. Cf. Epictetus's claim that if we fulfill our role, even a humble one, it is sufficient (1.2.33–35 and *Ench.* 24.4). I return to this issue in chapter 6.

Chapter Five

The Cases of Socrates and Heracles: Role Conflict and Identity

As we saw in chapter 1, Epictetus implies that our roles divide into two sorts (3.23.3–5), one sort is common to us as rational human agents (2.9.1–10) and another sort is more specific to us as individuals: "son, father, brother, citizen, husband, wife, neighbor, fellow-traveler, ruler, and subject" (2.14.8) and so on. Applied to Socrates—a figure to which Epictetus pays considerable attention—this division holds that Socrates had the common role of a human being, which includes the obligation to practice the canonical Stoic maxims such as treating externals as a matter of indifference. In addition, Socrates had the more specific role of philosophic teacher, which included such obligations as playing the gadfly and inflaming the jurors at his defense,[1] a role potentially shared by only a small sector of humanity.

While Epictetus's account of roles provides an innovative framework for Socrates's life, it confronts readers with a fresh difficulty about the status of Socrates's roles. In particular, do these specific roles (such as brother or gadfly) arise merely from the application of our universal, human role to some given circumstance? That is, does Socrates's role as gadfly arise simply because he has (in his view) received a divine order and thus his mission is nothing more than the human virtue of piety? Or, do these specific roles lay upon Socrates any special obligations that are not stipulated by or necessitated by our common human role? Does Socrates's role as gadfly represent a special obligation to cross-examine others, an obligation that is distinctive from his general obligation to be an ethical human being? And, in so far as Socrates's specific roles entail special obligations, might these obligations conflict? In turn, these questions about the status of Socrates's roles have significance for how (on Epictetus's view) we ought to evaluate our own lives and actions relative to Socrates's actions. At issue here is how all of our roles (both universal and specific) should come together to guide our actions and whether or not our specific roles can conflict.

In this chapter, I shall defend the view that we each bear many roles, that each role carries special obligations, and that such obligations may even conflict.[2] To support my view, I shall examine the cases of Socrates and Heracles, two cases in which Epictetus suggests some detail about how specific roles seem to feature in the practical reasoning of agents. We will begin by exploring a passage in which Epictetus sketches a layered picture of humanity, a picture according to which our practical reasoning must operate by analyzing our roles as two layers of obligations, our human role and our more specific roles. We will investigate how Epictetus exemplifies these layers through the trial of Socrates (or a Socrates-like figure). We will examine how Epictetus even implies that Socrates's role as gadfly was in conflict with his role as father and we will use that conflict to defend my conclusion that human agents have many roles. Then, we will examine a passage which provides further detail about how specific roles and their associated externals feature in our practical reasoning. I will argue that Epictetus appears to treat specific roles as a kind of fixed point so that, for example, Heracles is roused into action because he has the role of a hero and he is confronted with the necessary challenges to fulfill that role. Finally, I will show how my interpretation of roles extends beyond the examples of Socrates and Heracles.

THE LAYERS OF HUMANITY

Towards the end of *Discourses* 2.5, Epictetus takes up the view that we, as human beings, are attached to the cosmos just as a foot is connected organically to the body; and, just as a severed foot is no longer a foot, so a "detached" human would no longer be a human being (2.5.24–26). Immediately following this claim, Epictetus clarifies it by pointing out that we are citizens of the cosmos and citizens of a human city. He then concludes the discourse by examining the trial and condemnation of an individual who sounds like Socrates (2.5.27–29). In the section ahead, I shall attempt to unpack 2.5.24–29 in order to show that it provides a layered picture of practical reasoning according to which our calculations about our human role are distinct from our calculations about our specific roles. This analysis focuses on Epictetus's treatment of Socrates's universal role as a human being and the resulting conflict with his specific roles as gadfly and father. I demonstrate that one layer of reasoning does not "deflate" into the other and that role conflicts are possible.

To begin with, 2.5.26 asserts that human beings are members of two cities (*poleis*): "For what is a human being? A part of a city; first, [of that city composed] of gods and humans; and then, of that which is said to be as close as possible [*hôs engista*] [to that],[3] [the city] that is a certain small copy [*mimêma*] of the universal [city]" (2.5.26).[4] This passage regards us as citizens of the city of gods and humans, and it seems apparent that this citizenship refers to our cosmopolitan role as a human being. It also makes us members of a microcosmic city, such as Athens or Corinth, and gives us the many other roles that citizens assume there, such as senator or shoe-maker (cf. *Ench.* 24.4). Thus, what we can determine of Epictetus's understanding of the relationship between these two forms of citizenship holds great importance for determining what he thinks about the relationship between the universal role and specific roles.

Towards that end, let us first examine Epictetus's tantalizing claim that our political community is a "small copy of" and is "as close as possible" to the cosmic community. From comments he makes elsewhere, it seems that he sees city-states as "copies" of the cosmic state in as much as the citizens of both ought to obey a sovereign and act for the benefit of the whole:

> What, then, is the profession of a citizen? To keep nothing profitable in private, to plan about nothing as if he were detached [from everyone], but [to act] just as the foot or the hand, which, if they had reason and understood the construction of nature, would never exercise an impulse or a desire in any other way than by reference to the whole. . . . [Our place] is assigned from the arrangement of the whole, and the whole is more sovereign than the part, and the state more sovereign than the citizen. (2.10.4–5)

Indeed, whenever Epictetus discusses our cosmic (human) commitments in relation to our specific political commitments, he mirrors these same themes about reasoning holistically, fulfilling our function and obeying the sovereign (see 1.9.1–7 and 2.15.10). The state, then, is a copy (*mimêma*) that is "as close as possible" to the cosmos because the two have parallel components which are expected to perform the corresponding functions: a citizen ought to obey the sovereign just as a human being ought to obey nature, a citizen should benefit the whole just as a human ought to benefit the world, and so on. Features of my political citizenship arise from the part that I play in my specific city just as features of my cosmic citizenship arise from the part that I play in the world at large.

What emerges from the foregoing description is the fact that Epictetus seems to treat our cosmic and political stations as *hierarchical* but *distinct* cases of membership (as parts) in a whole.[5] He does not treat one as an instance of the other. Moreover, outside of the 2.10.4–6 passage on citizenship, Epictetus's picture of cosmopolitanism makes the distinction between cosmic and civic memberships even stronger. In his cosmopolitan view, Epictetus distinguishes our political citizenship from our cosmic citizenship, and he values cosmopolitanism over our more narrow commitments because it is our relation to nature that makes possible our civic communities

(1.9.1–7). Even though the universal form of citizenship is more fundamental, the sense of this priority is that we should meet our civic attachments *after* trying to meet our cosmic commitments. Further, Epictetus's picture of cosmopolitanism suggests that our specific commitments should never conflict with our cosmic ones, and if they did, we should follow our cosmic ones. Correspondingly, by distinguishing our specific roles from our cosmic role, Epictetus opens up the possibility that there may be a conflict among our specific roles. Such conflict would be impossible if all of our roles were mere extensions or applications of our human role because the universal role cannot demand *p* while its particular applications demand *q* and *r* such that *q* and *r* are in conflict.[6]

As a result of the hierarchical picture at 2.5.26, it seems that individuals ought to examine the layers of their communities, first cosmic, then civic. And, in fact, this is the picture of practical reasoning that Epictetus suggests throughout the *Discourses*. For Epictetus, individuals have layers to their attachments, with the highest priority layer constraining the choices and actions of the lower layer: first, individuals ought to obey the will of God in whatever form it may occur and they ought never to forsake their own (divinely given) capacity to reason or their own volition (*prohairesis*); second, so long as piety and rationality are preserved, individuals ought to pursue the requirements of their specific roles, such as the role of an Athenian or of a father.[7] As Epictetus says:

> For each of the things that come to be by us [i.e., by our agency], if we do not refer them back to anything, we shall act at random; . . . Furthermore, there is a common standard and a specific [standard]. First of all, in order that I [act] as a human being. What is included in this? Not [to act] as a sheep, gently but at random; nor destructively, like a wild beast. The specific [standard] applies to each person's pursuit and volition. The cithara-player is to act as a cithara-player, the carpenter as a carpenter, the philosopher as a philosopher, the rhetor as a rhetor. (3.23.3-5)[8]

Similarly, as he says at 4.12.15–16, "[we ought] to pursue nothing external, nothing belonging to others. . . . And next to this, [we ought] to remember who we are, and what our designation [i.e., role] is, and [we ought] to try to guide aright our appropriate acts in reference to the significance[9] of our relations" (4.12.16); that is, we first ought to fulfill our human obligation to treat externals as indifferent and then we ought to fulfill our specific roles or functions.

Beyond the language of copies, 2.5.26 also claims that we are members of both a cosmic and a civic city because we are human beings: a human is "part of a city; first, [of that city composed] of gods and humans; and then . . . [of the city] that is a certain small copy of the universal [city] . . ." (ibid.). In the next section, I shall argue that 2.5.26 implies a composite picture of humanity in which our possessing a *logos*, a specific body, and a specific place in the world lays the basis for role conflict.

THE CASE OF SOCRATES

To establish and clarify this composite picture of humanity, let us examine the passage that immediately follows 2.5.26 and which closes *Discourses* 2.5.[10] In it, Epictetus tries to explain the practical meaning of his remark about the communities to which we belong as human beings by examining the place of an accused person in the larger community around him:

> "Then [is it necessary] for me to be put on trial now?" Now then, [is] someone else to be sick with fever, someone else to be at sea, someone else to die, someone else to be condemned? For it is impossible in such a body [as ours], in this [universe] which encompasses us, among such fellow-inhabitants, that such things not happen, some to one man, some to another. It is your task, therefore, to come forward and say what you ought, to arrange these things as is fitting. Then that man [*viz.*, the judge] says, "I judge you guilty." [I reply], "Let it be well with you. I have done my part, and it is yours to see whether you have done yours." For there is some danger for that man [*viz.*, the judge], do not forget that. (2.5.27–29)[11]

Although Epictetus does not explicitly say so, I suggest that he is thinking of a figure like Socrates who is calmly asking whether or not he ought to be put on trial. There are at least two factors indicating that this is whom Epictetus has in mind. First, Epictetus discussed the trial of Socrates earlier in *Discourses* 2.5 as a way of clarifying the point that success or failure in court is a matter of indifference but one's trial behavior is not (2.5.18–21). Second, it would be altogether surprising for Epictetus to be invoking an individual contrary to Socrates, that is, a wicked man, because the passage would then say that it is necessary for some individuals to do wrong and thus be condemned.[12]

Given that Epictetus likely has Socrates in mind, we can elaborate on what is meant by the dual citizenship of a human being through the example of Socrates. On one level, Socrates is a human being and a citizen of the cosmos (1.9.1–9); he thus has the God-given faculty of volition (*prohairesis*), a faculty that must be preserved by concerning himself with what is under his control and not worrying about what is outside his control. Applied to his court case, this divine gift requires that Socrates has to treat as indifferent anything beyond his control, "Imprisonment, banishment, drinking poison, being deprived of his wife, leaving his children orphaned" (2.5.19; cf. 3.24.60–62, 4.5.1–7, and 4.1.159–169). Instead, Socrates had to manage what was under his control, his behavior, by not entreating or begging for his life or his family (2.2.15–20; cf. 4.4.21–23). On another level, Socrates is a particular human being who had to live among other human beings; he thus is a citizen of Athens, a husband, father, friend, and (Cynic-like) teacher. In other words, Socrates has many specific roles with their own obligations.[13]

Among Socrates's specific roles, Epictetus supplies the most detail about the roles of a father and of a Cynic-like teacher. Epictetus contrasts the obligations of these two roles, and I shall use his analysis to argue that these two roles are incompatible such that Socrates could meet the obligations of only one of them. In Epictetus's view, it is *de facto* impossible to be a Cynic and father because both roles are simply too demanding on one's time. On the one hand, a father has many home-bound obligations. A father ought "to demonstrate certain [services] to his father-in-law, to render [services] to the other relatives of his wife, [and] to the wife herself" and he must "care for the sick [and] earn an income" (3.22.70). Accordingly, "it is necessary for him [to get] a pot in which he prepares hot water for the baby in order that he bathe it in the tub; a little wool for his wife when she has given birth, olive oil, a little couch, a cup (the utensils immediately become more and more)" (3.22.71). Ought he not "bring little cloaks for the little children? Come, [isn't it necessary for him] to send them to the elementary teacher having little writing tablets, pencils, notebooks, and to prepare a little couch for them? For they are unable to be Cynics when they have come forth from the womb" (3.22.74).[14] Indeed, "if he does not [do these things], it is better to expose those [infants] who have been born than to kill them in this way" (3.22.74). In sum, a father is "tied down to the private appropriate acts" of everyday life (3.22.69; cf. 3.22.74). On the other hand, the Cynic's life is equally demanding because Epictetus treats the Cynic as a kind of Stoic priest who must commit to the austere life of ministering to the ethical character of others (3.22, see especially 3.22.45–50). Similarly, Epictetus presents the Cynic as a special king who must watch over all families (3.22.72) and as a universal doctor who regards everyone as a patient (3.22.72–73). Thus, a Cynic needs to be "free from distraction, wholly [applied] to the service of the god, able to go among [every] human being . . ." (3.22.69; cf. 3.22.81–82). He requires "leisure for [serving] the public" (3.22.72).[15] If we force a Cynic to concern himself with the appropriate acts of a family, he would have no time to be a Cynic; he would be "entwined by relations which he cannot transgress while preserving the role [*prosôpon*] of the fine and good man" (3.22.69). If we encumber a Cynic with family obligations, Epictetus complains, "consider how far down we have dragged our Cynic, how we have taken away his kingdom" (3.22.75).

Epictetus therefore concludes that a Cynic cannot fulfill the obligations of a private family without destroying his role as a Cynic (3.22.69; cf. 3.22.75). At the same time, a father "has a certain function which, unless he fulfills it, he has destroyed the father" (3.18.5). Hence, it seems apparent that Epictetus regards these two roles as in conflict. This conflict is crucial because Epictetus seems to absorb Socrates's role as gadfly into his paradigm of the Cynic's role. In the 3.22 discourse "On Cynicism," Epictetus says that a Cynic must "get up onto the tragic stage and speak [the words] of Socrates" (3.22.26) about our unfortunate obsession with external things and our neglect of the good. Epictetus also treats Socrates's mission as comparable to the station of Diogenes the Cynic (3.21.19). In addition, Epictetus does not portray Socrates as performing any of the tasks of a father; rather, he portrays Socrates as "holding up against a cantankerous wife and a senseless son" (4.5.33).[16] Accordingly, Epictetus's analysis of the roles of a father and a Cynic rather strongly suggests that Socrates's role as father is in tension with his role as gadfly.

Of course, Epictetus tries to minimize the tension between these two roles, but his setup is unable to eliminate it. Epictetus attempts to downplay the tension by pointing out that Socrates had *philia* for his own children (3.24.60–62) and that this *philia* is consistent with regarding family members as a matter of indifference (see above and cf. 3.3.5–10). In addition, Epictetus tells his students that they must "learn the [life] of healthy men, how slaves live, how laborers, how the genuine philosophers, how Socrates lived—that man [i.e., Socrates] lived even with a wife and children—how Diogenes, how Cleanthes studied and drew water[17] at the same time" (3.26.23) as though Socrates successfully carried both roles. And yet, where Socrates's family is concerned, Epictetus's approach remains concessionary: Epictetus here tells us that Socrates lived as a healthy man *even with* a family. Socrates could live a sound life because he understood that the character of his family was beyond his control. Epictetus explains that Socrates could endure Xanthippe dumping water on his head and smashing the cakes that he received because he regarded such things as matters of indifference (4.5.33).[18] Moreover, even if his family was beyond his volition (*prohairesis*), his treatment of his family was under his control (cf. 2.22.20). Perhaps Cleanthes successfully combined work and school—contemplating as he hauled water[19]—but Epictetus's account makes it difficult to reconcile the manifold tasks of a father with the demanding task of tending to the ethical character of humanity. As Epictetus says elsewhere, prospective philosophers must endure many hardships including leaving their families (3.15.11). While the Socrates of the *Phaedo* can send away his lamenting wife and small children from his final conversation with his students,[20] Epictetus will chastise a senator for running away from a sick daughter (1.11). Even for a senator, Epictetus finds it unnatural and unaffectionate to avoid care-giving for a sick child (1.11.20–26).[21] Nevertheless, for the Cynic-like Socrates, Epictetus appears to think that Socrates can neglect his family because his gadfly role entails a life outside the home caring for the ethical well-being of all of Athens (cf. 3.22.72–74); thus, in Socrates's final hours, he attends not to the false grounds for his wife's grief (since death is not an evil) but to the faulty beliefs of his grieving associates.

Aside from the treatment of the above conflicting roles, Epictetus adds to the distinctness of Socrates's specific role as gadfly through his discussion of Socrates's courtroom defense. Here, too, Epictetus brings out the competition between roles. For Socrates, his gadfly role will entail making orphans of his children; for another man, his role as father will entail defending himself while preserving his family. Epictetus makes this point in a passage where he uses his own friend, Heracleitus, as a foil to Socrates (2.2.15–20). Epictetus begins by saying that, if Socrates had wanted to preserve his external goods, he would not have provoked the judges (2.2.15–16). Epictetus then relates that Heracleitus was in a petty lawsuit about a piece of land and he copied Socrates's technique of explicitly rejecting entreaties precisely when they were expected in the peroration (2.2.17; cf. Pl. *Ap.* 34b–35d); naturally, Heracleitus destroyed his own case (2.2.18). Epictetus objects that it was useless for Heracleitus to do that; he should have made no entreaties but withheld boasting about it (ibid.; cf. 3.18.6–8). One should not behave as Heracleitus did, "unless it is the critical moment to purposefully antagonize the jury as it was for Socrates" (2.2.18).[22] "But," Epictetus concludes, "if reason [*logos*] persuades you that you should appear in court and outdo yourself to persuade [the judge] about your [lawsuit], then the things that follow [from what reason has determined] surely must be done while maintaining what is your own [*ta idia*[23]]" (2.2.20).

Epictetus does not tell us why it was time for Socrates to provoke his jury, but he does indicate that Socrates's very identity was at stake when it came to his behavior: "And how would he still be Socrates if he bewailed these things?" (4.4.22). And, we can surmise that Epictetus thought that inflaming the jury was a part of Socrates's role as gadfly. In so far as it was Socrates's role to be the radical who summons us to virtue, Epictetus implies that Socrates fulfilled that mission when he secured his own execution: "if we are presently beneficial, will we not be more beneficial to humanity after we have died when it was necessary and as it was necessary? And since Socrates is now dead, the memory [of him] is no less beneficial (or is even more beneficial) to humanity than what he did or said while he lived" (4.1.168–169).[24]

Although Epictetus offers no more detail at the end of *Discourses* 2.5 about the layers of our roles, the above way of understanding specific roles is confirmed by how Epictetus discusses particulars and the varieties of human experience:

> Do you not know that in the long course of time, manifold things necessarily happen; a fever gets the better of one man, a robber of another, a tyrant of yet another? For such is [the character of] what encompasses us, such is [the

> character of] the associates around us; cold and heat; unsuitable food; road travel and sea travel; winds and manifold crises; one man is demolished, another banished; one man is tossed on an embassy, another on a military campaign. (3.24.28–29)[25]

In much the same way, our own nature directly features in the sorts of roles that we take up—the sun is given its place in the heavens because it has the power to emit light and traverse the heavens (3.22.5–7), the bull heads the herd because of its muscle power (1.2.30–31), and even shoemakers take up their place in the city because our human bodies require shoes (*Ench.* 24.4).

For Epictetus, then, our humanity appears to be a composite fact because we have a share in reason (*logos*), which connects us to cosmic nature, and because we have a body in a certain place and time, which means that we are susceptible to illness and a variety of material needs and that we must live among others and the consequences of their actions. As a result, our humanity cannot act as one standard because it has *many* influences acting upon it. Thus, Epictetus does not say to agents, "Here is a universal (human) standard, apply it to your differing circumstances"; rather, he says, "The universe needs these different functions, so here are your specific stations" (cf. 1.29.26–28, 3.22.4–8, and 3.24.94–95).[26] It is this fact that is recognized by 2.5.26 and Epictetus's account of Socrates.

In sum, I suggest that Epictetus's treatment of Socrates substantively fills in the claim that we are first members of the cosmic city and secondarily we are members of a civic city. Granted, Socrates's human role had to be the fundamental layer and he had to preserve that role in order to be a good man in any of his specific roles (see 3.24.61); it remains the case that each of Socrates's specific roles entailed their own set of (potentially conflicting) obligations. Epictetus would surely prefer these specific roles to operate in harmony, but he nonetheless seems to recognize that some roles can conflict. On the one hand, Socrates was a father, a role which suggests that Socrates ought to have been present to his family and thus perhaps convinced the jury (*without* entreaties or arrogance) to release him. On the other hand, Socrates also had the role of a gadfly, a role that required him (as Epictetus sees it) to inflame the jury into issuing a death sentence. For a man without Socrates's role as gadfly, it is appropriate to avoid a conviction (within reason);[27] but, for Socrates, it appears that his missionary role won out over his role as a father. In this way, by treating practical reasoning as a layered process which reflects the composite features of humanity, *Discourses* 2.5.26 opens up the possibility for conflict between specific roles.

However, while 2.5.26 establishes that specific roles are a distinct (but subordinate) layer of practical reasoning, it turns out that Epictetus is willing to go further. Even though our human role is clearly the more fundamental, it appears that Epictetus regards our specific roles and their associated externals as ends-in-themselves in the deliberations of agents. He supplies this evidence in *Discourses* 1.6 to which we now turn.

THE CASE OF HERACLES

In this section, I want to consider in more detail how Epictetus believes that specific roles feature in the reasoning of agents and argue that he implicitly treats our specific roles as ends-in-themselves. He implies that stance in *Discourses* 1.6 where he discusses the realization of our capacities and suggests that we *need* the twists of fortune in order to realize our capacities and even to be who we were meant to be. As a case in point, Epictetus discusses the life of Heracles; he argues that Heracles would not have been Heracles without the hydra or lion and he examines the part played by those externals in Heracles's motivation for action. In examining *Discourses* 1.6, I will give a selective reading, emphasizing those points that relate specific roles to their associated externals.

Early in *Discourses* 1.6, Epictetus prepares his audience for thinking about the interdependence between externals and specific roles when he lays out a principle of providential design concerning the relationship between capacities (*dunameis*) and their respective objects:

> If God had made colors but had not made the faculty [*dunamin*] for seeing them, what would be the use [*ophelos*]?—None whatsoever—But, conversely, if God had made the faculty but what exists is not the sort of thing that is subject to the faculty of sight, in that case what is the use?—None whatsoever.—What then, if God had made both of these, but had not made light?—Even thus, there is no use [*ophelos*]. (1.6.3–6; cf. 2.23.2–6)

As a way of launching this argument, Epictetus continues with examples of human artifacts where the parts are designed to fit together (1.6.6–11). For our purposes, what is of interest here is the initial principle: if a faculty (*dunamis*) cannot be exercised, it has no use (*ophelos*). Epictetus does not here deny that a faculty could exist perennially dormant; rather, he finds it objectionable that divine design would allow for such waste. So, his claim is a maxim about the world's proper design: every faculty *should* have the corresponding conditions needed to realize itself.

On the basis of this claim, Epictetus turns to consider our human faculty for understanding. He argues that since God designs our faculty of understanding with the necessary conditions for it to be realized, we *ought* to actualize that faculty (1.6.12–29; cf. 2.23.3–10). Epictetus unfolds this principle about realization by examining the essential faculties of animals and human beings. He asserts that animals have the capacity to "make use of their impressions" and that we have the further capacity to "understand the use [of impressions]" (1.6.13). From this observation he infers that, for an animal, "it is sufficient to eat, drink, rest, procreate, and all other such things it is prescribed for each of them [to do]" (1.6.14). The ability to use external impressions explains the ability of animals to perform various survival functions (such as eating and reproducing) *and* it limits them to performing *only* those functions. By contrast, Epictetus reasons, since we have the capacity to do more than our animal counterparts, it is therefore not sufficient for us merely to perform our survival functions. Our capacity to understand requires us to behold Nature as an aesthete does a work of art (1.6.23–27). Accordingly, Epictetus also holds that not only should all faculties have the corresponding conditions to be realized but that all faculties *ought* to be realized.[28] As he summarizes it, "For of beings whose constitutions are different, the tasks [*erga*] and the ends [are different]" (1.6.16).[29]

To justify our obligation to realize our capacities (*dunameis*), Epictetus returns to the idea that Nature needs us each to play our parts. He holds that our roles were designed with reference to the whole and that our capacities were designed to allow us to fulfill our roles. To that end, 1.6 explains that animal and human capacities are so designed because God has a use for things to be that way (1.6.13). For animals, it seems that they are limited to survival functions in order to serve anthropocentric ends: to be eaten, to serve as pack animals, and so on (1.6.18). For human beings, Epictetus says that God "has introduced human beings to be a spectator of Himself and of His works, and not only a spectator, but also an interpreter of them" (1.6.19).[30] Epictetus provides no explanation of why God would need a spectator and interpreter or, quite surprisingly, why humans need God, but, for our discussion, we should see that Epictetus is further expanding his observations about capacities and the external world: each part (i.e., role) has been given the requisite capacities and the corresponding circumstances necessary to fulfill its place.[31]

After elaborating on our human capacity to understand, Epictetus applies the foregoing principles to an example about special capacities and their obligatory realization through preferred externals. The example concerns the labors of Heracles and seems to invoke his specific role as a hero (1.6.30–36). Epictetus does not explicitly say that Heracles has a specific role, but we have some grounds for thinking that Heracles does exemplify a special role (as does Socrates) because he matches Epictetus's treatment of the exemplary roles in *Discourses* 1.2. In 1.2, Epictetus uses the analogy of a bull in a herd of oxen who is aware of its own prowess and thereby takes up the role of defending the herd against a marauding lion (1.2.30–31).[32] In the herd of humanity, the labors of Heracles would make him the bull. Translated into human terms, Heracles's special role is to be a "commander and leader of all the earth and sea, the purifier of injustice and lawlessness, the bringer of justice and piety" (3.26.32).

Regarding Heracles, Epictetus wonders what "Heracles would have amounted to" (1.6.32) had it not been for his epic labors with beasts and evil men. For "what would he [*viz*., Heracles] do if no such things had come to be? Or is it not clear that he would have wrapped himself [in a blanket] and lain down to sleep?" (1.6.33). Moreover, Epictetus says,

> Well then, in the first place, he would never have become Heracles by dozing away his whole life in such luxury and ease; but even if he had, of what good would he have been? What would have been the use of those arms of his and of his other strengths, his perseverance and his nobility, had not such circumstances and materials roused him and exercised him? (1.6.33–34)

A sleeping Heracles, then, would either no longer be Heracles proper or he would be of no use.

Epictetus here develops his example in two somewhat incompatible ways. In one way, a sleeping Heracles would not really be a Heracles at all; he would be much more like Endymion than a legendary hero who performed epic labors.[33] Epictetus's point here appears to emulate Aristotle's argument that sleep cannot constitute happiness and so it cannot be the activity of the gods. "For what is the difference between sleeping an unbroken sleep from one's first day to one's last, say for a thousand or any number of years, and living the life of a plant?" (*Eudemian Ethics*, I.5 at 1216a3–6; Solomon trans.; cf. *NE* 1176a33–35). Thus, Aristotle says, "Still, every one supposes that they [the gods] *live* and therefore that they are active; we cannot suppose them to sleep like Endymion" (*Nicomachean Ethics*, X.8 at 1178b19–21; Ross and Urmson trans.). For Epictetus, a dormant capacity (in the form of a sleeping Heracles) suffers harm or destruction; an eye without exposure to light goes blind. In another (incompatible) way, Epictetus offers that a sleeping Heracles would retain his identity, but would be of no use. By this course of reasoning, a dormant capacity is not harmed by remaining dormant but may readily persist, never to be summoned. As in the case of eyesight and color, Heracles (and his capacities) would have been for naught without the proper external circumstances through which to realize them.

Between the two readings, Epictetus's language emphasizes the claim that a sleeping Heracles would, in some sense, no longer be Heracles. His phrasing "but even if he had" implies that the scenario of a sleeping Heracles retaining his identity is granted for the sake of an argument concerning realization, without conceding that such a scenario makes sense. In light of the Heracles example and the discourse leading up to it, therefore, it appears that the externals relevant to a role are necessary to the realization of that role; that is, the stage must be set for the role. Certainly, Epictetus's main point in this passage is one about providential design, but, by implication, he provides insight into Heracles's reasoning as a particular role-bound agent.

What is interesting from that perspective is the fact that Epictetus's argument does not focus on the material requirements of virtue as much as it does on the reasons for action. Epictetus could have argued that Heracles needed the lion in order to exercise his extraordinary courage and prowess just as a materialist picture of substance would say that shapes need matter in order to exist; "if *such a* [*toioutos*] lion had not come to be" (emphasis added, 1.6.32), Heracles would have had no object on which to realize his prowess. Although Epictetus appears to accept that point, what he chooses to emphasize here is the fact that, without such obstacles as the lion, Heracles would sleep; he does not say that Heracles would exercise himself on other activities.[34] Elsewhere, Epictetus praises the fact that Heracles traveled the world and made himself at home wherever he went (3.24.13–16) because "it was possible for him to pass his life happily wherever he was" (3.24.16);[35] but, in 1.6, it seems that Heracles *needed* the lion in order to take action.

We can see more clearly the meaning of this feature of Heracles's decision by briefly contrasting it with a fragment of a poem that purports to be from Aristotle. Fragment 675 of Aristotle[36] is a poem which is written in honor of virtue (*aretê*) and says that it is for the sake of virtue that Heracles underwent his labors. In the Aristotelian poem, Heracles was roused by virtue as an end in itself; that is, virtue itself brought him to complete his labors. By contrast, in 1.6.32, Epictetus claims that it is the challenge of the hydra itself that roused Heracles and virtue resulted from the confrontation; without such a challenge, Heracles would have been contented merely with sleep. Of course, Epictetus would surely think that Heracles wishes to be virtuous (and to express his humanity), but, in the passage, it is neither virtue nor vice that rouses Heracles—it is the hydra, the lion, and so on. And, Epictetus thinks that Heracles should not "prepare these [labors] for himself and seek to bring a lion into his own country," for that would have been "folly and madness" (1.6.35–36).[37] And yet, "since they did come to be and were found, they were serviceable for the sake of revealing and exercising our Heracles" (1.6.36).[38]

It is significant, too, that Heracles's choice matches with two of the life-or-death cases in *Discourses* 1.2, the discourse that announces and exemplifies Epictetus's account of roles. There, Epictetus relates the unusual case of an Olympic athlete who refuses medical castration even though it means that he will die (1.2.25–28);[39] for him, death was the appropriate choice, whereas for lesser athletes or non-athletes death is not appropriate. Epictetus also relates his own case in which he refuses the imperial order that philosophers shave their beards even though his decision puts his own life at risk (1.2.28–29; cf. 3.1.24). Epictetus explains that such action is "according to one's role [*prosôpon*]" (1.2.28). For the athlete, perhaps we may account for his decision on the grounds that a castrated athlete might be prevented by shame or custom from appearing in the nude public games or that, like

Samson shorn of his locks, he would lose his physical power if he became a eunuch. Nevertheless, just as Heracles without the lion, he should have been able to exercise his role as a human being; and yet, also like Heracles, he decided that his life as someone other than a great athlete was not a life worth living. For Epictetus, we may explain his astonishing choice due to the fact that he regards an untamed beard (and a rough cloak) as the proper accoutrements of the role of a philosopher (4.8.4–20; cf. 1.2.28–29 and 3.2.24). Even so, it is difficult to see how a beard is necessary for his role (surely Epictetus could think philosophically without it).[40] Thus, as with Heracles, Epictetus treats an external as a necessary component for fulfilling his specific role, as a fixed point upon which there is no compromise.

Moreover, similar to Epictetus and the athlete, Heracles faces a life-or-death decision, but the death involved is not of the body but of the person. If Heracles sat at home because there were no lions, Heracles would be Eurystheus (2.16.44). If he lay himself down to sleep, he would not be Heracles (1.6.33) but would be Endymion. Accordingly, the choice before him was to live a human life as another person or to be dormant. The presence of this choice distinguishes Heracles's case from the analogy of eyesight that began *Discourses* 1.6. On Epictetus's eye analogy, an eye in a world without light would be useless. It does not have the ability to choose another course of action; but, even if it did, it has no other function (other than sight) to take up; it cannot decide to perform the function of hearing. By contrast, Heracles has volition (*prohairesis*; cf. 4.10.8–16) and he has another function other than his role as hero—that of a human being—so it is indicative that Epictetus has him sleep when his heroic actions become impossible. On the basis of the athlete example and Epictetus's own example, it seems apparent that Heracles's identity is at stake because his role as hero is at stake and that that role is constitutive of who he is. And, from the perspective of his specific role, the de-personalized human life is less worthy than a life of sleep. What made his waking life worth living is the role that constitutes him, not as a human being per se but as a particular person.

BEYOND SOCRATES AND HERACLES

In view of the preceding discussion, it seems that Epictetus supplies two related considerations for claiming that we have multiple specific roles, that these roles generate specific appropriate acts, and that these appropriate acts can conflict. First, for Epictetus, it appears to be a basic fact about human beings that they are members of several different kinds of communities. It is because Socrates is a member of Athens and is a member of a specific family that he has the role of citizen and the role of father. Of course, Socrates's humanity makes possible certain kinds of community roles (such as that of "gadfly"), but his humanity is not sufficient by itself to explain his role in the civic community. As I have argued, each community membership constitutes a distinctive role with distinctive obligations. In this way, when we consider that Epictetus takes humans to be members of at least two sorts of communities (cosmic and civic) *and* that humans have many different capacities and functions to be fulfilled within a given civic community, Epictetus has good grounds to conclude that humans have many roles.

Second, Epictetus supplies us with an account of how specific roles relate to their associated externals. In the case of Heracles, his heroic role is not simply an extension of his human role. If it were a mere extension and if there were no hydra or lion, it would be wrong for Heracles to sleep because dormancy would make him more of a plant than a human. Without those feats, Heracles should find some other way to express his humanity. By contrast, I have argued that we can account for why Heracles sleeps and why he is awoken by appeal to his specific role. Heracles did not fight the hydra in order to express his humanity, rather he fights the hydra because he has the role of the "bull in the herd." Although it remains true that externals (such as mythic beasts) ought to be treated in a way that is consistent with one's humanity, Epictetus nonetheless gives a special place to externals because he seems to treat specific roles (and their associated externals) as constitutive of who we are and as ends-in-themselves.

NOTES

1. This is how Epictetus interprets Socrates. See 1.9.23–26 and 3.1.19–23; cf. the echoes in 1.16.21 and 3.24.99. Also cf. note 22.

2. Thus far in the literature, the most common response to these examples of specific roles has been the contrary interpretation. For example, two noted authors on the subject, Bonhöffer 1996 and Gill 1988 doubt that Epictetus awards specific roles such as father or philosophic teacher with a substantive place in the practical reasoning of individuals. Both scholars appear to believe that Epictetus endorses only one kind of role, our human one, with all other "roles" as the expression of our humanity in specific contexts and circumstances. Since this reading favors only one role, we might call it the "deflationary" reading since, in my view, it deflates all specific roles into one.

Bonhöffer endorses the deflationary reading because he treats those actions that fulfill our role as brother or friend as mere applications of our universal (human) obligations. For example, Bonhöffer 1996 deflates Epictetus's claim that a brother's role requires "deference, obedience, good speech, and never laying claim against your brother for any of the things beyond [the province] of choice" (2.10.8). Of this claim, Bonhöffer says that one "sees at once that these duties contain really nothing characteristic, but are essentially the same ones which generally hold good in dealings with human beings" (129). Thus, Bonhöffer does not appear to believe that different jobs will require different appropriate acts. This way of reading specific roles by Bonhöffer seems to be an application of his view that the Stoics have "the tendency . . . to obliterate and [make] uniform individuality . . ." (153). A version of this position also seems to be put forward by White 1983: "It does appear that [Panaetius], more than Epictetus, stressed the differences that might obtain among various people all aiming at the same ideal. For although Epictetus is concerned . . . with giving advice to imperfect human beings, he tends to assume that generally speaking the same advice will do pretty well for all of us" (7).

Bonhöffer's deflationary view finds a more recent counterpart in Gill 1988, who interprets two of the key discourses for his account of roles (1.2 and 2.10) in a deflationary manner. According to Gill, Epictetus's "advice to maintain [one's] own *prosôpon* is converted into the advice to maintain our universal *prosôpon* as human beings" (189). (Gill makes a weaker version of this claim, saying that specific roles "should, in effect, be subordinated to our common human role" [189]. This weaker claim is echoed by A. A. Long 2002, 232 and 237–241, and Annas 2007, 145–150.) Correspondingly, Gill argues that *Discourses* 2.10 is only interested in our universal role as human beings and that our roles such as ruler or guest "are, in essence, simply regarded as contexts in which rational moral agency can be expressed. . . ." (Gill 1988, 191). Gill suggests that for Epictetus these specific roles do not have "a weight and value of their own . . ." (192).

While this deflationary view is certainly plausible, it generates a number of difficulties for Epictetus's account of roles. Above all, Epictetus would not fulfill the stated purpose of his account. He announces that we can account for many different lives as different kinds of roles (*Ench.* 17); but, on the deflationary model, it turns out that we only need to reflect on our lone role as human beings. Similarly, it is puzzling that Epictetus bluntly tells us that we cannot all be like Socrates (1.2.33) because "all horses do not become fast" (1.2.34). Stranger still, Epictetus nowhere invokes our humanity in his analysis of Socrates or in the examples of roles in *Discourses* 1.2, even though the deflationary reading requires it to do the important work of the account. Indeed, on the deflationary reading, it is hard to see what a role even is.

Moreover, I suspect that what motivates the deflationary view (as I have termed it) is the expectation that the extraordinary individuals in *Discourses* 1.2 (and elsewhere) must be Stoic sages. Because the deflationary reading sees specific roles as mere ersatzes for the universal role, the deflationary reading must locate in Epictetus one ideal for all individuals to emulate—the wise man. See, for example, De Lacy 1977, 167. Or, as Hijmans 1959 says, "one may say that the Socrates presented to us by Epictetus shows, apart from his personal characteristics, all the attributes of the Wise Man of the Stoa, the ideal man, to whose full splendour most of us cannot attain" (76).

And yet, as I argued, the extraordinary individuals of *Discourses* 1.2 are not sages because they are called upon to perform different deeds. They certainly are role models, but as role models they have replaced the sage. I take up this issue again in the next chapter.

3. Oldfather 1928 renders this line in 2.5.26 as "and then of that which is said to be very close to the other," whereas Hard and Gill 1995 render it as "and next, of that to which you immediately belong." On Oldfather's reading, Epictetus indicates a close kinship between the cosmic *polis* and the human *polis*; on Hard and Gill's reading, Epictetus merely says that we are immediately proximate to our civic *polis*. Although, grammatically speaking, it might be debated what is being called close to what, there are good grounds for favoring Oldfather's interpretation as the more consistent. If we follow the Hard and Gill interpretation, we have made Epictetus say that our civic *polis* is nearer to us than the city of humans and gods. Unless we attribute to Epictetus the rustic and non-Stoic view that the gods inhabit a faraway place (such as Mount Olympus), it is difficult to make sense of this interpretation. For Epictetus, as for any Stoic, the cosmic *polis* envelops us; in fact, Epictetus forcefully asserts that our immediate and fundamental kinship is *not* to our civic *polis* but to the cosmic *polis* (1.9.1–7). Epictetus cites Socrates as an exemplar of this cosmopolitan kinship and he explains the primacy of our cosmic citizenship by reference to the fact that we are "interwoven with God through *logos*" (1.9.5). Indeed, this immediate kinship with the cosmos is even emphasized in lines before 2.5.26 when Epictetus urges that we ought to consider ourselves as "parts of the whole" (2.5.25). The cosmic kinship is also reflected in Epictetus's emphasis that we are surrounded by physical nature and all the random events of life (2.5.27 and 3.24.29). For these reasons, my translation takes Epictetus to say that the human *polis* is as close as possible to the cosmic *polis*. Alternatively, we could take the city that is as close as possible to be our own soul. Such a claim would follow Plato's *Republic* and would resonate with Epictetus's claim that we must first please God and then ourselves (4.12.12), just as 2.5.26 makes us first cosmic souls and then individual souls. However, it is strange to speak of our soul as that which is as "close as possible [to us]" when the soul should *be* us. In addition, the context does not seem to support it and Epictetus nowhere follows up on the idea that the individual soul is a *polis,*

perhaps on the grounds that it would entail the heterodox position that the soul is not unified (see L&S, 321).

4. See also 2.6.9–10 and 2.10.4–6, of which the latter passage is preceded by a discussion of our universal (human) role.

5. Cf. 3.24.34–36 where he speaks of Nature as a general ordering up troops, but he adds that "that General [i.e., God] and this one [i.e., an ordinary general] are not the same, either in strength or the superiority of character" (3.24.35).

6. Curiously, the subject of role conflict is rarely addressed in the literature on Epictetus and yet it is the natural question to ask of Epictetus's account (cf. Cicero's criticisms of Panaetius on this score; *De Off.* 1.152–161). Regarding role conflict in Epictetus, Annas 2007, 140–142, raises the problem of conflict between our universal human role and our more specific roles (such as son or councilor) and she concludes, quite rightly, that the two should work in concert (149–152). It is only Frede 2007, 167, who explicitly worries about the thorny problem of conflict between our specific roles, what we might call "horizontal" conflict. Frede agrees that our human role must take precedence, but he adds that there are many specific roles "instantiated in one individual human being" (ibid.) which may not mix. Frede, however, defers further discussion: "It is an important part of Epictetus's thought about persons, which unfortunately I have no time to address, that various roles or sorts of person do not mix (IV.2.10)" (ibid.). Sorabji 2006 equally notices that we "cannot combine different roles," but he draws the unusual inference that we thus each have a human role and a unique, individual role (162; cf. 163 and 167). In addition, his insistence on the uniqueness of our specific role appears to rule out any conflict of the sort that I am describing because his account appears to leave us with only one specific role per person.

7. Cf. 2.10.1–7; see also *Ench.* 24.4 in which we are told to take up whatever role in a city we can have while maintaining our (human) sense of shame. Interestingly, this priority system resembles Cicero's in that Cicero also clearly indicates that our human *persona* has ethical priority over our specific *personae*. Epictetus is less explicit, however, quite possibly because he seems to think that conflict between our humanity and a specific role is rare.

8. See chapter 1 for more discussion of this passage.

9. The use of *tas dunameis* here is curious. Oldfather 1928 translates it as "the possibilities of our social relations," whereas Hard and Gill 1995 translate it as "the rightful demands of our social relationships." I have followed LSJ which indicates that *dunamis* can mean "*the force* or *meaning* of a word" or "*the worth* or *value* of money." As a result, Epictetus is saying that we gauge appropriate action by reference to the weight or importance of each relationship.

10. In the next section, it is not my aim to develop Epictetus's complete account of Socrates or of Cynicism. I offer the example of Socrates and Cynicism as one of Epictetus's best examples of role conflict. Another instance might include the strange case of Crates's Cynic marriage or *kunogamea* (3.22.67–76; cf. Diogenes Laertius 6.96.1–15); Cynic marriage is discussed in chapter 7. Readers interested in a much fuller account of Epictetus's relationship to Socrates should consult Long 2002. Readers interested in Epictetus and Cynicism should consult Billerbeck 1978 and Schofield 2007.

11. Cf. 1.1.18: "'Then, [is it necessary] for me to be the only one to be beheaded now?' What then? Do you want everyone to be beheaded in order for you to have consolation?" See also 2.5.25, 2.10.4–6, and 3.24.28–29.

12. This would contradict Epictetus's claim that we are given volition (*prohairesis*) by the gods (1.1.7–9), a faculty that is strictly up to us (3.26.24 and 4.5.34) and which can be used for good or evil (1.25.1).

13. As implied by 2.5.18–21; see 3.24.60, 3.26.23, and 4.5.33 on Socrates's role as a father; 4.1.159–165 on his roles as father, husband, citizen, and soldier (cf. 4.5.1–7).

14. Throughout the litany, Epictetus frequently uses the diminutive, signaling a kind of annoyance at all the "little" tasks that are placed upon this Cynic-father.

15. In much the same way, Epictetus grants that even the position of high-level politician mixes poorly with family life: "You are stationed in a chief city and not in some humble spot, and you are forever a senator. Do you not know that it is necessary for such a man to manage his household minimally, and to be away from home much of the time whether ruling or being ruled or serving some ruler, whether serving in the army or sitting as a judge?" (3.24.36).

16. Epictetus straightforwardly accepts the apocryphal stories about Socrates's jealous and hostile wife, Xanthippe, and his ungrateful son, Lamprocles. Compare, for example, 4.5.33 to D.L. 2.36–37.

17. See D.L. 7.168–170, although Diogenes reports Cleanthes as working by night and engaged in philosophy by day.

18. As Oldfather 1928, vol. 2, 344, points out, these were gifts from Alcibiades; presumably, they were smashed by Xanthippe out of jealousy. See Athen. *Deip.* 14, 643 F.

19. Musonius *Diss.* 11 claims that farmers can study philosophy by listening to a teacher while they toil in the fields. However, Musonius cautions that "occupations which strain and tire the whole body compel the mind to share in concentration . . . upon the body"; and so, "it is not impossible for men to learn in addition to their farm work, especially if they are not kept at work constantly but have periods of rest" (Lutz 1947, 81–82 and 85).

20. Plato *Phaedo* 60a. Since Epictetus cites few details of Socrates's home life, I am extrapolating from the record about Socrates in order to bring out a relevant contrast. However, given that Epictetus seems to accept the entire record, whether Xenophon or Plato (see, for example, his quoting from the *Crito* in 1.4.24 and .31), my use of an example from the *Phaedo* seems warranted. Epictetus appears to quote from the *Phaedo* 77d at 2.1.15 and he seems to nod to the dialogue at 4.4.22 when he speaks of Socrates composing hymns while in prison, a detail that is recorded in *Phaedo* 60d and 61a–b. See also 2.13.24 which references Socrates's dialogues in prison. Epictetus's use of the *Phaedo* is discussed in Erler 2007.

21. On the challenges of mixing a senator's life with a family, see note 15.

22. While I think that Epictetus has grounds for concluding that Socrates is deliberately provoking the jury (e.g., his inflammatory demand for free meals as his punishment at Plato *Apology* 36b–38b), I am not entirely convinced of his interpretation that Socrates's role as gadfly requires such behavior. Rather, I suspect that, because Epictetus absorbs Socrates into the Cynic tradition (see 3.22.26, cited above), he sees Socrates's courtroom demeanor as akin to the scandalous behavior of the Cynics. For Epictetus, the outrageous behavior of a Cynic seems to have the goal of shocking us into an awareness of our own hypocrisy about virtue.

23. As with the translation of *idia* in 3.23.4 (see chapter 1), the resonance of this compact expression is difficult to render. Given that Epictetus uses *idios* to distinguish our more specific roles from our universal role in 3.23.4 and *idiôtikos* in 3.22.69 and 3.22.74 to distinguish our familial obligations from the public obligations of the Cynic, Epictetus might here be referring to Heracleitus's specific roles or his familial obligations. At the very least, *ta idia* picks out one's personal or private interests, including one's family, as opposed to what is public.

24. Reydams-Schils 2005, 48, helpfully notes that Musonius justifies Socrates's death on the grounds that one is "allowed to disregard one's current obligations, Musonius says, if through one's death one would benefit even more people." She points to Musonius fr. 29 in Lutz 1947.

25. Cf. 2.5.25 and 2.5.27, the lines which immediately surround the central passage we have been considering in this chapter: as an "attached" human, that is, as a human being living in the cosmic plenum among others, "it is appropriate for you now to be sick, now to be at sea and in danger, now to be at a loss, and sometimes it is possible to die before your time" (2.5.25). These lines are discussed in note 3. Also see 2.10.4–6.

26. Cf. how in 1.2.26 Epictetus explains the reasoning of the athlete who chooses death over castration, an explanation couched in terms of specific roles "as a man [*anêr*], Epictetus said, and as a man who had been proclaimed at the Olympic games and had contended for victory, who dwelled in such places, and had not merely been rubbed with oil in Bato's [wrestling school]."

27. Epictetus does not cite an example beyond his friend Heracleitus, but perhaps he would allow that Aristotle made the right decision to withdraw from Athens during the upswing of anti-Macedonian sentiment rather than to stay and risk a conviction (or worse).

28. Besides our human capacity to understand, Epictetus adds that we also have other (presumably allied) human capacities. He says, "have you not received capacities [*dunameis*] according to which you will bear everything that happens? Have you not received magnanimity? Have you not received courage? Have you not received endurance? And what care do I have for the things that can happen, if I am magnanimous? What will distress me or agitate me,

or seem painful to me? Shall I not use my capacity [*dunamin*] for what ends I have received it, but mourn and groan at what happens?" (1.6.28–29).

29. Given the different obligations among specific roles, it appears that Epictetus believes that his function argument applies not just to humans versus animals but to Cynics versus fathers and so on. He thus merges his account of roles with Aristotle's function argument (*NE* 1.7). I would suggest that Epictetus's variation on the function argument also provides us with an analogous way of understanding the potential role conflicts discussed in the previous section; for just as the function of reproduction may tragically come into conflict with the function of survival (in what biologists call antagonistic pleiotropy), so the functions of a father may conflict with the functions of a Cynic.

30. Although Epictetus develops those features with an emphasis on human beings (see, e.g., 1.2 and 2.10), his account in 1.6 suggests that he is open to the idea that non-humans have roles because they, too, have specific capacities and relations. This suggestion is further supported by Epictetus's use of analogies to animals when he explains certain special roles (e.g., 3.1.22–23, 3.22.6, and 3.22.99); see Stephens 1998.

31. For Epictetus, our specific roles concern jobs that we must do for our relations in the civic community (cf. *Ench.* 24.4) and, in this passage, it seems, that our human role concerns a job or jobs that we must do in relation to Nature. See chapter 1.

32. Epictetus several times uses the analogy of a bull for the role of a protective leader. See 3.1.22–23, 3.22.6, and 3.22.99.

33. Cf. Epictetus's line elsewhere: "If Heracles had sat at home, what would he have been? [He would have been] Eurystheus [the figure who commanded Heracles's labors] and not Heracles" (2.16.44). See also 4.4.22, discussed above, which says that a crying Socrates would no longer be a Socrates.

34. Indeed, note that Epictetus does *not* present us with the traditional story about Heracles at the crossroads where Heracles must choose between virtue and vice (cf. Cicero *De Off.* 1.118 and Xenophon *Mem.* 2.1.21ff.). For Epictetus's Heracles, the choice is between being Heracles and being Endymion or Eurystheus.

35. From other references to Heracles in the *Discourses*, it is clear that Epictetus expected Heracles to fulfill his human obligation to accept what the world assigns to him (3.22.57 and 4.10.10).

36. "Excellence [*Areta*], greatly striven for by mankind, / . . . For your sake Heracles, son of Zeus . . . underwent much, hunting your power" (F675 R from D.L. 5.7; translated by Jonathan Barnes and Gavin Lawrence).

37. If Heracles sought to create his own labors, he would, in effect, be doubting that God has beneficently designed a match between his circumstances and his talents; he would be usurping Nature (cf. 1.24.1–3). Nonetheless, there is a sense in which Heracles *does* seek the lion or the hydra: when he has no choice but to confront a beast, he piously assents to his circumstances, he wishes no others, and he rushes into the fray (3.22.57). Accordingly, Epictetus generalizes from Heracles's role to all our specific roles, explaining how the realization of our capacities must involve a willingness to meet whatever Nature sends our way: "Come then, since you perceive these things, pay attention to the faculties [*dunameis*] which you have, and while you behold them, say: 'Bring now, O Zeus, what circumstance You will; for I have equipment given to me from You, and resources for adorning myself through what happens'" (1.6.37). Similarly, if the foot understood that its job sometimes included getting muddy, it would seek the mud (2.6.9–10; cf. 2.10.5–6).

38. Epictetus's unusual treatment of Heracles's labors has also been recognized by Cullyer 2003 in her essay on *andreia* in Stoicism. Cullyer explains the passage by suggesting that Epictetus is synthesizing Stoicism with Greek conventions about the nature of *andreia*. While Cullyer's explanation is plausible, I have been arguing that Epictetus's account of Heracles is not so much about conventional norms of courage as it is about Heracles's fitting attachment to his specific role as a hero.

39. Cf. note 26.

40. Sorabji 2006, 161, helpfully explains that the origin of the philosopher's beard "is said to have lain in a misconception that arose when the clean-shaven Romans were smitten by a delegation from Athens in 155 BC of three bearded Greeks who were the leading philosophers

of the day. The Romans assumed that the beard was the mark of a philosopher." *Pace* Reydams-Schils 2005, 46, who associates the beard strictly with masculinity.

Chapter Six

The Role of Roles in Epictetus's *Discourses* 1.2: Three Interpretations

In the previous chapters, we explored the basic structure of Epictetus's account of roles. We saw that we all bear a human role as well as a wide variety of specific roles such as "son, father, brother, citizen, husband, wife, neighbor, fellow-traveler, ruler, and subject" (2.14.8; cf. 3.2.4, and 4.6.26). We also examined the connection that Epictetus draws between roles and appropriate action as well as his recognition of role conflict. Throughout the preceding chapters, I have frequently made use of the examples of roles that Epictetus cites in *Discourses* 1.2, a discourse that is his longest discussion of roles among all his scattered remarks. I have used those examples as reasonably as possible, but I have certainly acquired a number of interpretive debts along the way. In *Discourses* 1.2, Epictetus moves through a compressed series of examples in order to elucidate his claim about determining reasonableness and goodness by reference to our role. And yet, as Epictetus proceeds through *Discourses* 1.2, it becomes increasingly unclear precisely how roles are being invoked in order to explain what is reasonable and good. Is he contrasting the right and wrong way to fulfill a role, is he contrasting better and worse courses of action, or is he contrasting equally valid but different roles?

Fortunately, owing to the work of the previous chapters, we now have the resources to fully address the role of roles in *Discourses* 1.2. At the same time, I intend my analysis to reaffirm my claim that, on Epictetus's view, individuals have many roles and that these roles are substantive enough such that they may conflict.[1] To make my case, this chapter will examine three interpretations of the roles presented in *Discourses* 1.2—a deflationary interpretation,[2] a concessionary interpretation, and an egalitarian interpretation. I will begin by analyzing the problem posed by *Discourses* 1.2 in greater detail and then analyze the strength of each interpretation by means of successive readings of *Discourses* 1.2; I shall conclude in favor of the egalitarian reading as the best interpretation.

THE PROBLEM OF EPICTETUS'S ETHICAL ROLES IN *DISCOURSES* 1.2

Epictetus commences *Discourses* 1.2 by announcing a principle about what rational agents can and cannot tolerate (1.2.1–4). He asserts that rational agents cannot tolerate what is unreasonable but they can tolerate what is reasonable (*eulogon*); indeed, such agents are even attracted to what is reasonable. Epictetus illustrates his point with the seemingly paradoxical examples that we can endure a whipping or even endure being hanged if we feel that it is reasonable. To a Stoic audience, Epictetus's claim would likely resonate with the standard definition of an appropriate act as one that admits of a reasonable justification (*eulogon apologian*).[3] The admissibility of a reasonable defense is significant because it applies to the action itself; accordingly, even plants and animals are not precluded from performing appropriate actions because rational observers can explain plant or animal actions as reasonable by reference to their respective natures (L&S, 59B; cf. 59C). It makes sense for a flower to open its petals in direct sunlight in order to nourish itself and therefore its action is appropriate. From the perspective of that definition, we can see that Epictetus is already adding an interesting point about the psychology of rational agents: their resistance or attraction to an action is driven by what they feel (*pathêi*) is reasonable (1.2.3). While plants and animals can have a surrogate who supplies the reasonable account for them, Epictetus informs us that we, as rational agents, must locate the reasonableness in our own actions because we cannot tolerate doing what we find unreasonable.

Following that insight, Epictetus observes that what is reasonable or unreasonable differs from person to person (1.2.5). The force of his observation, however, is somewhat perplexing. Epictetus is not, of course, recommending that we merely follow what appears to us to be reasonable for he subsequently tells us that our picture of what is reasonable must harmonize with nature (1.2.6). And yet, it is not clear if such harmonization should or would make what is reasonable the same for every person. On the one hand, Epictetus seems to imply that it should be so universalized when he tells us that, because what is reasonable differs for different persons, "we need education most of all so that we learn to adapt . . . our preconception of what is reasonable . . . to the particular instances" (1.2.6; cf. 1.22.9). What is reasonable should vary according to the particulars, and not, so it seems, according to the person. On the other hand, Epictetus also implies that the application of reasonableness may vary from person to person when he dissects the very notion of what is reasonable and says that reasonableness itself is judged on the basis of what is external and what befits one's own role (*prosôpon*). These externals are surely made up of preferred and dispreferred things; while nature inclines us to prefer life over death or the well-being of our family, there is at least some variation from person to person in that we each prefer our own families above the families of another. In much the same way, Epictetus refers to judging by what befits each one's (*heautou hekastos*) role, as though there might be differences in roles from person to person.

The difficulty of understanding what Epictetus means here is made frustratingly worse when he tries to illuminate these claims by means of a perplexing series of binary examples concerning the slave who resists versus the slave who obeys, the senator who speaks out against Caesar versus the senator who sits in silence, and so on. As Epictetus proceeds through these examples, he does not tell us precisely what roles he has in mind or how many roles are at stake in each case. Epictetus's very first example is sufficient to demonstrate this ambiguity. Epictetus offers us the case of a person who has been ordered to hold the chamber pot for someone else (1.2.8–11). Epictetus explains that one individual will see it as reasonable to hold the chamber pot when he considers that he will be beaten if he does not hold it (1.2.8); another individual will find it intolerable (*aphorêton*)[4] to hold it or witness someone else hold it (1.2.9). The individual in question then asks Epictetus if he should hold the chamber pot, but Epictetus does not answer. Rather, Epictetus reviews the obvious fact that there will not be any punishment if the order is obeyed. The anonymous interlocutor then tells Epictetus that it does not befit him to hold the chamber pot. Epictetus replies to this individual that it is up to the recipient of the order to consider the question because "you are the one that knows yourself, of how much you are worth to yourself and for how much you are selling yourself. Different men sell [themselves] at different prices." (1.2.11). The ensuing examples are equally ambiguous.

Herein is the difficulty: what role or roles are at stake in this example? What do they contribute to our ethical reasoning? Since Epictetus declares that roles are a factor in determining what is reasonable, it is pressing to know the answer; in turn, we could thereby decipher what work a role is supposed to do for each person. And yet, rather than discussing roles, the chamber pot example focuses on outcomes such as being beaten versus being fed which the Stoics treat as mere preferred indifferents.[5] It is therefore unclear what work a role does in the example, especially since none are named.

In response to this ambiguity, I will examine three possible readings of the examples: (1) a deflationary reading—in each dyad, there is only one role-type and it is to be identified with the agent who takes the dramatically resistant action; the other agent fails to follow this role-type at all; thus, the role in question is none other than that of a sage-like figure, whereas the individual who fails this role does so because he is ignorant of what is reasonable and he is wicked; (2) a concessionary reading—in each dyad, there is only one role-type and it is to be identified with the agent who takes the "lesser" course of action; accordingly, the resistant action represents an appropriate action as dictated by Stoic ethics, whereas the more passive role-bound action is offered as a "second best" alternative for agents who are unable to perform the ideal appropriate act; (3) an egalitarian reading—in each dyad, there are two role-types and both have relative merit; accordingly, what matters is that agents discover and fulfill the role which fits. I will examine the difficulties with fitting each of the first two interpretations to the text of *Discourses* 1.2. On the basis of the shortcomings in the first two interpretations, I will argue that the last interpretation is the most consistent reading of 1.2 as a whole.

A DEFLATIONARY INTERPRETATION

Let us begin our analysis with the first interpretation and investigate *Discourses* 1.2 on the assumption that Epictetus is offering us an account of the Stoic wise man in the guise of a dramatic role. This interpretation is initially quite plausible because every example in this discourse follows the same pattern: an individual who resists some pressure[6] is contrasted with an individual who folds under pressure. And, if we assume that Epictetus has Stoic wise men in mind, we naturally surmise that he identifies these ethically exemplary figures with the acts of resistance (e.g., refusing Caesar's order) while treating their counterparts as pusillanimous or ethically compromised. Indeed, on this reading, Epictetus appears to deploy each of the binary examples in order to show us that we can calculate what is reasonable by reference to externals (such as being fed or not) *or* that we can calculate it by reference to the role of the exemplary figure. In addition, given the magnificence ascribed to these model figures, it would seem that Epictetus wants us to regard the role-bound path as ethically superior. In fact, it would even seem that Epictetus is merely rephrasing standard Stoic doctrine: actions that seek what is preferred are appropriate but remain indifferent (cf. 2.5.19) and without ethical worth;[7] by contrast, actions that (quoting Stobaeus) "acquire the additional properties of firmness and tenor and their own particular fixity" (L&S, 59I) are truly good. In the language of *Discourses* 1.2, the latter actions are the actions which befit our role (*prosôpon*). Of course, both what is external and what befits our role inform what is reasonable but, as Epictetus says, "we need education most of all so that we learn to adapt . . . our preconception of what is reasonable . . . to the particular instances" (1.2.6). I take it that such education would require us to study what befits our role.[8]

With this interpretive template, the examples of *Discourses* 1.2 prove manageable but rather condescending. If we return to the chamber pot example (1.2.8–11), we can say that Epictetus intends the example to glamorize resistance to a demeaning command and to show us that it is only a Stoic sage who would face a beating with equanimity. In addition, we must say that ignoring a beating (which is a matter of indifference anyway) is virtuous. Also, we make Epictetus implicitly disapprove of slavery by exalting a kind of civil disobedience. Nonetheless, the example focuses on an individual who feels ambivalent; this cowardly figure feels that holding the chamber pot would not befit him (1.2.11) and yet, he is painfully aware of the consequences of such disobedience since "he considers only [*monon*] that . . . he will get a beating" (1.2.8). The use of *monon* here suggests that perhaps the ambivalent individual is guilty of tunnel vision. To this person, the one who does not yet unqualifiedly feel that it is reasonable to resist the demeaning command, Epictetus tells the obedient slave that he should not sell himself cheaply. In this way, Epictetus appears to offer an inferior alternative to an individual who lacks the courage to perform the correct action and refuse the shameful order. For such a person, Epictetus suggests that, if he must compromise, at least try not to compromise about something worth little.

The next two examples follow the same pattern. First, we encounter Florus who has been ordered by Nero to participate in a spectacle (1.2.12–18), an activity which any Roman noble would consider unbecoming. Such obedience would be distasteful, but disobedience to Nero would carry a heavy price, either punishment or death. Florus reveals his inner turmoil to Agrippinus, who intends to resist Nero's command. As Florus debates the matter with Agrippinus, Agrippinus ominously warns Florus that "once a man stoops to the consideration of such questions, voting on the value of externals, he is very close to those who have forgotten . . . their role [*prosôpon*]" (1.2.14). Agrippinus goes on to explain that he himself refuses to obey Nero's invitation because he sees himself as like the purple stripe on a senatorial toga. Although he is speaking metaphorically, it seems safe to say that Agrippinus is picking out his role (*prosôpon*).[9] His job in resistance is to stand out from the rest. Like the slave in the previous example, Florus is fixated on externals as his measure for what constitutes a reasonable action whereas Agrippinus has transcended them so that only his sage-like role informs his sense of what is reasonable. Obedience is so unreasonable to Agrippinus that he does "not even debate it" as an option (1.2.14). By contrast, it would seem that Florus lacks the strength to resist and he seems inferior because his obeisance is described as plain vanilla assimilation, like the white part of a toga (1.2.17–18). Our sense of Agrippinus's superiority is heightened when we consider that the Agrippinus cited here is probably Paconius Agrippinus, a Stoic who was known for his opposition to tyranny.[10]

In the next example, Helvidius Priscus is presented as debating with Emperor Vespasian, who is threatening Helvidius to stay silent in the senate or else be beheaded. Like Agrippinus, Helvidius was known for his opposition to tyranny and we imagine that Vespasian does not want to hear criticism of himself or his regime in the senate house. However, Helvidius explains to Vespasian that, so long as he (Helvidius) remains a senator, he will speak out regardless of what is threatened. Helvidius appeals to a standard Stoic trope about how we are mortal and the appropriate response to an inevitable death is to die without distress (1.2.21). Epictetus justifies this intransigence with the same language as Agrippinus: he is the purple stripe on the senatorial toga and his role is to be "set forth as a beautiful example to the rest" (1.2.22). Epictetus closes this example by contrasting Helvidius to an anonymous senator who would obey Vespasian's order to stay away from the senate. Epictetus does not explain why this individual would obey, but the preceding cases suggest that this anonymous senator would obey because he is narrowly focused on what is preferable (namely, his own life). Epictetus appears to affirm that this anonymous senator has taken the inferior path when he says that Vespasian would not need to forbid such a man because the anonymous senator would "either sit like a jug, or, if he spoke, [would say] what he knew Caesar wanted, and would pile up besides still more" (1.2.24).

Epictetus rounds out his examples with two even more compressed and ambiguous cases, but they unfold just like the previous instances. First, he discusses an Olympic athlete who has suffered an injury and has been told by a doctor that he must undergo castration or he will die (1.2.25–28). The athlete refuses castration, and Epictetus explains that his death was appropriate given his status. Epictetus does not explain the decision further but, as suggested in the previous chapter, it is likely that he thinks that a castrated athlete would somehow lose his masculine power. Second, Epictetus discusses his own case where the Roman emperor has ordered philosophers to shave their beards or else be beheaded. Epictetus proudly explains his refusal to obey even though he is taking a potentially fatal risk (1.2.28–29). He asserts that his action is befitting his role (1.2.28). As he explains elsewhere (and as we saw in the previous chapter), Epictetus regards a beard and rough cloak to be the essential uniform of a philosopher (3.1.24, 3.2.24, and 4.8.4–20). In both cases, death is regarded as indifferent because, on this interpretation, their preconception of what is reasonable has been brought into conformity with nature (cf. 1.2.6). Each unflinchingly risks death because each apprehends their role and such apprehension makes even death reasonable—so long as such a death would preserve their role.

After these examples, according to the deflationary interpretation, the discourse finishes with a generalized review of the fact that we need education in order to be ready to fulfill this role (1.2.30–32). The discourse also offers some encouragement to those who are not exemplary (1.2.33–37)—they should not give up their diligence "from despair for [not attaining] the highest" (1.2.37). Epictetus insists that we are indeed born to become like Socrates (1.2.34), that is, for becoming wise, but he recognizes that few men realize that potential.[11] In more traditional Stoic language, Epictetus is instructing those who are making progress not to give up their quest to one day perform perfect appropriate actions. To summarize, then, as Phillip De Lacy frames this interpretation, *Discourses* 1.2 organizes individuals "in terms of their position on an ascending scale that terminates in the sage. Those who differ from the sage are his inferiors."[12] When it comes to judging what is reasonable and therefore what is appropriate, *Discourses* 1.2 demonstrates that it is ethically superior to judge by what befits one's role (rather than by preferred indifferents). More specifically, it appears that the content of that role looks like the Stoic sage and we may perhaps identify it simply as our role as rational agents, that is, as human beings. Epictetus is thus not endorsing a diversity of roles for he is requiring everyone to fill the same role-type; he is reaffirming the standard Stoic view that only the sage is truly good while all others, including those who are making progress, are ignorant. And, in fact, this interpretation is how Epictetus's role ethics has sometimes been read.[13]

This interpretation has an important advantage in that it tries to treat the impressive characters of *Discourses* 1.2 as sage-like figures and thus Epictetus sounds like a standard Stoic. However, this interpretation also has a critical disadvantage in that it fails to make sense of the concept of a role. Epictetus begins *Discourses* 1.2 by stating that we find actions reasonable according to our roles, but the preceding interpretation requires that everyone's role be exactly the same and thus it eliminates any value to Epictetus's initial claim that reasonableness varies according to role. Apparently, reasonableness does not vary at all because roles do not vary at all. Indeed, although Epictetus uses the term "role" (*prosôpon*) in the singular,[14] he does not talk about it as though it is a single and universal maxim. At 1.2.7, he is quite explicit about referencing *each one's role* (*prosôpon heautou hekastos*); similarly at 1.2.30 he refers to the role of each person (*prosôpon hekastos*). In the same way, when Agrippinus warns Florus about his actions, he instructs Florus not to forget his private (*idiou*) role (1.2.14), not a common (*koinos*) role.[15] Perhaps we could say that we each have that one role which happens to be exactly like everyone else's role; and, given that we share our humanity in common, we could say that Helvidius and Agrippinus are sage-like exemplars of a human role. And yet, Epictetus does not appeal to our humanity in

1.2 in order to justify various courses of action; what he appeals to is a *role*, held by some but not by others.

Furthermore, if we take the view that Epictetus is contrasting sage-like figures with those who are ignorant or making progress, we must take these exemplary figures (and even Epictetus) to be very bad advisors. When Florus wonders whether or not he should debase himself by appearing in Nero's spectacle (1.2.12–18), Agrippinus tells him to enter. If, however, Agrippinus properly represents how rational human agency should be expressed in the context of Nero's order, Agrippinus should have told Florus to resist the command. Similarly, Epictetus seems to have sanctioned ignorant action when he explains that not every horse becomes fast (1.2.34) and so not everyone can be like Socrates.

Finally, although it is entirely plausible that Epictetus views a figure like Socrates as a sage, Epictetus does not distinguish between the examples in *Discourses* 1.2 along the lines of ignorance versus wisdom (the exclusive possession of the Stoic sage). In standard Stoic terms, the wise man has right reason (*orthos logos*) and from this perfect state of knowledge, he always says and does what is right (L&S vol. I, 367);[16] by contrast, the ignorant have—at best—only a reasonable defense of their actions. Between these two, the external action may often be the same (cf. Cicero, *De Fin.* 4.15); they differ in the epistemic state behind the action. But, this contrast between the wise and the ignorant is not the operative contrast in Epictetus's distinction between Agrippinus and Florus, between the purple stripe and the white toga; rather, the operative distinction in *Discourses* 1.2 is between extremely challenging appropriate acts and less challenging appropriate acts. Granted, the exemplary individuals of *Discourses* 1.2 act without doubt and they appear automatically aware of their own prowess (1.2.30–32). In addition, the self-assurance of extraordinary individuals appears to arise from a high sense of self-worth just as the self-doubt of ordinary individuals appears to arise from a diminished sense of self-worth (and perhaps even a failure to accept their own self-worth). But, when Epictetus proceeds to instruct ordinary individuals about their self-worth, he does not exclude them from experiencing certainty nor does he does imply that certainty about their self-worth or their role would transform them into extraordinary individuals. Rather, if the ordinary slave had a sense of certainty, it would mean that he would hold the chamber pot as unhesitatingly as the extraordinary slave would refuse to do so. Likewise, Florus would not require an exhortation from Agrippinus about whether or not to enter the festival; instead, he should calmly enter the event as required by his own sense of self-worth.

A CONCESSIONARY READING

It is out of these problems in the first interpretation that the second reading is generated. This second interpretation holds that there is only one role in each pair but it is to be identified with the agent who takes the lesser course of action; accordingly, the resistant action represents a perfect appropriate action as dictated by Stoic ethics, whereas the more passive (role-bound) action is offered as a "second best" alternative for agents who are unable to perform the ideal appropriate act. I take my inspiration for this reading from R. Kamtekar,[17] who appears to treat the roles of *Discourses* 1.2 as a second best way for calculating what is right. She holds that we turn to roles when we cannot infer the will of nature (Kamtekar 1998, 148).[18]

This concessionary reading has the advantage that it can absorb the very criticisms leveled against the first interpretation. In this second reading, Epictetus is offering a two-tiered ethics; on the highest tier, one acts like "Socrates and such men" (1.2.33) and performs the sort of actions that "we are born for" (1.2.34). These are the actions which befit us as human beings. On the second tier, Epictetus recognizes, somewhat hesitantly, that "the great and magnified deed, perhaps, befits others" (1.2.33) so he offers us an ethics based on roles. And, because this is offered as a concession, Epictetus is concerned to advise us that we settle as minimally as possible, that we do not sell ourselves cheap (1.2.11 and 33). By acting according to our role, we will at least be acting in a way that admits of a reasonable defense and thus be acting appropriately; and yet, because these actions are "second best," we can accommodate the standard Stoic point that even appropriate actions fall short of the perfect actions of a sage.[19] Additionally, this interpretation can easily explain the fact that Epictetus implies that we have many roles because his examples reveal that there are such: slave, ordinary senator, and athlete.

We can see the effectiveness of this interpretation especially as applied to the example of holding the chamber pot. Concerning the slave or servant who receives the order (1.2.8–11), Epictetus begins, as we saw, by straightforwardly explaining that it is preferable to be fed and not to be beaten; thus, if the slave measures his action against those consequences, he should fulfill his master's order to hold the chamber pot. Since what is external is part of determining what is reasonable, the slave should find it reasonable to hold the chamber pot. And yet, the slave in question hesitates. According to the concessionary interpretation under examination, the slave detects that the superior action is to resist the command because the command does not befit himself and yet he also recognizes that it befits a slave to obey his master. The slave presses this point to Epictetus, but Epictetus avoids assigning a role to the slave, perhaps because it represents the lesser alternative: "It is necessary for you to 'add to the bill' in your inquiry, not I. For you are the one who knows yourself, of how much you are worth to yourself . . ."

(1.2.11). When Epictetus renews this same advice at the end of the discourse, he adds that one should not sell oneself cheaply (1.2.33). In the context of the concessionary reading, we must surmise that the slave should aspire for the most dignified role that he can (perhaps as a servant of higher rank than chamber servant), even though it is already the second best option to fulfill the demeaning slave role at all. Above all, the slave should not rush to hold the chamber pot simply because it is the path of least resistance.

While that analysis works quite well for the example of the slave, we encounter some difficulty in transferring it to the example of Florus, who has been ordered by Nero to appear in a public spectacle (1.2.12–18). Like the example with the slave, Florus may believe that the best action is to resist Nero's demeaning order, but he finds himself unable to resist because the penalty would be a beheading. Unlike the slave example, however, Agrippinus does not hesitate to tell Florus what to do. As Florus hesitates, Agrippinus does not comfort Florus with the thought that it is only Florus who knows himself. Instead, Agrippinus chastises Florus, telling him that "once a man stoops to the consideration of such questions, voting on the value of externals, he is very close to those who have forgotten their private [*idiou*] role [*prosôpon*]" (1.2.14). Most importantly, Agrippinus seems quite confident about what Florus's role is: Florus is not a purple stripe but rather is a white thread which should assimilate and have nothing which stands out relative to the other threads (1.2.17–18).

In this way, when Agrippinus attributes a role to Florus with the toga analogy, Agrippinus has implicitly attributed a different role to himself. That is, Florus is not being offered a second best alternative; rather, he is being instructed on his role and how it differs from Agrippinus's role. Just as Florus has the role of the white thread, so Agrippinus has the role of the purple stripe. The same point and the same metaphor is also drawn out in the succeeding example of Helvidius Priscus (1.2.19–24). Helvidius even pinpoints his obligation to speak out on his office as senator when he offers Caesar the shameless solution of stripping him (Helvidius) of senatorial rank and thereby removing the obligation to speak (1.2.19). Indeed, there is good evidence to suggest that these exemplary figures interpret their actions as based on some special role—as we saw when we reviewed the first interpretation. The athlete chooses to die because he was an Olympic-class competitor (1.2.26), while Epictetus refuses to shave off his beard in the face of an imperial order to do so because he is a philosopher (1.2.29). In the case of the chamber pot example, the individual who finds it intolerable to fulfill the order is probably also the bearer of a role, perhaps the role of a figure like Diogenes the Cynic who was sold into slavery and yet insists on giving orders to all human beings (Diogenes Laertius, 6.29–30).[20]

AN EGALITARIAN INTERPRETATION

Once we grant, however, that each scenario contrasts two roles, the exemplary and the ordinary, we are over halfway to the third interpretation that I want to defend.[21] According to this last interpretation, there are two roles and both have relative merit; what matters is that agents discover which role befits each person (cf. *Ench.* 37). The challenge for this interpretation is to explain why Epictetus would assert that the reasonable and unreasonable differ for different persons according to their role (1.2.5–7)—and yet eulogize the role that refuses obedience as magnificent and glittering (1.2.17–18) while insulting the anonymous obedient senator for being likely to flatter Caesar (1.2.24). Similarly, it must explain why Epictetus would concede to the slave that "different men sell [themselves] at different prices" (1.2.11) but identify that act with the vice of selling one's choice (*prohairesis*, 1.2.33). Finally, it must explain why Epictetus would concede that he will not be better than Socrates (a figure he much admired) but plead that it would be sufficient if he himself is not worse than Socrates (1.2.36–37).

Without an answer, we would be forced to recommit to the first interpretation in which *Discourses* 1.2 is simply a hymn to the Stoic sage. However, we should not retreat to the deflationary interpretation because Epictetus hints at an egalitarian picture of these disparate roles in his very description of the role of the purple stripe. Of Agrippinus, Epictetus says that the purple stripe is "a cause to the others of *their seeming to be fitting and beautiful*" (1.2.18); of Helvidius, Epictetus says that the purple stripe is "set forth as a beautiful example to the rest" (1.2.22). Yet given that few of us are a Milo (a great athlete) or a Croesus (1.2.37), the purple stripe surely cannot be the exact model for the white threads unless the aim of the whole toga is to become purple. The purple stripe must therefore serve as a non-literal model of what it means to fulfill a role with audacity. As Agrippinus is able to confidently act without having to debate his actions (1.2.14; cf. 1.1.28–32), so we should diligently apply ourselves to our own pursuits (1.2.37)—whatever they may be. These exemplary figures are not models in the material of their actions because their actions do not befit most of us (1.2.33). Instead, they are a model in the *manner* of their actions: they do what is appropriate without a tremor and without distress (1.2.21; cf. *Ench.* 30). They are models for *how* agents should fulfill any role.

It is instructive to compare the scenario of holding the chamber pot to Epictetus's treatment of the trial of Socrates versus the trial of Epictetus's friend, Heracleitus (as discussed in chapter 5). For their respective trials, it is clear that they should treat the outcome as a matter of indifference, whether conviction *or* acquittal, and that this indifference is required by their role as human beings. So, too, with the slaves and the demeaning order, the outcome must be a matter of indifference, whether beatings *or* holding the chamber pot. Thus, when Epictetus begins the example of the slave in *Discourses* 1.2, he first explains to the slave the two sets of preferred goods that are at stake (1.2.8–10). Yet, this answer does not satisfy the slave. What the slave wants to know is whether it is beneath himself to hold the chamber pot (1.2.11). As in the Socrates and Heracleitus example, external goods are not sufficient to determine what to do. What they need to know is their specific role—to bait the jury or to persuade the judge. So it is with the slave. The matter is to be resolved by determining what his specific role is, the role that is consonant with who he is. Intriguingly, Epictetus demurs from answering; instead, he advises the slave not to sell himself cheap. In the context of his account of roles and our elucidation of it, I suggest that this means that the slave not fail his human role by obsessing over external goods *and* that he not assign to himself a specific role that is other than the role that he can and ought to fill (cf. *Ench.* 37). It is for the slave himself to determine if the role of a slave genuinely belongs to him or if, for example, he is a figure like Diogenes the Cynic who can be bought as a slave and yet insist that his role is to govern humanity (D.L. 6.29–30). Under one role, the slave should obey; under another, he should resist.

This interpretation of the slave scenario is similarly consistent with the example of Heracles's role. As in the Heracles example from chapter 5, it is not circumstance that necessarily determines one's role for it is the role itself which determines whether a circumstance is relevant to action. One's circumstances may be insufficient because there are many avenues through which we can express ourselves as human agents. For Heracles, it is his role as hero that gave the lion and the hydra their central importance. Thus, for the slave, what matters is that he find the right role. Of course, it should be a matter of indifference to the slave whether he is a servant or a senator, but once he knows which role applies, it is not a matter of indifference to fulfill his given role. And, to find his role, Epictetus says that the slave will have to rely on self-knowledge for "you are the one who knows yourself" (1.2.11). Just as Heracles must recognize who he is, that he is neither Endymion nor Eurystheus, so the slave must come to know what role makes him who he is. It is up to the slave to determine what role that is. So long as he endeavors to fulfill that specific role while preserving his role as a human being, the slave can be secure in the fact that his endeavors are sufficient (cf. 1.2.36 and *Ench.* 24.4). Thus, the slave who recognizes that his role is that of a servant should obey, not in a pusillanimous fashion, but with as much grace (and perhaps humor) as he can muster. In much the same way, at 2.6.6–8 and 3.24.44–49, Epictetus explains that there is nothing shameful in the act of a client saluting his patron so long as the salutation is not given in a lowly spirit. Epictetus even grants that the salutation may have to be offered while the door is being slammed in the client's face. Although this client presumably does not suffer as much as the slave holding the chamber pot, Epictetus manages them similarly because he emphasizes that we should ignore any indignities (which are mere preferred indifferents) in order to do what is appropriate to a role.

Applied to the other binary cases of *Discourses* 1.2, what this interpretation suggests is that Epictetus is not concerned by the fact that it befits Florus to obey Caesar. Rather, Epictetus is troubled by the fact that Florus dithers about what to do because that is when he has forgotten his role (1.2.13–14); "For once a man stoops to the consideration of such questions, *voting on the value of externals*, he is very close to those who have forgotten their private [*idiou*] *prosôpon*" (emphasis added;1.2.14). By fluctuating about his role, it would seem that Florus is acting like a child (see 3.15.12–13). Accordingly, Florus has sold his own capacity to choose (cf. 1.2.33). Epictetus is also worried that once Florus recognizes his role (whatever it is), he may still sell himself short by vacillating or groveling. Similarly, the anonymous senator who is contrasted with Helvidius ought *not* to thank Caesar when he is ordered to stay away from the senate house or flatter Caesar when he is ordered to stay silent.

So, too, Epictetus cannot perform the same actions as Socrates, but if he fulfills his role as philosopher, he will not be worse (1.2.36–37). Epictetus's claim here is significant because he expresses himself in such a precise way about the prospects for his character. Referring to himself in the third person he says, "Epictetus will not be better [*kreissôn*] than Socrates; but if I am not worse [*cheirôn*], that is sufficient [*hikanon*] for me" (ibid.). On the deflationary reading, Epictetus is being highly rhetorical here about wishing to be as good as a sage like Socrates. On the one hand, there is no such rank as "better than Socrates" since no one can be better than the sage Socrates; Epictetus raises that impossibility only to indicate (rather circuitously) that Socrates is the top of the heap. On the other hand, when he expresses a desire not to be worse, the deflationary interpretation must say that Epictetus means that he wishes to be equal to a sage. But, such an interpretation tortures the line in order to take away the impact of its humbly worded conclusion that it is sufficient *for him* not to be worse. Not good *simpliciter* nor great, but "sufficient for me."

If we stay true to the humble conclusion and read the line, not as an out of character rhetorical flourish, we must read the statement as an extremely cautious expression of hope from the man who just reminded us that not all horses become swift nor do all dogs become keen trackers (1.2.34).[22] Indeed, we must read Epictetus as being similarly cautious about what anyone has achieved or can achieve. On this non-deflationary view, Epictetus is saying something quite startling when he declares that he will not be better than Socrates because he is granting that such a rank is meaningful and we are left to assume that it is the genuine Stoic sage. Epictetus is thereby cautiously implying that no one has become a sage, not even the great Socrates (although he must have been one of the closest). In turn, Epictetus is admitting that he will not be a sage since it is virtually guaranteed that he will not be better than Socrates, but it is sufficient for the philosopher Epictetus not to be worse than a man like Socrates. Alternatively, A. A. Long suggests that Epictetus's ambitions are even more humble and he renders the line to say "Epictetus will not be superior to Socrates, but if I am not too bad [*ou cheirôn*], that is enough for me" (2002, 240).[23] Although it is more natural to interpret Epictetus as saying it is sufficient to be "not worse than Socrates," either translation is consistent with my point that Epictetus does not expect us to all be sages or even to be heroes. And similarly for those who will never surpass a great athlete like Milo or be richer than Croesus (1.2.37). Epictetus has still set the bar high because we must not compromise our self-worth, but he has lowered it just enough such that we each have hope to become the best version of ourselves in accordance with our roles, not impossible versions of historic figures.

And, in order to become the best versions of ourselves, we must discover our roles and fulfill them without a tremor and without distress. In turn, we must come to know ourselves and what we are worth (1.2.11), we must become accustomed to adding our roles into our considerations about our actions (1.2.28), and we must "undergo a winter training" so as to prepare ourselves and "not . . . spring randomly into what is improper" (1.2.32). Such a process would be assisted by an education in which we "learn to adapt, in conformity with nature, [our] preconception of what is reasonable and unreasonable to the particular instances" (1.2.6). In short, we must make a habit of our roles (cf. *Discourses* 2.9), whatever they may be.

One last mystery remains. In each set of examples, there is the dramatic act (performable only by the "purple stripes") and there is the plain act (performable by the many). While it seems clear enough that the purple stripe represents a role, it is puzzling that Epictetus chooses to discuss these plain acts in terms of the preferred goods that are at stake. Given that external goods are merely preferred and serve as the material upon which virtue is applied, it is exceptionally puzzling that the "plain" actors worry about them and even need to be warned against obsessing over them. This problem would seem to support the first interpretation.

However, this difficulty dissolves when we see that Epictetus holds there to be a special, reciprocal relationship between roles and what is preferred.[24] As in the first interpretation, the appeal to our role is more important than the appeal to what is external, but the appeal to preferred externals is not irrelevant: "in respect to judging the reasonable and the unreasonable, we employ not only the value of external things but also of what befits one's own role" (1.2.7). In particular, when a role is firmly apprehended, it shapes what the role-bearer finds preferable or not. Epictetus comes quite close to making that very point at the opening of *Discourses* 1.2 when he tells us that if someone feels it reasonable to be hanged—an activity which should normally be dispreferred—he will straightaway hang himself (1.2.3). Epictetus says that, when we find an activity reasonable, we are attracted to it (1.2.4). In other words, when we find some external reasonable, we find it preferable. Elsewhere in the *Discourses*, Epictetus makes this point by declaring that a foot by itself prefers to stay clean, but if it could understand its part (i.e., role) in the whole, it would seek to get dirty (2.5.24–26 and 2.10.3–6).

By the same token, it would seem that our feelings about externals might very well be an indicator of our role. In the case of the slave, if we take it that the role of a slave entails a special obligation to obey one's master (apart from one's obligations as a human being), then Epictetus's responses about beatings and starvation are apparently designed to think through the terms of that role as well as to consider whether the individual in question has that role at all. If the slave finds it reasonable to hold the chamber pot, then he should accept his role and obey the master's order. If the slave finds it intolerable to hold the chamber pot, then this individual finds the action unreasonable and apparently does not see himself as a slave. This resistant figure should, therefore, prepare himself to receive the beatings that will follow from his refusal of the order. On this reading, *Discourse* 1.2 allows that we have many sorts of roles with many sorts of obligations.

Of course, Epictetus would surely not permit us to decide on the basis of what is external alone; this is why Helvidius warns Florus not to fixate on external goods or else he may have forgotten his role (1.2.14). Nonetheless, a review of what externals are at stake might help the slave to understand whether he sees himself as a servant, just as a similar sort of review might help Florus understand whether he is a white thread. If he finds entry into the festival to be intolerable, that would be a clue that he is not a white thread. But, as it stands, he finds a beheading intolerable, so it is probably on that basis that Agrippinus recognizes Florus's role as a humble official and instructs him to enter.

Although this egalitarian interpretation is not immediately evident from the abbreviated examples of *Discourses* 1.2, I suggest that it makes the most sense of the evidence. And, if this egalitarian interpretation is correct, we should not be lured into concluding that *Discourses* 1.2 is an idealization of the sage or a concession to those who cannot measure up. Instead, *Discourses* 1.2 reveals itself to be as much concerned with the nameless slave who must hold the chamber pot as it is with Helvidius who must resist Caesar because both figures are capable of determining what is reasonable by calculating what befits their respective roles. So long as each person dispassionately does what is required of his or her role, it is sufficient (cf. 1.2.36). As Epictetus elsewhere says, it does not matter whether you can outfit your city with public baths (as a nobleman) or outfit your city with shoes (as a cobbler), if you perform your function, it is sufficient (*Ench.* 24.4). To all of these role-bound individuals, Epictetus's point is simple but difficult to realize: know your role and never "give up [your] diligence" in fulfilling it, certainly not "from despair for [attaining] the highest" (1.2.37).

NOTES

1. In chapter 7, we will finally consider what resources Epictetus offers for resolving role conflicts.
2. See my initial notes in chapter 5 where I attribute the denial of substantive roles and of role conflict to an interpretation that I label as deflationary.
3. See chapter 3.
4. The term *aphorêton* (unendurable; 1.2.9) is a strong term for what is intolerable.
5. E.g., Epictetus's own claims at 4.1.137–138.
6. This resistance is what Gill 1988, 187, aptly calls "the rigorous response."
7. Stobaeus, 2.65–68, Diogenes Laertius, 120–124, and Cicero, *De Finibus*, 3.70.
8. Note that the second subject (*topos*) of Epictetus's model for education involves the study of roles and appropriate action (3.2.4 and 4.10.13).
9. See chapter 2.
10. See Griffin 1984, 173. The Florus here might be Gessius Florus; he was the procurator of Judea and was blamed for creating conditions that led to a revolt (see 101 and 233).
11. Although Socrates predates Stoicism, he was absorbed by the Stoics as an idealized instance of Stoicism (cf. 2.16.35–36, 3.21.17–20, and 3.22.26).
12. De Lacy 1977, 167.
13. See Bonhöffer 1996, 129; Gill 1988, 189; Hijmans 1959, 76. These passages are also quoted and cited in the notes to chapter 5.
14. With one exception, Epictetus uses the term *prosôpon* only in the singular, suggesting either that the customary philosophic use of the term is in the singular or that he characteristically discusses roles through individual examples. He uses *prosôpa* at 4.2.10 to refer to different characters in a context where the plural seems unavoidable.
15. See the discussion of *idios* in chapter 1.
16. There are some grounds to think that Epictetus agrees with this claim; cf. 2.22.4 which implies that only the *phronimos* has *epistêmê*. See also 2.17.33 and 3.2.5. Nonetheless, this distinction is explicitly not at play here in 1.2.
17. Kamtekar 1998, 148–151.
18. It is possible that Dobbin 1998 falls here, too, although his interpretation may be a hybrid of the deflationary and the concessionary readings. Nevertheless, I find it difficult to identify Dobbin's precise stance on roles. In his helpful commentary, Dobbin treats the purple stripe as an instance of "outstanding virtue" (80) comprised of "acts of moral supererogation . . . not strictly required" (84). Yet, he adds that the example of the purple stripe "shows what is possible when the factor of self-worth comes into play; and helps inspire actions that, if not as bold, at least partake of some of the same independence" (81). And, he suggests that, as trainees make progress towards that outstanding virtue (85–86), their progress may admit degrees of virtue (89–90). Finally, when the elite athlete (i.e., a purple stripe) chooses death over castration, Dobbin treats it as an instance of the human role (79–80 and 84–85), an identification which surely singles out the athlete's decision as the pinnacle of human virtue.
19. According to Stobaeus's definition, an appropriate action is one which "when it has been done, admits of a reasonable [*eulogon*] justification [*apologian*]" (L&S 59B). On perfect appropriate actions, see L&S 59F, Cicero *De Finibus* 4.15 and *De Officiis* 3.13. See chapter 4.
20. For Epictetus's admiration of Diogenes the Cynic, see 3.21.19 and 3.26.23. Note that Epictetus apparently does not expect us all to be Cynics; see *Discourses* 3.22. As in chapter 2, I take Epictetus to regard "Cynic" as itself a special kind of role not suited for all.
21. A. A. Long might be a defender of the egalitarian interpretation although I suspect that he would adopt a more confined version of the position. Long 2002 approaches the egalitarian position when he analyzes the slave and the chamber pot example (*Disc.* 1.2.8–11; 239–240)

and he urges that Epictetus is not criticizing the slave. As Long properly points out, holding a chamber pot is a matter of indifference. And, he adds that what Epictetus aims to criticize is doing whatever one can in order to gain or avoid an object of indifference. Moreover, "Epictetus cannot tell anyone what a person is worth in the person's own eyes, but he is entitled to argue that when we weigh up the material advantages or disadvantages of any contemplated action we are also engaging in a trade-off with our characters" (239). Long does not apply this interpretation to the remaining examples of *Discourses* 1.2, however, and it does not appear that he would follow my claim that role fulfillment is not merely a form of Stoic progress but is a good. Finally, as I argued in the previous chapter, with the exception of Frede 2007, I appear to be alone in endorsing the possibility that Epictetean roles may conflict.

22. See Epictetus's even more startling claim that it is not possible for us to be without error (4.12.19).

23. Long 2002, 240, notes that the text here has sometimes been emended in order to avoid making the ordinarily humble Epictetus put himself on the same level with Socrates. Long solves the dilemma by preserving the text while creatively retranslating the line.

24. Long 2002 suggests that "Epictetus verges on heterodoxy when he claims . . . that 'natural' and 'unnatural' are evaluative distinctions that pertain only when we look at our lives in 'detachment' from our social and global contexts" (201); Long adds that "Epictetus seems to be saying that it is as natural . . . for one's foot to be dirty, and therefore the so-called preferred indifferents are inadequate guidelines for influencing one's conduct as a well-reasoned local and world citizen" (202). While I agree with Long that Epictetus diverges from standard Stoicism here, I do not think that Epictetus is raising doubts about the utility of preferred goods because their preferred status is context dependant. Rather, I think that Epictetus is demonstrating that preferred goods differ according to our roles; hence a foot by itself (which is not really a foot) prefers to be clean, but a foot attached to the body properly prefers to get dirty as a part of its job in walking.

Chapter Seven

Resolving Role Conflicts

In this chapter, we approach the limits of Epictetus's account of roles and address the difficult issue of conflict among specific roles, between my role as a brother and my role as, say, a teacher. We are at the very limits of Epictetus's account because he seems to have positioned us to recognize role conflicts, but he provides no explicit resolution of them. In fact, even Epictetus's recognition of role conflict is more tacit than explicit. Aside from the previous two chapters, we have been building towards this issue from early in our analysis of Epictetus. In chapter 2, I argued that Epictetus saw specific roles as different from each other so that it is imperative that we select the right role (*Ench.* 37). As Epictetus says, "But different characters [*prosôpa*] do not mix in this fashion; you cannot act the part of Thersites and that of Agamemnon too. If you wish to be a Thersites, you ought to be humpbacked and bald; if an Agamemnon, you ought to be tall and handsome, and to love those who have been made subject to you" (4.2.10; cf. 3.22.5–8 and *Ench.* 24.4). But, what would happen if an individual were forced to play both parts, like the ailing Philoctetes who was built to be an aristocrat like Agamemnon but suffered a mangled body like Thersites? In chapter 4, we considered the scenario in which two brothers fight over an inheritance (3.3.5–10), and we saw how Epictetus resolves that conflict by reminding us that externals are a matter of indifference. And yet, that resolution only works in cases where one agent's role conflicts with another agent's role. What should we do if we happen to be saddled with two incompatible roles? Epictetus would surely wish our roles to cohere, but he owes us an account about how to harmonize them.

Although I take the view that Epictetus fails to provide a clear-cut solution to role conflict, he has not left us without resources to think through role conflict. In this chapter, I will argue that Epictetus supplies us with three cases that shed light on how we may resolve role conflict. The first two cases can reasonably be read as instances of conflict between specific roles and I shall examine how Epictetus manages them. The third case concerns the possibility that even a single role could entail conflicting obligations and I will argue that such conflicts must be resolved from "outside" the role.

THE EXTRAORDINARY SLAVE

We return briefly to the two individuals who are ordered to hold the chamber pot in *Discourses* 1.2. In chapters 5 and 6, we considered what we can learn from Socrates's roles and what his situation means for an ordinary slave who must obey his master's order to hold the chamber pot. In this present section, I want to consider what Socrates's situation means for the extraordinary individual who resists the order. For as in the case of Socrates, the slave who resists the order is apparently saddled with *two* roles and Epictetus similarly resolves the conflict by putting one role above the other. On the one hand, this individual has received the order to hold the chamber pot, suggesting that he bears the role of a servant or slave. On the other hand, this extraordinary individual who plans on resistance apparently also bears the role of the "purple stripe in the white toga."[1]

We can imagine three roles that would put the extraordinary individual in a position to confront the order to hold the chamber pot: (1) The extraordinary individual is a citizen who receives an order from a mad caesar like Nero; (2) This extraordinary individual is a slave; (3) The extraordinary individual is a free-standing member of someone's retinue and witnesses the offending order. In each instance, the demands of two specific roles come into conflict. For the citizen, it is appropriate to obey as a citizen but inappropriate as the "bull in the herd." For the slave, it is fitting to obey, but since he is also an extraordinary individual (perhaps he is a deposed aristocrat or, as suggested previously, a figure like Diogenes the Cynic), he ought to resist.[2] For the staff member, it is presumably proper to stay silent, but as the "purple in the white toga," it is proper to intervene.

In his follow-up remarks, Epictetus appears to resolve the conflict by searching out which role the two individuals genuinely identify with themselves. For extraordinary individuals, Epictetus expects such identification to be immediately apparent (1.2.30). Although Epictetus seems to use self-worth to pick out what role a servant identifies with and is ideally fit for,[3] it seems plausible that the question may be answered by other features of the self.[4] Any feature of the self is relevant so long as it helps the slave to come to see what is reasonable (*to eulogon*) for him to do. The idea of identification brings both these points together—the role we identify with is naturally going to make the appropriate actions implied by such a role make sense and seem reasonable to us.[5] Hence, if the slave identifies with his position it makes sense to him that he ought to avoid a beating, so he is best fit for the slave role. If, by contrast, he identifies with the role of the extraordinary individual, it does not make sense to him to hold the chamber pot and so he is best fit for an extraordinary role.[6]

Even though Epictetus's resolution initially appears to allow for choice because he characterizes self-worth as something "for you to add to the consideration, not I" (1.2.11), he blocks that possibility because he expects that we must locate the role that truly fits (cf. *Ench.* 37). A lowly slave can not choose to do the work of an extraordinary individual because he does not have the power to bear it any more than the extraordinary individual can bear to hold the chamber pot (1.2.8–9). Just as prospective athletes ought to consider their physical prowess because their very role is at stake if they are unable to perform it, so here. Accordingly, Epictetus's advice cannot be that we may choose to consider self-worth or not; rather, his remark at 1.2.11 must mean that it is up to our own initiative for each of us to introspect and identify what our own self-worth is since that is the operative and necessary capacity in these two conflicting roles. Epictetus cannot perform that consideration for us because, as he says, "you are the one that knows yourself" (ibid.). Thus retranslated on this basis, 1.2.11 says that "it is necessary for you [to do the work] to introduce this [*viz.*, self-worth] into the inquiry [about your role], not me." What he is demanding is that we place a premium on honesty with ourselves, a premium altogether consistent with Epictetus's emphasis on self-knowledge. And, once we introduce this honest reflection with ourselves, Epictetus apparently expects that we will eventually be able to resolve upon one role or the other.

THE FAMILY MAN AND CYNIC MARRIAGE

As formulated, Epictetus's appeal to identification works reasonably well for conflicts where individuals identify unequally with two competing roles. It solves the conflict on the assumption that the role we identify more with is the role that is the better fit. In this case and the next, we shall examine conflicts where that procedure would be inappropriate or inapplicable. First, we shall see that Epictetus's procedure works well only in cases where two roles necessarily conflict, where one role demands x and the other demands $\sim x$. But, in cases where two roles conflict contingently, it remains possible that the conflict be solved by creatively shuffling the contingent circumstances.

In the present case, we shall return to Epictetus's treatment of the conflicting roles of a Cynic and a family man because Epictetus grants special circumstances under which these two roles may avoid conflict and be chosen *together*. For such cases, role conflict is resolved, not by appeal to a procedure, but on a case-by-case basis. Indeed, applying the above procedure in these special cases would yield an undue role amputation. As we saw in chapter 5, Epictetus argues in *Discourses* 3.22 that a Cynic's role and the role of a married or family man are incompatible. Against the possibility of a married Cynic, Epictetus argues that it is de facto impossible to be a Cynic and family or married man because both roles are simply too demanding on one's time. Hence, a Cynic who happens to have siblings must choose one role over the other (presumably, the role of the Cynic).

However, throughout Epictetus's discussion, he is plagued by the example of Crates the Cynic's marriage, an example that his students appear to raise continually (much to Epictetus's annoyance). Although Epictetus stresses that this instance is a (special) circumstance (3.22.76), his management of the strange possibility of a Cynic marriage or a Cynic family reveals a limitation to his handling of role conflict. In reply, Epictetus considers both a hypothetical case of a Cynic family (3.22.67–68) and the real case of the marriage of Crates the Cynic (3.22.76). We shall review these two special cases where Epictetus allows that an individual may take up both roles and speculate under what contingent circumstances that is possible and what these exceptions imply for roles more generally. We shall see how, by altering the conditions or the details of these roles, Epictetus makes it unnecessary (or even inappropriate) to choose one role over another.

Epictetus considers the hypothetical instance of a Cynic who is also a family man when he confronts the question of "will marriage and children be undertaken by the Cynic as a matter of prime importance?" (3.22.67).[7] Given Epictetus's argument about the competing tasks of home life and a Cynic's life, we would expect Epictetus to deny a family to Cynics. Surprisingly, he instead supplies an imaginary scenario in which a Cynic could have his own family:

> If, replied Epictetus, you grant me a city of wise men [*sophôn*], . . . there will be nothing to prevent him from both marrying and having children; for his wife will be another person like himself, and so will his father-in-law, and his children will be brought up in the same fashion. (3.22.67–68)

Of course, Epictetus quickly reminds us that this hypothetical scenario does not represent "such an order of things as the present" (3.22.69). Nonetheless, the concession grants that we can alter the conditions under which this family exists in order for an individual to live the life of a Cynic *and* fulfill the obligations of a private family.

Epictetus's rationale seems to be that if a Cynic's compatriots are themselves Cynics, they will not need the same services as ordinary individuals. Thus, a Cynic's day is not tied down by the need to visit parents, to send funds to a brother, or to rush children off to school. In this hypothetical city, Epictetus is not exactly clear about how a Cynic's children are themselves Cynics, especially given his remark that children "cannot be Cynics from the moment they leave the womb" (3.22.74). Perhaps, Epictetus thinks that children in a Cynic society would be born with the tough nature of their parents, or at least they could be quickly socialized to live under such conditions;[8] or perhaps they are raised in some sort of communal manner not unlike Plato's *Republic* (457c–e), thus easing the burden on individual parents. Under any of these special conditions, a Cynic could still have a private family because his familial obligations would be nominal and would not interfere with his Cynic lifestyle. In a sense, he would have a family without having a family. More precisely, he would have a family in one sense (blood and legal relations) but not in another sense (a myriad of obligations); the relationship remains, but its objects have changed, thus removing the contradiction between the Cynic and the family man.

In addition, Epictetus confronts the real instance of Crates, a married Cynic.[9] Epictetus manages the example in a fashion similar to the previous scenario, but he adds more detail:

> "Yes, but Crates married."—You are mentioning a special circumstance which arose out of erotic love [*ex erôtos*], and you are assuming a wife who is herself another Crates. But our inquiry is concerned with common marriage [*koinôn gamôn*] apart from special circumstances, and in this way, we do not find that marriage, under the present conditions, is a matter of prime importance[10] for the Cynic. (3.22.76)

As in the previous case, Epictetus has altered the object of the relationship so that Crates's wife, Hipparchia, is another Cynic (cf. D.L. 6.96.1–15). By implication, she did not need from Crates the sorts of things a woman of the world would need; she could live the same ascetic life by his side. Although they remained husband and wife, their spousal obligations were evidently changed by the fact that Hipparchia also adopted the Cynic lifestyle. What is more interesting is the fact that Epictetus establishes that their relationship is unique by pointing out that it was based on *eros*, which contrasts with the more customary arranged marriages.[11] An arranged marriage is one presumably orchestrated for reproductive, economic, and perhaps even semi-political purposes; such aims bind the husband and wife into a host of obligations, from the need to establish a functioning household with offspring to maintaining all the proper relations with parents, cousins, siblings, and so on (cf. 3.22.70). On the other hand, an erotic marriage is based solely on the desire to be with one's companion, a desire that seems only to require compatible lifestyles. Thus, while a Cynic marriage and a "common marriage" share the basic relation of a husband and wife, the nature of the relationship appears altogether different. So, as before, by altering the object of the relation, and by altering the demands of the relationship itself, Epictetus allows for a Cynic such as Crates to keep to all of humanity as his family while being joined in his efforts by a wife. As a result, a Cynic could *only* be married in the way that Crates was; he could not survive a "common marriage," that is, a marriage "under the present conditions" (3.22.76). Perhaps if Xanthippe had been a Cynic, Socrates could have solved his competing roles in exactly the same way.

It is unfortunate that Epictetus did not say more nor offer similar examples where individuals creatively resolved conflicts between two roles instead of choosing one role over the other. Nonetheless, it seems that we can make a few inferences based on the examples of Cynics. First, Epictetus leaves himself in the position of saying that we cannot predict when conflicting roles may in fact be resolved; such resolutions must be discovered on a case-by-case basis. His discussion begins with a firm argument against joining the roles of a Cynic and a family and yet he accepts Crates's creative solution. Although we are able to infer from Epictetus the rule that Cynics may marry another Cynic and they may have children if they can be reared with minimal obligations, Epictetus does not try to systematize any further guidelines for such an exception. Moreover, Epictetus does not confront the claim that Crates and Hipparchia had a child together and that their child was not produced in a city of wise men,[12] a circumstance that does not fit the conditions just outlined. Instead, Epictetus simply limits himself to calling Crates's case a "special circumstance" (3.22.76). As a result, to remain consistent, Epictetus must say that role conflict is sometimes a circumstantial truth which we can only recognize and resolve on an individual basis. At best, we can say that when we confront the question of whether or not to assume two seemingly incompatible roles, we must do so by appealing to our own circumstances and capacities as well as to the precise obligations of the roles themselves. Frequently, the two roles (Cynicism and marriage) will prove to be incompatible, but, sometimes they will not.

Second, Epictetus seems to treat the relation of marriage as a fixed point; it does not appear that Crates had a choice about the fact that marriage requires a shared lifestyle any more than Epictetus's hypothetical city of wise men had a choice about the fact that parental roles require caring for the young. However, it does seem that there is some flexibility about how roles are applied to particular circumstances.[13] Crates had the choice of whether or not to marry, but in choosing to marry Hipparchia, he had to have a marriage based on an erotic partnership and the obligations that that entails rather than a common marriage and its socio-economic obligations. While Crates acquired the fixed role (*prosôpon*) of husband in the relation (*schesis*) of marriage, the details of his obligations depended upon the application of his role to the particulars (in this case, Hipparchia). For the city of the wise, they have the choice of whether or not to produce offspring and perhaps even a choice about how precisely that offspring was to be reared but no choice about the obligation to rear their children.

Finally, Epictetus's treatment of Cynic marriage provides yet another affirmation that our specific roles carry a weight that is all their own. Epictetus does not discuss them as though the Cynic considers his special circumstances (as a man with certain special gifts) and decides that his humanity requires of himself that he forgo marriage. In fact, it is not at all clear how a Cynic's humanity (which emphasizes preserving his volition) helps him to decide between the circumstance of his talent for living as an ascetic teacher and the circumstance of his real family relations (siblings, parents, extended family, etc.). Instead, Epictetus seems to see the Cynic and ordinary individuals in similar circumstances: both have siblings and parents, both are born into a social world with many potential relations, including marriage. And yet, in Epictetus's account, the Cynic's role seems to *override* one set of his circumstances, namely, the likely existence of siblings and parents.[14] In effect, he has two competing functions or roles in relation to the same circumstances. Moreover, Crates's creative solution was not produced by folding his specific roles into his universal human role. Rather, without any appeal to his universal role, Crates seemed to treat both of his specific roles (as a Cynic and as a married man) as fixed points to be resolved on their own terms.

THE MANY CONFLICTING JOBS OF SAILORS AND SOLDIERS

The maxims offered by the preceding two cases do assist in resolving a number of role conflicts, but they fail in a very specific instance: irremediable conflicts between two specific roles in which an individual identifies equally with each role. Epictetus does not seem to consider such an instance, and it is possible that he would have argued against such conflicts as implausible or impossible.[15] Nonetheless, it seems *prima facie* clear that individuals can experience equally divided conflicts between two or more roles, so we should expect Epictetus to have an answer. The case of Agamemnon's conflict between sacrificing his army and sacrificing his daughter is, quite possibly, one where an individual could feel so torn. Is the only solution a kind of psychological exercise in which we lay Agamemnon on the psychiatrists's couch to examine which role he must surely identify with more, even if it is only by a hair's breadth? No. Instead, I want to argue that such a conflict cannot be solved definitively from *within* role theory; Agamemnon cannot solve it by an examination of his role as father or commander, or an examination of his identification with either role. The "solution" must come on a meta-level, by an outsider's choice (whether a commander's or God's). I shall argue that this approach is suggested by Epictetus in a passage where he considers soldiers and sailors who are confronted with a conflicting set of choices about the exercise of their roles (3.24.31–35). Although the passage does not appear to have been intended by Epictetus to take up the question of role conflict, it nonetheless implies that while roles can help us recognize certain conflicts, such conflicts may be resolvable only by an "outside" order.

The passage I will be analyzing rather clearly follows up on Socrates's claim in the *Apology* that his philosophic life is a kind of campaign (28e–29a). Epictetus weds this claim to his role theory and explains that, because we cannot fulfill every specific role, we each must take up some specific part. He analyzes both the roles of soldiers and sailors and addresses what appears to be a conflict among their roles. Beginning with the role of a soldier, he writes: "Do you not know that the business of life is a campaign? It is necessary for one to mount guard, another go out on reconnaissance, and another out to fight. It is not possible for all to stay in the same place, nor is it better so" (3.24.31). Epictetus here divides the appropriate acts (or perhaps sub-roles?) of the soldier and emphasizes that they are mutually exclusive. Epictetus goes on to argue that we each should therefore stick by our specific post because, if we do not, no one will play their part and the army will fall apart—"no one will dig a trench, no one will construct a palisade, or watch through the night, or risk his life fighting, but they will seem useless soldiers" (3.24.32). In this way, it appears that Epictetus pictures soldiers regarding several necessary tasks as potentially unpleasant with none as particularly choice-worthy. The example presents us, at least implicitly, with a conflict between the role of a guard, a sapper, an infantryman, and so on—a conflict between incompatible options that are all unpalatable. After the soldier, Epictetus considers the case of a sailor and he is likewise concerned to persuade us each into playing our specific parts; but, in doing so, he sets up the same sort of example, that of a sailor who is confronted with many different and competing tasks or roles. To be a good sailor, you must be willing to do any nautical task or job, you must even be ready to switch from one to the other, but you cannot do them all (3.24.33). Thus, the sailor is also implicitly presented with a conflict between the role of lookout, rower, assistant, and so on—a conflict between incompatible options that are all necessary.

For both the soldier and sailor, Epictetus recognizes that they cannot fulfill every military or nautical role at the same time *and* he recognizes that this problem must be gotten past if the army is to stay together or a ship is to set sail. There are practical reasons why the conflict must be solved. However, what is interesting for us is how Epictetus appears to solve the conflict. In his summation to these two cases of competing roles, Epictetus implies that they are resolved by the order of their commander, which when applied to the world at large, means God: "So also in this world; each man's life is a kind of campaign and a long and complicated one at that. It is necessary for you to maintain the [station] of a soldier and do each separate act at the bidding of the General, if possible, divining what he wishes" (3.24.34–35). In the first half of this passage, I take it that Epictetus is demanding that we stand by our roles while admitting that they involve complications, particularly the complications of competing roles and even sometimes shifting tasks (3.24.31–33). In the second half, Epictetus suggests that, just as sailors and soldiers know which task or role to take up from among many conflicting choices because their commander has instructed it, so we, too, should look to our commander (namely, God) to take up the post that God orders.

Epictetus's answer admits an important limitation on role theory. In both the soldier and the sailor example, the question of which role or obligation to take up next is *not* solved by an examination of what it means to be a guard or a sapper, a boatswain or a lookout. Instead, the conflicts in question are solved by fiat of the commanding officer who parses out each role. Of course, the concept of a role would allow a sailor to appreciate that he cannot take up the role of both lookout and rower at the same time. Nonetheless, in cases where both roles are needed and no sailor has a special calling or talent for either, the conflict between the two must be solved by an external command. And, this fact makes sense. If we cannot solve a role conflict internally (by examining the internal nature of a role), then we can only solve it by an external principle, by fiat, or by command. Insoluble role conflict is solved on a "meta-level," outside of the specific roles in question. In this way, we see what roles can, and more importantly, *cannot* tell agents.

Given that roles arise as a result of God's provenance and design, it should be no surprise that Epictetus resolves conflict by appeal to divine command. However, by relying on that strategy, Epictetus exposes himself to a problem about what we ought to do if we are *unable* to determine what God wishes. Although the *Discourses* 3.24 passage is quick to warn us that we must try to divine God's wishes (3.24.34–35), Epictetus admits that we should do that "if possible" (3.24.35). Should we be unable to determine what God wishes when circumstances are otherwise equal, Epictetus leaves us with no clear alternatives. Epictetus could argue that we will always be able to determine what God wishes, but that seems unlikely given the uncertainty and hesitation experienced by ordinary role-bound agents (see *Discourses* 1.2). As a result, Epictetus must at least counsel that, in such ambiguous cases, we must choose the best alternative that we can from among our conflicts. While Epictetus certainly wishes us to follow nature, it is nonetheless true that our own judicious choice would end a conflict between two roles and allow us to get back to action. In this last form of role conflict, what is required is that we solve the conflict on the "meta" level, outside the confines of roles themselves.

ROLE CONFLICT AND THE LIMITS OF ROLE THEORY

In the preceding cases of conflict between specific roles, I suggest that we have approached the limits of Epictetus's role theory, the Okeanos that circles his practical ethics. Not only is role conflict wider than Epictetus suggests,[16] it is largely left to inference what Epictetus's strategies are for resolving conflicts between specific roles. Indeed, it is particularly in the last case of irremediable conflicts that role theory shows its limits because roles there only serve to reveal conflict, not solve it. Because conflicts between roles do happen, it seems that Epictetus ought to have said more about them than he does. But, if I am right about the third case of role conflict, it appears that he only could have said so much. Role theory is a way of reasoning about our appropriate acts. In most cases, we can identify our roles and our roles can identify all our appropriate acts; in cases where it is not (namely, in unsolvable conflicts), roles are nonetheless sufficient to *start* our thinking about appropriate acts and to outline what issues a reasonable agent must address. Roles may not always provide the answer to a conflict between being a good son and a good brother, but they do define the basis on which our practical reasoning must proceed.

NOTES

1. On this latter role, see chapter 2.
2. In chapter 5, I suggested that this resistant servant sounds like Diogenes the Cynic. In Diogenes Laertius's account, Diogenes the Cynic was a slave who rebuked his "superiors" (Diogenes Laertius 6.30; see Epictetus *Disc.* 2.13.23–26 and 4.1.29–32, 114–117, and 151–158).
3. Epictetus does so through the terms *kat'eme* and *axios* (see chapter 2).
4. E.g., a young man could decide between the summons to head off to war versus the obligation to stay home and tend the farm on the basis of whether or not he believes he has a special talent for one activity versus another.
5. Cf. 1.28.1–6 where Epictetus says that just as no man can assent to what he knows to be false, so no man can do what fails to be *kat'eme*. Although 1.28.1–6 does not explicitly name *to eulogon*, the idea of following what is true is a good analogue for following *to eulogon*.
6. The idea here resembles Harry G. Frankfurt's notion of moral necessity, that if we really identify with a certain course, we cannot do anything but that. See Frankfurt 2003.
7. Prime importance (*proêgoumenôs*): Although the term *proêgoumenôs* is a bit unusual, it appears to refer to those acts that are ordinarily considered *kathêkon*, like honoring one's parents. For this curious term, cf. 3.7.25–36 where Epictetus divides duties into three obscure categories: "first, those concerning being, those concerning particular existence, and the principle ones themselves. . . . What are these [principle things]? To be a citizen, to marry, to beget children, to revere God, to care for parents, in a word, desire, avoidance, choice, refusal, to do what is necessary of each one of these acts, and that is, in accordance with our nature." Even though this opaque passage has caused some stir in the literature (Oldfather 1928, vol. 2, 56; Bonhöffer 1996, 170–171; Dyck 1996, 4–8; Long 2002, 257; Sandbach 1989, 55; and De Lacy 1977, 169), for our purposes, we need only see that *proêgoumena* seems to pick out all the important, customary social and religious obligations a Greek or Roman would associate with a good man.

8. Note that Diogenes Laertius, 6.88–89, reports that Crates the Cynic and his Cynic wife Hipparchia had a child: "Eratosthenes tells us that by Hipparchia, of whom we shall presently speak, he had a son born to him named Pasicles, and after he had ceased to be a cadet on service, Crates took him to a brothel and told him that was how his father had married. The marriage of intrigue and adultery, he said, belonged to tragedy, having exile or assassination as its rewards; while the weddings of those who take up with courtesans are material for comedy, for as a result of extravagance and drunkenness they bring about madness" (Hicks translation).

9. Crates himself seems to have called his marriage to Hipparchia a *kunogamia* or "dog wedding" as LSJ translates it. See Clemens Alexandrinus, *Stromata*, 4.19.122, Tatianus, *Oratio ad Graecos*, 3.3.4, and Theodoretus, *Graecarum affectionum curati*, 12.49.8.

10. *Proêgoumenon*: on this term, see above.

11. I owe this point to Oldfather 1928, vol. 2, 156–157.

12. See D.L. 6.88 and Reydams-Schils 2005, 130.

13. Compare this to what Epictetus says about our preconceptions (*prolêpseis*), that they are "common to all men, and one preconception does not contradict another" but contradictions can arise in "the application of our preconceptions to the particular cases" (1.22.1–3).

14. Note that Epictetus does not require that all Cynics be orphans.

15. Epictetus could have argued, for example, that a benevolent deity would not allow for such a poorly planned event. Alternatively, perhaps Epictetus would have found reasons to argue that individuals do not plausibly experience role conflicts that are *equally* and *perfectly* divided.

16. Witness, for example, the surplus of characters facing conflicting demands in Greek and Roman myths, stories surely known to Epictetus.

Chapter Eight

Cicero's Account of Panaetius's Four *Personae*: A Theory of *Decorum*

Over a century before Epictetus, Cicero outlined a theory of the four *personae* (roles) in the *De Officiis* (On Duties) according to which agents determine what activities are consistent with the virtue of decorum (or seemliness) by reference to their roles. Although Cicero himself was an avowed Academic skeptic (and therefore deployed arguments pro and contra as a kind of epistemic cleanser; L&S 68S), he was sympathetic to the ethics of Stoicism.[1] Moreover, Cicero based the first two books of the *De Officiis* on an earlier but now lost work by the Stoic Panaetius, *Peri Tou Kathêkontos* (Concerning Proper Function). Cicero wrote the *De Officiis* in lieu of his intended visit to his son, Marcus,[2] and was apparently forced to construct the work somewhat hastily. Cicero intended his own book to guide not just his son Marcus[3] but young men of his position.[4] Cicero's hasty writing certainly led to some gaps in the structure and logic of his presentation,[5] but it also afforded readers a less varnished perspective on Cicero as he tried to advise young Marcus from within the framework of Stoic ethics. As a result, we contemporary readers have the unique opportunity to see Cicero in the position of philosophic advice-giver much as Epictetus took up a similar position in his *Discourses* (as recorded by his pupil Arrian). Both Cicero's *De Officiis* and Epictetus's *Discourses* still have an immediacy and urgency as they attempt to show the practical side of Stoic ethics for Greek and Roman audiences in need of advice. And, both figures take up role ethics in the service of that cause.

Because Epictetus's role theory is later than Cicero's theory of the four *personae* (roles) and because Epictetus's remarks on roles appear so fragmentary, some scholars have looked to Cicero's earlier and more organized account of (Panaetean) roles in order to provide a framework for analyzing Epictetus.[6] P. A. Brunt, for example, believes that Epictetus is a direct intellectual descendent of Panaetius (Cicero's source)[7] and thus he treats Epictetus as an appendix to Cicero and Panaetius. R. Sorabji appears to concur by noting that "much of this [Panaetius and Cicero's account of roles] is repeated by Epictetus in the next century."[8] M. Frede suggests that Epictetus divides roles "not quite in the same way that Panaetius does" but proceeds to find strong parallels between Cicero's fourfold division and Epictetus's roles.[9] By contrast, P. De Lacy denies that Epictetus was influenced by Panaetius, but he nonetheless uses Cicero's account entirely to frame his picture of Epictetus.[10] Whether on historical or intellectual grounds, Epictetus has thus often been analyzed by outlining Cicero's more systematic treatment and then by comparing and contrasting it with passages from Epictetus.[11]

However, by adopting such a strategy, we artificially make Epictetus seem like Cicero and we lose important details of Epictetus's account because Epictetus's account includes more types of roles and is more organic than Cicero's fourfold scheme. My aim in this book has been to reconstruct Epictetus's account of roles on its own terms, neither speculating on its possible antecedents nor harvesting it for observations about personhood or personality.[12] Instead of treating Epictetus as a sequel to Panaetius (as expressed by Cicero), my goal has been to give Epictetus his soliloquy. Moreover, when we release Epictetus's account from the confines of Cicero's, Epictetus's account reveals itself to be both ambitious and distinctive within Stoicism. First, as we shall see in this chapter, Epictetus incorporates much more into our human role than the requirement to exhibit the virtue of *decorum* (as Cicero frames it). For Epictetus, the human role amounts to a reformulation of the Stoic account of virtue. Second, unlike Cicero, Epictetus resists saying that we have a fixed number of roles; Epictetus will only affirm that we have a human role and many specific roles. This fluidity to his account of roles has certainly been noticed,[13] but I have gone much further and argued that Epictetus manages our many roles by *replacing* any sort of categorization scheme (as found in Cicero) with a set of criteria by which agents can identify their roles. For Cicero, role identification is relatively straightforward since he tells us that we have exactly four *personae*; but, because Epictetus's account is less schematic, the identification of all of our roles becomes more challenging. In turn, Epictetus highlights role-identification because he treats it as a form of self-analysis. Finally, as we shall see ahead, Cicero appears to develop the metaphor of a role in a way that is quite different from Epictetus's account. At root, Cicero understands our roles merely to be the public parts that we perform with *decorum* (propriety) in front of an audience; Epictetus understands our roles to be the function that we play in the cosmos and in our local human communities.

My aim in this chapter, therefore, is to separate Epictetus from Cicero (and Panaetius), not on historical grounds about whether one influenced the other but on the philosophical ground that Cicero's theory is merely a theory of *decorum* (the virtue that concerns what is socially pleasing), whereas Epictetus's role theory is a theory of ethics in general. In turn, I intend the account of Panaetian roles to provide a useful contrast for highlighting Epictetus's originality.

To make my case, this chapter will examine Cicero's account of our four roles: (1) humanity, (2) personality, (3) social standing, and (4) career choice.[14] I shall argue that Cicero's account is motivated by his picture of the virtue of *decorum* (propriety) and that these *personae* operate as criteria for discovering what is proper. I will follow that account of Cicero's theory by arguing that, while he recognizes *personae* as the main tools for *decorum*, he also recognizes other tools that accomplish the same end; these latter tools will complete my case that Cicero's role theory limits itself to *decorum*.

THE CONTEXT OF CICERO'S ROLE THEORY IN THE *DE OFFICIIS*: THE VIRTUE OF *DECORUM*

Although Cicero explicitly takes up the topic of roles (*personae*) at *De Officiis* 1.107, his discussion relies upon the subjects that precede it. That is, his role theory assumes his account of the virtue of *decorum* (propriety).[15] As Cicero sees it, *decorum* includes "a sense of shame [*verecundia*] and what one might call the ordered beauty of a life, restraint and modesty, a calming of all the agitations of the spirit, and due measure in all things" (1.93). If we generalize from these cases, we can say that *decorum* is centrally concerned with shame (*verecundia*) and conversely with what is fitting (*to prepon*) and pleasing to others (1.98; cf. 1.126). This context is crucial to my argument that Cicero's role theory is offered as a tool in the service of *decorum*, not as an all-encompassing ethical theory in its own right but as a heuristic for discovering what are proper appropriate acts.

On the heels of his characterization of the virtue of *decorum* (1.93–96), Cicero connects the virtue of propriety to roles (*personae*) by comparing a gentleman's search for propriety to the poet's search for what is fitting.[16] By showing how the poet and the gentleman parallel *and* diverge, Cicero makes clear what he thinks an ethical *persona* is and what it ought to accomplish in relation to propriety. To connect *decorum* to *personae*, he writes:

> We say that poets "observe what is proper" when what is said and done is worthy of the role [*persona*]. If Aeacus or Minos [judges of Tartarus] were to say, "Let them hate provided that they fear," or, "The father himself is his children's tomb," it would seem improper, because we believe them to have been just men. When Atreus [a wicked king] says it, however, there is loud applause: the words are worthy of his role [*persona*]. . . . Poets, therefore, will

> look to what is suitable and proper for a huge variety of roles [*personarum*] . . . (1.97–98)

Accordingly, one's own propriety, one's own harmonious arrangement of parts, "arouses the approval of one's fellows" (1.98).[17] Cicero thereby establishes a kind of craft-analogy between poetry and virtue (cf. 1.114, 129 and 145–147), according to which what is true of the general operation of an art or craft is true of virtue.[18] In turn, he transforms his analogy of the poet and gentleman into an analogy between poetry and nature. Nonetheless, while both poetry and virtue (i.e., following nature) seek what is fitting and produce what is pleasing to others, Cicero limits the craft-analogy because poets must determine what is proper even for evil roles (1.98), but there should be no evil roles in real life.[19] While poets search for propriety among many kinds of roles,

> . . . nature has imposed on us a role [*personam*] that greatly excels and surpasses that of other creatures. Poets, therefore, will look to what is suitable and proper for a huge variety of roles [*personarum*], even wicked ones [*vitiosis*]. But our parts [*partes*] have been given us by nature: since they are ones of constancy, of moderation, of restraint, of a sense of shame. . . . (1.97–98)

Strictly speaking, Cicero does not differentiate poetic roles from ethical ones on the ground that nature could never permit something as pernicious as evil *personae*. Instead, he emphasizes that our natural role is assigned rather than chosen, but it so happens that nature has assigned us such upright roles as constancy, restraint, and so on.[20]

For Cicero, then, we are to imagine that the gentleman is a kind of ethical poet, in search of what is fitting and what arouses approval concerning the role that nature has assigned to him. But, what is that role? Cicero answers, in effect, that it is not one role (*persona*), but many.

THE FOUR *PERSONAE*: THE WARDROBE OF *DECORUM*

Although Cicero will assert that there are four *personae*, he introduces them in pair: first, the *persona* based on reason (*ratio*) and the *persona* based on one's own nature or type; second, the *persona* based on circumstance and the *persona* based on choice. At 1.107, Cicero formally inaugurates the theory of the *personae* and its first pair, where he treats the two as the gift of nature:

> [W]e have been dressed, as it were, by nature for two roles [*personis*]: one is common [*communis*], arising from the fact that we all have a share in reason [*rationis*] and in the superiority by which we surpass the brute creatures. Everything honorable [*honestum*] and proper [*decorum*] is derived from this, and from it we discover a method of finding out our appropriate acts. The

other, however, is that assigned specifically to individuals [*proprie singulis*]. (1.107)

We shall analyze these two roles in turn (human and one's nature) and then examine the second dyad of roles.

i. The *Persona* of Humanity (*Ratio*)[21]

After the first pair of *personae* is introduced, the discussion moves immediately into the details of the second *persona* concerning one's own type. Strangely, Cicero never returns to the subject of the *persona* based on reason (*ratio*) nor does he explain his silence. Indeed, he does not even supply a cognomen for the first *persona*, although 1.107 naturally suggests that it should be termed the human role because its scope concerns (human) reason as opposed to brutishness. This oversight has caused some confusion for interpreters, but I suggest that, perhaps because of the hastiness of its construction,[22] the *De Officiis* intends the preceding discussion of *sôphrosunê* (moderation, an aspect of propriety) at 1.100–106 to be the domain of the first *persona*.[23] This hypothesis is likely since Cicero identifies the first *persona* with our human capacity for reason (*ratio*) in 1.107 and he defends moderation (*sôphrosunê*) as the rule of reason (*ratio*) in 1.100–106. Nonetheless, while this earlier passage will provide Cicero with an account of the first *persona*, it will prove to be a problematic and incomplete account. And yet, without such a reading, Cicero's notion of the universal role remains a largely uninformative placeholder.

In characterizing moderation (*sôphrosunê*) at 1.100–106, Cicero fluctuates, somewhat problematically, between two related—but not necessarily co-extensive—pictures of temperance or moderation: keeping one's place and keeping due proportion. Initially, moderation (*sôphrosunê*) is described along fairly Platonic lines, meaning the rule of the rational part (*to logistikon*) of the soul over the spirited and appetitive parts (389d–e; 430e–434c; 442e and 442c–d).[24] In propriety, "reason commands and impulse obeys" (1.101; cf. 1.141).[25] This claim means that moderate agents should be "free from rashness and carelessness" and should not do anything "for which he cannot give a persuasive justification [*causam probabilem*]" (1.101; cp. 1.103).[26] They should, therefore, resist the rule of impulse, which is immoderate and therefore ugly (1.102).

In addition, since reason is shared by all (1.107), this picture of moderation as keeping one's place translates into the maxim that moderation means keeping our human station as opposed to the station of an animal. And, interestingly enough, Cicero briefly strikes just such a note when he discusses moderation about pleasure and argues that it is bestial to be carried away by pleasure (1.105–106; cf. 1.96 and 3.119). Accordingly, it is unworthy of our "upright" station as humans to indulge in pleasure or to permit luxury (1.105); likewise, "bodily pleasure is not sufficiently worthy of the superiority of man" (1.106). In this way, when he says that moderation means asserting the rule of reason over the passions, we can read him to mean that we must act according to reason, not passion so that we keep our place as humans, not beasts.

Within the same general discussion, moderation is also characterized in terms of seeking the mean, a characterization which Cicero underutilizes in connection with his theory of the *personae*. This portrayal and oversight emerges in Cicero's analysis of leisure and pleasure.[27] A gentleman, he says, is "neither extravagant nor excessive" (1.103) and exhibits a "certain proportion" (1.104; cf. 1.133) in his humor, leisure, recreation, and entertainment.[28] Similarly, pleasure is described in terms of seeking a middle ground, so "if there is anyone who assigns some worth to pleasure he must take care to keep his enjoyment of it in proportion" (1.106).[29] Cicero provides a few examples, but they do not provide much insight into how we are to discover the mean. Instead, Cicero appears especially concerned to convince us that this mean is "by nature" (1.102 and 1.103) and that it matches the characteristically Roman virtue of *gravitas* (1.103–106), but he shows no concern about how to connect the mean to the *persona* based on reason. Cicero could have followed Aristotle's lead here by extrapolating the mean "relative to us" which is "not the same for everyone" (*EN* 1106a29f.);[30] thus, although Aristotle denies that we can use the mean to distinguish between human and animal behavior, Cicero could so use it and argue that the mean is discovered by reference to our human *ratio* as opposed to any of our animal features. Accordingly, if we piece together some of Cicero's own language, he could argue that, because we have *ratio*, "we have not been created by nature . . . for jesting and play" (1.103); the mean amount of humor is that which is kept within the bounds of our free time after we humans have "given time enough to weighty matters" (ibid.). Just as Aristotle's temperate athlete chooses a different mean than a non-athlete about how much meat to consume relative to his training goals, so Cicero's gentleman should seek the appropriate amount of humor and leisure relative to his human functions (as opposed to the idyll of specific animals). While such appeals are far from philosophically complete, it would nonetheless have helped Cicero to define moderation more consistently and to connect it more clearly to the first *persona*.

By searching out the ways in which Cicero's remarks on propriety can be connected to his theory of the *persona*, not only are we able to supply an account of the first *persona*, we also have the added benefits of extending Cicero's remarks about moderation and bringing together the two strands of moderation. At root, he says that the first *persona* arises "from the fact that we all have a share in reason [*rationis*] . . ." (1.107). On the one hand, humans can act in a proper manner about their own *ratio* if they recognize "the superiority by which we surpass the brute creatures" (ibid.), that is, if they act by reason, not passion. On the other hand, humans can also act in a proper manner about their own *ratio* if they measure the mean by reference to the place they have in the world and the place that reason has in their life. If we exhibit both, we shall exhibit the propriety that is true of our reason (*ratio*) and therefore true of our first *persona* as human beings.

ii. The *Persona* of Personality

The second *persona* is introduced together with the universal role because it, too, is given "by nature" (1.107). In contrast to the more universal basis of the first *persona*, the second *persona* "is assigned specifically to individuals [*proprie singulis*]" (ibid.). However, while it is tempting to term this *persona* the individual role in Cicero's fourfold schema, such a term would prove to be a misnomer because Cicero's category-type examples make clear that he is thinking of character types assigned to individuals, not individuals who possess *sui generis* character types.[31] Accordingly, the second *persona* is a role which belongs to individuals as members of a class, not as unique, irreplaceable individuals with unique, unrepeatable properties.[32] Of course, it may be that only numerically one individual takes up some specific *persona* at any given time, but such a fact is contingent, not necessary. Because this *persona* refers to a character type that is more specific than the first *persona*, it is perhaps most accurate to term the second *persona* a "specific role."[33] However, because of the content of this role and because the third and fourth *personae* equally count as specific or particular, I will frequently label the second *persona* as the *persona* based on personality.

After his initial introduction of the first two *personae*, Cicero proceeds to identify this second role with "differences in men's spirits [*animis*]" (1.107), differences which appear to amount to issues of temperament. Indeed, he gives a sizable list of brief examples that reveal aspects of one's personality: "Lucius Crassus and Lucius Philippus had plenty of wit . . . but in the same period Marcus Scaurus and the youthful Marcus Drusus were showing exceptional seriousness . . ." (1.108; cf. 1.133) and so on, throughout 1.108–109. Although his list is by no means an exhaustive or even satisfactory account of personality, its constituents nonetheless amount to features that we would now call personality traits: wit (*lepos*), seriousness (*severitas*), jolliness (*hilaritas*) and its opposite, ambitiousness (*ambitio*), geniality (*festivitas*), irony (*simulatio* / εἴρων), craftiness (*calliditas*), forthrightness (*simplicitas*), perseverance (*patientia*), and graciousness [*comitas*] and its opposite.[34]

Although these examples seem rather clearly to identify personality as the basis upon which the second *persona* rests, most commentators have, to varying degrees, either downplayed or denied the idea of personality here and have instead tried to discover a broader basis for the second *persona* such as cognitive abilities or physical talents. Brunt says that the second *persona* "arises from the individual's special inborn endowments, which he must develop to the full so far as they are compatible with virtue, and his natural disabilities, which limit what he can do . . ."[35] Stephens 1998 writes that "The second *persona* in Cicero's theory arises from a being's particular strength, talents, and abilities. Some have unique bodily excellences, while others have special mental or emotional powers."[36] Likewise, Bonhöffer understands the second *persona* in terms of abilities more generally and so he says that "Panaetius [as represented in Cicero's *De Officiis*] understands by the *propria natura* the physical and mental individuality of the human being, which entails that one person distinguishes himself more in this virtue, another more in that virtue" (10). Most interesting is Gill 1988, who says that the second *persona* concerns "our individual nature and talents" (175) and "distinctive talents and attitudes" (177),[37] but he stresses that "Cicero's project is . . . that of isolating characteristics that serve to make people (at least, some people) *distinguished*, that is, accomplished and notable in society" (181; cf. 171).

However, against these commentators, I shall argue that Cicero's discussion fails to provide good grounds for concluding that the second *persona* involves anything more than personality types. To begin with, commentators frequently point to Cicero's analogy of wrestling and running in 1.107 to connect the second *persona* to abilities more generally, but it is not clear whether Cicero intends the analogy to show that physical talents are included, and that, even if he did intend to include them, the analogy nonetheless minimizes physical talents relative to non-physical differences. In his introduction to the second *persona* at 1.107, Cicero writes: "For just as there are enormous bodily differences (for some, as we see, their strength is the speed that they can run, for others the might with which they wrestle; again, some have figures that are dignified, others that are graceful), similarly there are still greater differences in men's spirits" (1.107). Most commentators have taken this analogy to mean that the second *persona* concerns physical abilities, but the analogy is offered in the form of an argument to establish that there are extremely wide variations in individual spirits and thus it leaves open whether or not physical differences are meant to be included in the second *persona*. Nonetheless, if Cicero intended the analogy to show that physical differences factor in the second *persona*, he shows that while asserting that physical differences are far less important than spiritual ones. In fact, when he proceeds to fill out the second *persona* with his long series of examples, he cites only differences in spirit and never returns to the subject of physical prowess, suggesting either that physical differences are a minor part of the second *persona* or no part at all.

Several other passages seem to promise that abilities in general constitute the second *persona*, but they fail to deliver. In 1.109, Cicero initially seems to imply that other factors may come into play: "There are countless other dissimilarities of nature and conduct, which do not in the least deserve censure." However, this expression comes at the end of his extensive list of examples about personality, so it is unclear whether Cicero narrowly means other types of personalities or whether he broadly means countless other types of abilities (physical or intellectual). Likewise, at the opening of 1.114, Cicero tells us that "everyone should acquire knowledge of his own talents [*ingenium*]." Although it is difficult to translate *ingenium* here, Griffin and Atkins 1991 are too broad by translating it as "talents." Talents suggests something like a special ability for speaking or for singing, features which Cicero invokes in the fourth *persona*, not here. Moreover, following the *Oxford Latin Dictionary*, this term seems to be limited to mental qualities like temperament or mental prowess.

Perhaps the best case against my reading of the second *persona* is offered by Gill 1988. Like many other commentators, Gill's broad remarks about this *persona* tend to connect it to abilities in general (175 and 177). He also questions whether or not the second *persona* should be connected to personality at all (180–181).[38] Instead, he says, Cicero's focus is much narrower, aiming at conventional concepts of social success: "Cicero's project is not that of isolating *distinguishing* or individuating characteristics (that is, features that make any one individual different in personality from any other). Rather it is that of isolating characteristics that serve to make people (at least, some people) *distinguished*, that is, accomplished and notable in society" (181; cf. 171). In other words, Cicero is "concerned, though implicitly, to identify features that enable certain men to succeed in the various 'competitions' of social, political, and military life" (182).[39] As evidence, Gill finds competition in the contrasting pairs of character types listed by Cicero, and he also points to Cicero's examples of crafty (even deceitful) military generals, examples which Gill believes show that Cicero is not interested in personality but rather in what made them famous (182; Gill 1994, 4633, reaffirms this claim).[40]

On behalf of Gill's reading, it is indeed true that Cicero's initial examples of the second *persona* are presented as a series of famous individuals who fall into contrasting pairs. But, while Gill is right that Cicero elsewhere shows a concern for glory (see e.g., 1.38 and 1.78), we must not forget that role theory is in the service of *decorum*, a virtue which is inherently public-minded, and that it is natural that the second *persona* would exhibit some concern for reputation. Moreover, what that contrasting structure shows is not competition but a kind of parallel lives according to which men excelled with opposite personality traits: "Lucius Crassus and Lucius Philippus had plenty of wit . . . but in the same period Marcus Scaurus and the youthful

Marcus Drusus were showing exceptional seriousness . . ." and so on (1.108). It is undeniable that these contrasting pairs exemplify personality traits, but what is especially interesting is that these men succeeded with *opposing* (and sometimes extreme) personalities, so it is difficult to read this as a guide about what features a young man ought to emulate in order to succeed socially. Instead, because each man succeeded and preserved what was proper by following his own temperament, the examples appear designed to convince us that what matters is that we remain true to our (second) *persona*. Certainly, Cicero emphasizes famous individuals who have successfully chosen proper actions in line with their personality, but as Gill himself admits (1994, 181), this follows the Roman tradition of using *exempla* (extraordinary men); it does not assign fame or social competition to the second *persona*. Accordingly, while it is true that the *examples* focus on distinguished cases, the *theory* of the *personae* does not preclude ordinary cases.[41]

Gill also cites Cicero's examples of cunning generals or politicians, such as Hannibal and Themistocles (1.108), as evidence that the second *persona* merely concerns what makes a man famous. Gill's argument is not entirely explicit, but his implied argument appears to be that, since craftiness is included in the second *persona* and is very nearly a dishonest means to success,[42] it cannot be that the second *persona* concerns a virtue like propriety. Rather, it concerns what makes men succeed competitively. But, Gill is again mistaken to find competition in the example and to assume that Cicero must think of wiliness as a vice as opposed to yet another feature of personality. First, as with the other pairs of examples, Cicero stresses that men have succeeded by craftiness (1.108) and by straightforwardness (1.109), so it is unlikely that he is giving advice about how to succeed. Instead, as before, he is stressing the great varieties of *personae* that men can have; some have a *persona* that calls for trickery, others transparency. Second, it is not clear that Cicero intends us to think of trickery as a vice. While craftiness presumably counts as a vice in the Judeo-Christian tradition, it does not appear to have been a vice in the Graeco-Roman tradition. Indeed, honesty or truth-telling is *not* listed as an *officium* or a virtue in the *De Officiis*. Not only were certain heroes famed for their deceitful cunning (e.g., Ulysses), Cicero expressly points out that Socrates, the ethical hero of ancient philosophers, was widely known for his deceptive irony because he "put up a pretence whenever he spoke" (1.108). Finally, as Gill himself grants (183), Cicero saw the deceitful shrewdness of some Roman generals as supporting the survival of the state, a goal Cicero surely endorses (1.84).

Having argued that the second *persona* appeals to temperament or personality, I must now consider what Cicero thinks the notion of a personality can and cannot do. I shall begin by examining the two ways in which Cicero limits what is permissible to do on the basis of the second *persona* because it will set the stage for what surprising appropriate acts Cicero thinks propriety and temperament can address, including especially the suicide of Cato. He first limits what we can do on the basis of personality by subordinating the second *persona* to the first so that what is proper relative to temperament must be within the bounds of what is proper relative to *ratio*.[43] This limitation appears in 1.110 as an extension of the principle that reason must rule:

> Each person should hold on to what is his [*sua cuique*][44] as far as it is not vicious [*non vitiosa*], but is peculiar [*propria*] to him, so that the propriety [*decorum*] that we are seeking might more easily be maintained. For we must act in such a way that we attempt nothing contrary to universal nature; but while conserving that, let us follow our own nature, so that even if other pursuits may be weightier and better, we should measure our own by the rule of our own nature. For it is appropriate neither to fight against nature nor to pursue anything that you cannot attain. Consequently, it becomes clearer what propriety is like, precisely because nothing is proper "against Minerva's will," as they say, that is, when your nature opposes and fights against it.

Here, Cicero invokes the *sôphrosunê* (moderation) of the universal role that "reason commands" (1.101) and argues that reason forbids as improper anything that is contrary to nature, but he charges the second *persona* with the task of picking from among the many activities that are within the bounds of *decorum*. In this way, he treats one's own nature as a genuine basis for determining what is proper, but he rules out the possibility that the second *persona* (personality) permits us to do wrong,[45] just as he ruled out much earlier the idea that there may be evil roles (1.98).

Cicero also limits the permissiveness of the second *persona* by ruling out erratic behavior on the grounds that we must have consistency over time and with oneself, that is, "an evenness both of one's whole life and of one's individual actions" (1.111).[46] Such a maxim is important because, as Gill 1994 interestingly notes, if we fail to pursue a consistent life, we, in a sense "fail to have a life, or to be one person at all" (4626).[47] By advocating consistency, Cicero solidifies the concept of a personality as something long term, something that appeals to the general temper and history of one's psyche rather than anything as flexible or fickle as one's mood or daily humor. So, for example, ambitious individuals should take the bold path, even in moments when they feel beaten down because consistency demands it. In the same way, we should remain true to our own personality at each moment; we should not try to "copy someone else" (ibid.) or to be who we are not. Accordingly, naturally serious individuals should not try to act like comedians.[48]

Although Cicero limits what we can do on the basis of personality, he nonetheless appears to think that the second *persona* has some robustness such that it can address the propriety of how we manage our social encounters and even address the grave matter of suicide. To see this, we will look at

Cicero's brief account of Ulysses and Ajax and his extended account of the suicide of Cato. In the cases of Ulysses and Ajax, Cicero pairs them in order to contrast how the two men took opposing courses of action in accordance with their second *persona*: "How many things Ulysses suffered during his lengthy wanderings! He both was a slave to women . . . and was willing to be accommodating and pleasant to everyone in everything he said. . . . On the other hand, Ajax's spirit was such, we are told, that he would have preferred to seek death a thousand times than to endure such things" (1.113). Through this brief passage, Cicero reframes their famed temperaments in terms of *personae*, with Ulysses having the *persona* of many ways and Ajax having the *persona* of rigidity.[49] On the basis of their *personae*, it is proper for Ulysses to be yielding to both Circe and Calypso, but it is proper for Ajax to be magisterial throughout all his relations; Ulysses could endure much more than Ajax because of the differences in their personalities (1.113). In both cases, their *personae* prescribe proper actions that cover the manner of their relations to others.

On an even more serious level, Cicero analyzes Cato's suicide, drawing a connection between Cato's *gravitas* and the appropriateness of his act:

> Indeed, such differences of natures have so great a force that sometimes one man ought to choose death for himself while another ought not. For surely the case of Marcus Cato was different from that of the others who gave themselves up to Caesar in Africa? Indeed it would perhaps have been counted as a fault [*vitio*] if they had killed themselves, for the very reason that they had been more gentle in their lives, and more easy-going in their behavior. But since nature had assigned to Cato an extraordinary seriousness [*gravitatem*], which he himself had consolidated by his unfailing constancy, abiding always by his adopted purpose and policy, he had to die rather than look upon the face of a tyrant. (1.112)

Commentators have generally downplayed this as an example of Cicero's *persona* theory by instead connecting it to consistency, greatness of spirit, and the Stoic doctrine of suicide. However, I shall move against these commentators by arguing that Cicero uses the Cato example to connect a feature of Cato's personality (his *gravitas*) with his *persona* in order to justify the *decorum* of his suicide.

Against my position, commentators have generally connected the Cato passage to the Stoic doctrine on suicide without connecting it to role theory. Understandably, because the passage concerns suicide, commentators have explicated the passage in terms of the standard Stoic (and Cynic) argument that suicide can be reasonable (*eulogon*) for the Stoic sage or wise man under the right conditions.[50] Indeed, as Cicero himself elsewhere summarizes it in the *De Finibus* through the mouthpiece of Cato: "It is the appropriate action to live when most of what one has is in accordance with nature. When the opposite is the case, or is envisaged to be so, then the appropriate action is to depart from life. . . . Thus the whole rationale for either remaining in or departing from life is to be measured be reference to those intermediates [i.e., preferred indifferents] . . ." (3.60–61). Accordingly, this passage has understandably been interpreted by reference to standard Stoic views about the sage as well as Cato's own virtue. As J. M. Rist says,

> Cicero's description [at 1.112] is so laudatory that it may be said that he is already building the legend of Cato the Sage. . . . Cato's situation after the triumph of Caesar was different from that of other people. His character was marked by extraordinary dignity (*incredibilem gravitatem*), and he had strengthened that dignity with unceasing consistency. This looks like the description of the Stoic wise man, and, if that is what Cicero intended, he is justifying Cato's death solely on the ground that Cato was wise. For the decision of the wise man to take his own life is *ipso facto* a reasonable decision. Briefly, then, we say that in Cicero's Stoic treatises and in his comments about the Stoic Cato there is no significant variation on what the early Stoics taught about suicide . . . (245)[51]

In much the same way, Rist also explains Cato's suicide (as described in 1.112) by reference to the Cynic view that true Cynics can commit suicide in order to preserve their freedom (237–238).[52] In either case, Cato's decision is grounded not in his own *persona* but in the universal doctrine of Stoic or Cynic suicide.

Certainly, it is understandable that Rist has read Cicero in this way, but what is apparently missed is the fact that 1.112 proves oddly mismatched with the standard Stoic doctrine on suicide. While the standard doctrine emphasizes the external circumstances under which suicide is appropriate, Cicero here defends Cato's position as unique for reasons *internal* to Cato, namely, that Cato was naturally and constantly[53] "serious" whereas other men were "easy-going." As Dyck aptly points out, the relationship between suicide and circumstances has here been severed: "Cicero/Panaetius has spoken of the change in *officia* with a change in external circumstances ([in *De Officiis* Book I] §§ 31–32). Here external circumstances are the same . . . but a different decision is justified by a difference in the nature of the individuals" (*Commentary*, 282). This is not the classic defense of suicide, especially as Cato the Stoic was made to articulate it in the *De Finibus* (3.60–61; see above).[54]

To put this point in another way, Cicero ostensibly appeals to *two* separate justifications for Cato's suicide, but commentators have mistakenly conflated them into one. In Cicero's picture, Cato's suicide seems to rest on a two-tiered set of criteria, first a Stoic one concerning the (external) circumstances under which suicide is appropriate and then a Panaetian one concerning the *persona* for which suicide is proper.[55] In this way, Cato's first decision was whether his circumstances warranted suicide and Cicero discusses those external requirements at *De Officiis* 1.31–32 and *De Finibus* 3.60–61. But, once Cato decided that suicide was consistent with his circumstances, he could then consider the Panaetian standard about whether it was suitable for his own nature (his *persona*) to commit suicide. Since he found that his own *gravitas* made facing a tyrant intolerable, it was appropriate and fitting for him to commit suicide. By contrast, as Cicero notes, there were those who were in similar circumstances to Cato's and so met the Stoic standard for suicide, but because they found their own *personae* were "gentle" or "easy-going" (1.112),[56] they did not satisfy the second, Panaetian standard and thereby they would have been extreme for realizing the *officium ex tempore* of suicide. In sum, the Panaetian standard of 1.112 has mistakenly been read by some commentators as an expression of the typical Stoic standard for suicide.

Interestingly, while Dyck agrees that Cato's decision for suicide in 1.112 hinges on his *gravitas*, his own analysis lays too much emphasis on the way the passage connects to an earlier discussion about consistency; as a result, he does not connect it to the larger context, to Cicero's analysis of the *persona* based on "one's own," that is, on one's personality. Thus, for example, Dyck says that Cicero's passage on the *personae* of Ulysses and Ajax "lacks a connection with the foregoing [analysis of Cato] . . ." (Dyck 1996, 283). However, it is surprising that Dyck downplays the connection to Cicero's *personae* since he himself grants that the reasons given for Cato's suicide in 1.112 are internal. Moreover, it seems rather clear that the Cato example is offered as a way of continuing the discussion of the place of temperament or personality in one's *persona*. In citing Cato's *gravitas*, Cicero is grounding Cato's decision in a matter of temperament. This grounding certainly picks up on a feature which belongs to Cato's "own nature," the defining feature of the second *persona* (1.107).

Nonetheless, even while granting that Cato's decision was based on his own *gravitas*, some commentators still downplay *persona* theory in 1.112 by stressing the admiring tone of the passage, a tone which seems to offer up Cato's suicide, not as a role-bound decision but as an ideal for all. As Gill 1988 says, although Cicero's *persona* "framework promotes an attitude of neutrality as regards the two types of personal style (whether *gravis* or *facilis*), the phrasing and emphasis in Cicero's comments clearly, though implicitly, indicate his admiration for Cato's *gravitas* . . . " (186). In effect, Gill is suggesting that Cicero's tone transforms what ought to have been a private virtue into a universal virtue, one much like greatness of spirit. And, as Gill aptly notes, magnanimity is dismissive of private concerns, is aristocratic, and it calls out for one kind of life.[57] It pulls against the idea of a private *persona* according to which Cato would ground his suicide on features private to himself, features quite possibly not shared by others. In this way, Gill worries that the Cato example breaks free of the *persona* theory and is transformed into a principle to be imitated by all.

While Gill's point is a sensitive reading of Cicero's tone, it does not erase the substance of Cicero's appeal to *persona* theory. Although Cicero cannot resist eulogizing Cato and holding up his example for us to admire, Cicero's praise focuses Cato's constancy and hostility to tyranny. He can cite those features as universal and praiseworthy even while he justifies Cato's suicide with the fact that Cato had a distinct temperament (i.e., a different *persona*). Moreover, it is important to note that Cicero does not fault himself or others for lacking Cato's *gravitas* nor for abstaining from suicide under (external) circumstances similar to Cato. Thus, Cicero's admiring tone ought to be read as consonant with his *persona* theory: Cato is impressive because it was hard for him to be absolutely consistent about his own *persona* and because consistency was much easier for those whose temperaments did not require suicide, whereas Cato was consistent at the cost of his life.

In terms of the Cato, Ulysses, and Ajax examples, it appears that what the second *persona* can do is a factor of what *decorum* can do. This facet makes sense given that, as I have argued, roles are a tool for calculating *decorum*. Certainly, the second *persona* does not override the other virtues, nor can it contradict what is appropriate for a human being (the first *persona*).[58] But, within those confines, it still has some surprising scope. Cicero can even make suicide an issue of *decorum*, so long as the suicide is fitting and it arouses the approval of others. Moreover, this feature of suicide dovetails with what already appears to have been the prevailing conventions of the time: under the right conditions, Cicero and his Roman contemporaries found suicide to be a suitable exit[59] especially in contrast to execution, a disgraceful punishment intended for common criminals. Cicero and his Roman audience could understand even Cato's suicide as rooted, at least in part, in the virtue of *decorum*.[60]

By connecting the second *persona* with one's own temperament and by using it as one of the criteria for determining what is fitting, Cicero plausibly situates "one's own" within his picture of practical reasoning, but he does so while creating a tension with standard Stoic psychology. On the one hand, the Stoic picture of emotions suggests that we ought to be able to change our temperament, but Cicero's picture suggests that temperament is unchangeable. From the standard Stoic perspective, Cicero cites examples of the second *persona* (like seriousness or geniality) that seem like versions of the passions so criticized by the Stoics (cf. L&S 65E). For example, a Stoic could read jolliness as an appetite for talking excitedly with others and seriousness as the passion of being distressed at the levity of others. Thus, they could reason, personality is nothing more than a kind of emotional appetite or distress, an "irrational stretching [desire], or pursuit of an expected good" or "an irrational contraction, . . . a fresh opinion that something bad is present"

(Andronicus, L&S 65B). And, since passion is an "impulse which is excessive" (Stobaeus, L&S 65A) and since "all impulses are acts of assent" (Diogenes Laertius, L&S, 33I), impulses can be changed by giving or withdrawing assent.[61] As Epictetus advises, we can affect the sociability of our temperament by revising our view of the situation:

> You are impatient and discontented, and if you are alone, you call it isolation, but if you are with people, you call them schemers and bandits. . . . But you ought, when staying alone, to call that peace and freedom, and to look upon yourself as like the gods; and when you are with a number of people, you should not call it a crowd or a mob or an unpleasant thing, but a feast and a festival, and so accept everything contentedly. (*Discourses*, 1.12.20–21)[62]

While Epictetus does not use the formal language of the Stoics, his point is easily adaptable: withdraw your assent from the judgment that social encounters are unpleasant and your passions (temperament) will not be sour.

Even though Cicero does not explicitly address the matter, his text supplies good grounds for concluding that our personalities are an inflexible given. To begin with, the second *persona* is explicitly described as given "by nature" (1.107). Although Cato had to "consolidate [his *persona*] by unfailing constancy," it was nonetheless "assigned by nature" (1.112). In much the same way, he emphasizes that we should not try to "copy someone else's nature" (1.111),[63] suggesting that we cannot change our temperament. As he says most explicitly: "For they [*viz*., actors] do not choose the best plays, but those that are most suited to themselves. Those who rely on their voice choose the *Epigoni* and the *Medus*, those who rely on gesture, *Melanippa* and *Clytemnestra*. . . . If an actor, then, will observe this on stage, will not a wise man observe it in his life?" (1.114). While these prohibitions are joined to the reasonable claim that we should follow our own nature (e.g., 1.113), they prevent us from changing ourselves through imitation. In effect, we are warned not to try Cato's path if it is not in our nature, for not every actor gets the best part and so we cannot all become like Cato.

Of course, Cicero could escape this particular problem by denying Stoic psychology[64] or by drawing a fuller picture of temperament, separating it from the passions. But, while we would like more detail from Cicero, his discussion at 1.107–1.114 only goes far enough to establish with reasonable clarity that the second *persona* concerns one's personality and that its power and limitations rest on how Cicero situates *decorum* in his ethics. He wraps up his account by stressing the connection between *decorum* and one's own *persona* (1.113) and by revisiting the stage analogy, summoning agents to pursue their roles with the same care as actors (1.114). In making this appeal, he returns to the analogy that launched his discussion of role theory (1.97–98) *and* the two *personae* that are based on nature (1.107). With this ring structure, Cicero poetically signals that his discussion of the first two *personae* is finished.

iii. The *Persona* of Circumstance

In parallel structure with the first two *personae*, human nature and one's own nature, Cicero introduces the last two *personae*, circumstance and choice, as a pair (1.115). As is frequently noted, these roles are not foreshadowed in the introduction of role theory at 1.107 and so these two roles have felt to many like an afterthought or even an intrusion, leading to speculation that this material is Cicero's own invention.[65] Dyck 1996, for example, terms these two roles a "surprise" (285) and goes so far as to say that the "the third and fourth *personae* differ from the first two in not being moral determinants" (ibid.). But, I think that Gill is right to hold that "Cicero's advice [here] is, broadly speaking, moral"[66] and to stress a continuity between these ideas and earlier Stoicism: "The third and fourth (taken in conjunction with the first) reflect a long-standing Stoic idea that the performance of the 'appropriate acts' (*kathêkonta*) correlated with one's role and social status and the proper practice of an acceptable mode of life (*bios*) form the material of ethical development" (4606).[67] Moreover, Cicero himself may have understood this pair of roles as the logical counterpart to the first pair because the last two are based on what is changeable (*viz*., chance or will) and the first two are based on what is unchangeable (*viz*., nature). He hints that this is the taxonomy he has in mind at 1.120, when he discusses an apparent conflict between nature and circumstance and, by implication, their corresponding roles: "it sometimes appears that fortune, like some mortal, is struggling with immortal nature." With this claim, he picks up on the traditional opposition between chance (*tychê*) and nature (*phusis*),[68] and I suspect that Cicero believes that this is the operative distinction between the second pair of roles and the first pair.

Although Cicero's account interweaves the *persona* of circumstance and choice, they are distinguishable enough so I shall separate them and discuss each in turn. Indeed, concerning the *persona* of circumstance, what remains difficult is not how Cicero distinguishes it from the *persona* of choice but what sort of circumstances he thinks are relevant, a subject that has generated some speculation. He initially says that circumstantial roles are "imposed by some chance or circumstance" (1.115),[69] suggesting that any circumstance is relevant, from an accident in the forum to whoever happens to be in one's family. But, Cicero's own examples focus almost overwhelmingly on political offices and citizenship, suggesting a much narrower scope to this *persona*. I shall argue that although Cicero characterizes this *persona* in terms of circumstances, he limits these circumstances to ones that concern our social standing or reputation. I shall begin with the clear-cut cases of the third *persona* in order to form a model that will guide us for deciding what other cases may belong to the third *persona*.[70]

In his usual fashion, Cicero initially explains the *persona* of circumstance by way of examples: "Kingdoms, military powers, nobility, political honors, wealth and influence, as well as the opposite of these, are the gift of chance and governed by circumstances" (1.115). He later appears to unpack some of these roles when he discusses "the appropriate acts of magistrates, of private individuals, of citizens, and of foreigners" (1.124):

> It is, then, the particular function of a magistrate to realize that he assumes the role of the city and ought to sustain its standing and its propriety, to preserve the laws, to administer justice, and to be mindful of the things that have been trusted to his good faith.
>
> A private person, on the other hand, ought first to live on fair and equal terms with the other citizens, neither behaving submissively and abjectly nor giving himself airs; and secondly to want public affairs to be peaceful and honorable. For we are accustomed to think and say that such a man is a good citizen. It is the appropriate action of a foreigner or resident alien to do nothing except his own business, asking no questions about anyone else, and never to meddle in public affairs which are not his own. (1.124–125; cp. 1.149)[71]

Cicero's list of examples suggest that he primarily associates circumstantial roles with public offices and citizenship. In his subsequent unpacking at 1.124–125, he continues the political theme by emphasizing the public aspects of roles that would reasonably have private dimensions: even the *officia* for a private person *and* a non-citizen guest concern civic relations.

Aside from the obvious political dimension, there is a noticeable gap in Cicero's initial set of examples and his expansion—the station of social "inferiors" or at least the relationship these offices have to such persons. As Griffin and Atkins 1991, point out, "guest-friendship (*hospitium*) and guardianship (*tutela*) receive only brief mention elsewhere (I.139, I.64, III.61, III.70), and clientship is only noted as a relationship regarded as so humiliating by those of any social standing that they would rather die than enjoy patronage or be called clients (II.69 with n.1)" (xxii–xxiv).[72] Although Griffin and Atkins's point may be overstated because Cicero states that the *persona* includes high offices and "the opposite of these" (1.115), they remain correct that Cicero generally focuses on positions of an elite kind.

While it is tempting to read Cicero's initial description and examples of the third *persona* as purely political, such a reading fails to capture his inclusion of wealth and his exclusion of lesser but equally civic stations, such as that of a freedman. However, what does make sense of this mix of examples is the role of social standing or reputation. To begin with, it seems rather clear that he would interpret wealth and influence as an issue of social standing. Similarly, his other examples at 1.115 can be read as revealing an interest in offices of high prestige. In much the same way, when Cicero unpacks some of the examples at 1.124–125, he focuses on the fact that various agents must preserve their proper place, which, it seems, means that they must preserve their public repute. A magistrate must preserve the standing of his city through law and order; a citizen must preserve his repute by insisting on his own *libertas*; a foreigner must preserve his status by keeping his peace. But such standing would be destroyed by the magistrate who breaks the law, a citizen who submits or dominates, or a foreigner who casts aspersions. Finally, it appears that social standing even makes sense of the fact that Cicero does not discuss slaves, clients, and other menial positions because, to him, they have no standing.

In addition, it makes sense that Cicero would invoke social standing as a feature of at least one of the *personae* because, as I have argued, he frames role theory in terms of a search for what is suitable and, for him, what is suitable entails a certain public-mindedness. So, Cicero naturally focuses on the arena most associated in his mind with a concern for our public life: social standing. In this way, although Cicero sets up the third *persona* as the circumstantial role, what concerns him is the public nature of circumstantial roles, not whatever private implications this *persona* may have. On these grounds, the circumstantial *persona* might best be called the *persona* of public status or social standing.[73]

If I am right in my characterization of the third *persona*, we have a model that will help us to determine what other examples from the *De Officiis* may and may not fall under this role. I will first consider one case that does not fit this model and I will follow that with two cases that are good candidates for inclusion in the third *persona*. To begin with, it has troubled some commentators that family roles appear to have been overlooked by Cicero, especially since family roles naturally seem a part of our given circumstances. For example, Griffin and Atkins 1991, imply that Cicero's circumstantial roles include family roles and they note that this is a change from earlier Stoic positions which place familial obligations under the concept of justice (49 fn. 1).[74] While it is true that family roles qualify as a matter of circumstance and they may even affect our social standing (such as a good marriage), they do not seem to be included by Cicero under the third *persona*. Moreover, the Griffin and Atkins suggestion is quite problematic because Cicero *already* discussed family obligations in his account of justice, beneficence, and fellowship (1.50–58), just as earlier Stoics did, making it redundant and out of place in the third *persona*.

Aside from the above instance, Cicero seems to supply two additional examples that qualify as circumstantial matters relating to one's public standing or reputation: age and money-making. We have good grounds for including age in the third *persona* because of the subject's location in the text as well as the themes of Cicero's analysis. First, he discusses appropriate acts relative to age at 1.122–123, right before his fuller discussion of the obligations of magistrates, citizens, and foreign guests, subjects that he openly declared (at 1.115) to be instances of the third *persona*. Unless Cicero is digressing, the proximity of his account to the third *persona* suggests that he intends age to be a part of his account of this *persona*. Second, for Cicero and his audience, age would certainly qualify as a circumstantial matter that has a strong bearing on social standing, with youths seeking it and elders having earned it, Cicero advises as one would expect. For the young, he offers the advice that it is proper to obey their elders, to train their body and mind, and to guard against the excesses of youthful passion. For the aged, he urges that it is proper to counsel the young and the state, to stay intellectually active,[75] and to avoid the dangers of luxury. In both cases, his advice mainly concerns the sorts of proper activities that would improve or maintain one's standing as a good Roman, young or old. Indeed, the discussion of age can be read as an extension of the public offices initially listed as instances of the third *persona* because youth is the station *before* civic office and old age is the station *after* civic office.[76] In this way, the third *persona* pertains not just to a civic appointment but to the entire "career" of our public status.

In addition, much later in the text of *De Officiis* (at 1.150–151), Cicero discusses the various avenues for making a living and he uses the concept of propriety to decide what ways of earning a living are fit for free men (*liberales*). This topic seems like a good candidate for inclusion in the third *persona* because his account of money-making appears to connect the topic to social standing. While I will suggest that Cicero argues about propriety here in a problematic way, the subject nonetheless remains a likely candidate. Moreover, the subject of wage-earning also makes some sense of Cicero's inclusion of wealth in his initial examples of the third *persona* (1.115). For Cicero, wealth features here in the form of social class and it shapes what forms of wage-earning are proper. But, without that angle on wealth, its inclusion in the third *persona* is unnecessary as Cicero already discussed it in his lengthy account of liberality at 1.42–60.

Cicero first sets to work on the forms of gainful employment he considers dishonorable. His account appears motivated by what he believes would harm one's social standing and he therefore warns against such forms of employment as unworthy of free men (*liberales*). According to Cicero, dishonorable employments are any that involve disrepute among men (e.g., usury[77] or collecting dues), payment for labor (which amounts to contractual servitude) rather than for skill, wholesaling (because it requires deceit), and handicrafts and craft-work (especially those that cater to pleasure, such as performance) (1.150). While Dyck 1996, worries that this list "makes no attempt to distinguish justified from unjustified *odium*" (333), I suggest that, if I am right that social standing defines the third *persona*, Cicero has a quite clear standard for what distinguishes them—social approval. And, not surprisingly, it is precisely that criterion which he appeals to when he explains that these professions are inappropriate and improper: except for his belief that trade requires dishonesty,[78] these professions are generally dismissed because they "incur the dislike of other men," are "demeaning," and "they are least worthy of approval," and so forth. (1.150).

Next, Cicero considers honorable (i.e., socially reputable) ways of earning a living, but he apparently further divides this category according to social standing, reserving some types for ordinary free men but not for those of the highest social standing, the aristocrats. He writes that honorable ways of earning a living "require greater good sense or else procure substantial benefit, for example, medicine, architecture, or teaching things that are honorable . . ." (1.151). As opposed to payment for physical labor, he proposes that it is acceptable to be paid for a unique skill (1.150; see 2.12). He also allows that large-scale importing and exporting for trade "is not entirely to be criticized" (1.151) so long as it is done with honesty; and, if it is not genuinely done for profit, we even have "every right to praise their occupation" (ibid.).[79] The distinction between large- and small-scale trade is not entirely clear,[80] but it is clear that these occupations "are honorable for those who belong to the class that they befit" (1.151), meaning that these type of jobs are still improper for true aristocrats. As Griffin and Atkins 1991, note, the forms of livelihood listed here are "Not suitable to the upper classes" (58 fn. 4).[81]

Cicero finally considers the most honorable way of earning income, the way he thinks best suits the upper class—agriculture; "there is no kind of gainful employment that is better, more fruitful, more pleasant and more worthy of a free man than agriculture" (1.151). Of course, we should remember that he is not here recommending that aristocrats put their hands to the soil or plow, but rather, in so far as aristocrats need to earn income, they should head their own large farm, the kind of farming he discusses and commends in *The Elder Cato* (ibid.; cf. *De Off.* 2.89).[82]

What emerges here is a division of labor according to social standing: those without any standing are tracked into unpleasant labor; those with some are tracked into acceptable skill-based or large-enterprise jobs; those with a great deal ought to be heads of large farms, distant from dirtying their hands in day-to-day affairs. This categorization works by drawing a connection between social standing and what is proper, and this suggests that it belongs to Cicero's account of the third *persona*. However, Cicero's tacit categorization remains problematic. In the case of the "lowest" forms of wage-earning, Cicero argues that physical labor is unfit for a gentleman because it is disreputable, but, unless he wishes to say that the third *persona* does not apply to the lower classes, he must accept the absurd consequence that it is proper for low-class men to seek disreputable forms of employment.[83] In much the same way, he provides general grounds for defending skilled labor, but he nonetheless argues that it is improper for aristocrats to partake of admittedly honorable professions.

To avoid this tension, Cicero ought to have found reasons internal to the various professions why only certain individuals may honorably practice them. As we have seen in the previous chapters, Epictetus does just that by invoking ability as a criterion according to which those with the skill for physical labor ought to take up manual work with pride (*Ench.* 24.4). To a certain extent, Cicero could have reasoned about the third *persona* in a similar way had he followed the theatrical metaphor behind role theory to its natural conclusion. His *persona* theory is generated from the metaphor of actors on stage, and the third *persona* can be seen as capturing the idea that role-bound agents have an audience (society) to which their actions play. Accordingly, Cicero naturally understands this *persona* in a very "stage-like" way, in terms of how we appear before a large audience—not how we are in private. But, if we continue the stage metaphor, every actor has a place, even those who play the role of Clytemnestra or Creon. And, when translated into real life, the stage metaphor suggests that circumstances force us into many types of roles, whether high office or wage labor. On this basis, what Cicero ought to say about the third *persona* is that we should preserve our social repute and our *decorum* by not prostrating ourselves either before Caesar or our own vizier.

iv. The *Persona* of Choice

As a component of the second pair of *personae*, this fourth and final *persona* also concerns what could be otherwise. While the *persona* of circumstance or social standing concerns what happens to us, the fourth *persona* is one "which we assume for ourselves by our own decision" (1.115).[84] For Cicero, this role incorporates both the choice of a career or avocation (which is not the same as wage-earning) and the choice of those virtues in which to excel: "assuming a role that we want [*velimus*] ourselves is something that proceeds from our own will [*nostra voluntate*]; as a consequence, some people apply themselves to philosophy, others to civil law, and others again to oratory, while even in the case of the virtues, different men prefer to excel in different of them" (ibid.). I shall discuss these two in the reverse of Cicero's order, saving Cicero's lengthier discussion of career choice for last.

In the case of choosing a virtue in which to excel, Cicero does not elaborate any further on this surprising claim, neither here nor through the remainder of his account (1.115–121). Nonetheless, on the face of it, it seems that this component of the fourth *persona* can apply both to the Stoic sage and to those who are making progress towards sagehood. Applied to the wise man, it is possible for him to "excel" in a particular virtue by applying himself to genres of action that summon a particular virtue. A wise soldier "excels" in courage just as a wise judge "excels" in justice. Applied to those who are making progress, it is possible for them to express one virtue more than another and so it is possible for them to focus on one of the four virtues as a path to excellence in all four virtues. While we do not know whether this element of Cicero's *persona* theory was a part of Panaetius's own *persona* theory, we do know that Panaetius seems to have thought that we may choose our path to virtue so that some pursue courage while others pursue temperance—all with the aim of achieving complete virtue.[85] According to Stobaeus,

> Panaetius said what happens in respect of the virtues is similar to a single target set up for different archers, which contains within itself lines of different colors. . . . For just as these people [*viz*., archers] make hitting the target their highest end but propose to achieve it in different ways [by hitting different colors], so all the virtues make being happy their end which consists in living in agreement with nature, but they achieve this in different ways.[86]

Extrapolating from this analogy, we can say that, as imperfect archers, then, we may improve our skills by practicing every detail of shot mechanics, missing the target entirely until we suddenly hit a bull's-eye *or* we can accept that we each hit different lines of the target, continually working towards the perfect shot. And, by making the choice of virtue a *persona*, Cicero is advising us that the latter is the path of *decorum*. In other words, because each of the virtues are proper in themselves (1.93–94), Cicero thinks it is more proper to be second class in one virtue than fourth class in all of them.

Aside from our choice of virtue, what truly concerns Cicero in the fourth *persona* is our choice of career. For Cicero, our career is not necessarily the same as the wage-earning that is a part of the third *persona*; wage-earning is what we have to do, a necessity which we should make proper by minimizing it, whereas a career is what we choose to do, a vocation which we should make proper by maximizing it. So, as Cicero exemplifies it, "some people apply themselves to philosophy, others to civil law, and others again to oratory" (1.115). This career pursuit is important, as he says later, because, "just as in each specific thing that we do we seek what is proper according to what and how each of us has been born . . . we must exercise much more care when establishing our whole way of life, so that we can be constant to ourselves for the whole length of our life, not wavering in any of our appropriate acts" (1.119).

Having defined this *persona*, Cicero proceeds to analyze how to choose a proper path in life. His remarks are rather haphazard, but I shall argue that he seems to offer two separate approaches, each of which depends on the endowments of the individual making the choice. In both approaches, he wants our career *persona* to bring glory, just as we would expect from a theory that aims at the approval of others, and both employ our own nature as a check on our career choice. Our career options, however, are uncovered by different strategies, depending on our own powers. For most individuals, he generally advises that they imitate the professions of their ancestors, but for a rare, talented few, he advises that they directly examine their own nature.

In the first path, Cicero's remarks appear to be aimed at those who are uncertain about their career choice and so he advises them to look to their ancestors. Although his advice initially appears only as a series of sociological observations about career choice and ancestry, its aim seems to be to persuade by example. Cicero observes that those "whose fathers or ancestors won glory in a particular field generally devote themselves to excelling in the same way themselves" (1.116). He cites famous examples of those men who followed their fathers in rhetoric, law, or the military and who subsequently won glory for themselves. By contrast, he says, some individuals do not follow their ancestors and they are usually "men born of unknown ancestors who aim for great things themselves" (ibid.). While he does not explicitly say that we ought to imitate our ancestors, his examples praise those who do and therefore imply that we should follow our ancestors's careers in so far as their path was glorious. Moreover, he confirms this reading when he later refers back to this section, writing that "I said a little earlier that we should imitate our ancestors . . ." (1.121).

Interestingly, Cicero does not explicitly justify his advice that we ought to look to our ancestry by appealing to the general Roman idealization of *mos maiorum*, the legacy of one's ancestors (as he does elsewhere; cf. 1.121 and 2.65–66), although such justification may be implicit in his praise of famous ancestors. Instead, Cicero appears to defend his advice on the grounds that our career decision is both extremely important and very difficult. It is important, he says, because the decision is about "who and what we wish to be, and what kind of life we want" (1.117).[87] And yet, as he sensitively observes, that decision is "the most difficult thing of all; for it is as adulthood is approaching, just when his counsel is at its very weakest, that each person decides that the way of leading a life that he most admires should be his own. The result is that he becomes engaged upon a fixed manner and course of life before he is able to judge what might be best" (ibid.). Cicero underscores the pressure of this decision by contrasting it with the legend of Hercules at the crossroads as he contemplates his own path in life. Such a leisurely opportunity "could perhaps have happened to Hercules 'sprung from the seed of Jupiter,' but it is not the same for us" (1.118).[88] Understandably, then, we "imitate those whom each of us thinks he should, and we are drawn to their pursuits and practices" (ibid.). In most cases, this means that young adults look to their parents who have already given much advice and set an example. Of course, young adults can hit upon "the right path of life . . . by good fortune or by the goodness of their own nature" (ibid.), but, given the odds against it, the force of the passage suggests that we ought to look to our parents (cf. 1.119) since where they had success, ours is likely to follow.[89]

As a safeguard on this advice, Cicero adds that we should not follow our ancestors "if our nature is not strong enough to be able to imitate them in certain respects" (1.121).[90] So, for example, he cites the son of the Scipio Africanus (the elder Africanus) who won glory by leading Rome to victory in the Second Punic war; but Scipio's son suffered from poor health and therefore could not follow his father's military path. Similarly, Cicero advises that if we find ourselves unable to defend or prosecute in court, we should not follow an ancestor into the law. Accordingly, nature acts as a check on the appeal to our ancestry.

By contrast, Cicero notes that it is possible that an individual is gifted with the right set of capacities, education, and circumstances to approach the inquiry in much the same way as Hercules. Such an individual is "an extremely rare type of person who is endowed with outstanding intellectual ability or a splendidly learned education, or both, and who has also had time to deliberate over which course of life he wants above all to follow" (1.119). For these kinds of individuals, Cicero does not appear to think that looking to their ancestors is necessary or relevant. Instead, he says that "all counsel ought to be referred to the individual's own nature" (ibid.).[91] While most men must consult their ancestry and look to their own nature as a check, the gifted individuals in question here consult only their own nature.

For those rare individuals who must find their fourth *persona* based (solely) on their own nature, Cicero offers some brief advice by explaining how we ought to take our own nature into account. First, he says that we should give more weight to our own nature than to our fortunes[92] because nature "is far steadier and more constant" (1.120; cp. 1.114). Cicero is here probably thinking of a case like Themistocles who, according to legend, was not of privileged birth but knew that he was destined for a privileged command in the military. Against the odds of fortune, Themistocles held to his knowledge that he was fit to be a commander. Second, Cicero also asserts that if we discover that our current career is in conflict with our own nature, we should change it—even if circumstances work against us. In fact, if circumstances oppose us, he simply advises that it is more proper to effect the changes gradually (ibid.) and that "every care must be taken so that we appear to have done so with good judgment" (1.121). As with the previous point, no examples are provided,[93] but he would perhaps agree with the career change made by Thucydides, who found himself unable to continue pursuing the military career that he wished for and so transformed himself into a historian instead.[94]

In both strategies, what is interesting about Cicero's account is the fact that it announces itself as an account of career choice, but it focuses very little, if at all, on choice. In theory, this subject admits of choices, at least between options that are equally viable given our ancestors or our talents.[95] And yet, while Cicero says that this *persona* is up to us and he appears to understand that, as Dyck 1996, neatly expresses it, "the choice of profession is perhaps a human being's major act of social self-definition" (287), Cicero instead focuses on our uncertainty about careers, on the practical problem of finding this role, and advises how we may assure ourselves glory or, at least, success. Even in the case of exceptionally talented individuals, while Cicero is in a prime position to emphasize self-definition, he focuses instead on how to achieve propriety through constancy to our own nature. And, perhaps this is precisely what we should expect of Cicero because he inaugurated *persona* theory as a tool in the service of *decorum*. By emphasizing propriety of careers rather than the choices, Cicero's account of the fourth *persona* remains consistent with the very root of his role theory.

DECORUM AND THE LIMITS OF THE FOUR *PERSONAE* THEORY

At the end of his interwoven discussion of the third and fourth *personae*, Cicero confidently declares that his account of role theory is finished: "We have thus pretty well discovered what our appropriate acts are when the questions are 'What is proper?' and 'What suits different roles [*personis*], circumstances, or ages?' Nothing, however, is so proper as preserving constancy in everything that you do and in every plan that you adopt" (1.125).[96] But, Cicero subsequently goes on to offer more advice about what does and does not exhibit *decorum* (1.126–149), producing a difficulty about the status of that discussion in relation to his *persona* theory. According to Dyck 1996, this latter discussion deals with "some aspects of the πρέπον considered by the older Stoa" (299), but it nonetheless appears to extend the *persona* theory for "the simile of the playwright (§§ 97–98) really controls the whole presentation of decorum, the first half comprising the determination of the *persona* of the individual (§§ 105–25), the second half the actions, words or movements that are to be matched to that *persona*" (ibid., 300). By contrast, while Gill 1988 agrees that 1.121f. follows older Stoic doctrines, he finds the section to be an irrelevant redundancy; he says, it "seems . . . to represent a survival of the older type of Stoic *praecepta*,[97] retained here (in a kind of appendix) although Panaetius's more elaborate four *personae* theory makes it rather irrelevant" (176; see also 194). However, while Dyck and Gill are correct in discovering the footprints of older Stoic doctrine here, I shall argue that 1.126–149 neither extends nor repeats Cicero's *persona* theory; instead, 1.126–149 supplies additional criteria for proper action which are not based on roles.

To make my case, I will not try to summarize Cicero's rather jumbled[98] advice at 1.126–149. Instead, I will highlight *how* he attempts to ground his advice and show that he grounds it without appeal to roles. In so far as general maxims can be extracted from his untidy discussion, Cicero relies on three main grounds: (a) nature, (b) social norms, and (c) order (*eutaxia*).[99] I shall briefly examine these three standards and argue that Cicero treats them as fresh criteria for determining what is proper.

(a) Cicero appeals to nature to reject public nudity and to explain what parts of the body should be hidden as well as what bodily functions should be done but not discussed (1.126–127). His argument relies on a traditional Stoic picture about the teleological aims of (cosmic) nature rather than our *persona* as human beings (the first *persona*). Cicero asserts that "nature herself is our mistress and our guide" (1.129) and he presents the sort of "structural-anatomical" arguments found in the medical writers: some body parts have an "honorable appearance," so nature has crafted those to be visible; others have an "ugly and dishonorable look," so nature has crafted them to be covered (ibid.; cf. 1.131). For the same reasons, Cicero claims that we should reject the Cynic's scatological activities as contrary to nature (1.128).[100] Thus, while Cicero's account examines the nature of our human body and could have extended the idea of our human role (the first *persona*), he instead relies on the designs and intentions of cosmic nature.

(b) Cicero appeals to social norms by enshrining the approval of others, but while he could have treated this as an instance of the third *persona* (which concerns social standing), he worries more generally about approval regardless of social standing.[101] Cicero comes closest to connecting social approval to his *persona* theory when he talks about the proper design for a house. He says that "One's standing ought to be enhanced by one's house, but not won entirely because of it; the master should not be made honorable by the house, but the house by the master" (1.139). In this way, house design ought to augment but not overtake our social standing, a maxim remarkably similar to the third *persona*. However, Cicero does not explicitly make this connection and he proceeds to use social approval to generate a litany of maxims true of all individuals, regardless of role. For example, on a lighter note, Cicero tells us that "singing in the forum" is improper because it is "strongly discordant with civilized behavior" (1.145).[102] Presumably, Cicero thinks this applies as much to Cato the politician as to Lucilius the baker. Cicero is most explicit about the maxim of social approval in 1.126 when he says that the standards for propriety of body also contain "a concern to win the approval of those with and among whom we live" (cf. 1.98, 126, 130, and 143). Indeed, Cicero is so concerned with the approval of others that he stresses that we must guard how we appear to others: we must act so that "we appear to have done so with good judgment" (1.121);[103] "We must take particular care to be seen to respect and have affection for those with whom we share conversations" (1.136). Accordingly, we can find proper actions by looking to the reasoned judgment of others (1.147), that is, to the *mos maior-*

um and *publicis moribus* (cf. 1.129 and 1.148).[104] Just as artists take (informed) public criticism into account, so we should take into account what others have to say (1.147). Likewise, we should look to "custom and civic codes of behavior, as they themselves constitute pieces of advice" (1.148).[105]

(c) Finally, Cicero appeals to order (1.126) or orderliness (1.142) which concerns fitting actions to circumstances, a standard which could extend his *persona* theory but which Cicero seems to go out of his way to make its own standard. According to Cicero, orderliness is best understood as the Greek *eutaxia* rather than the Latin *modestia* (1.142). *Eutaxia*, he says, is "the arrangement of things in appropriate and suitable places: and they [the Stoics] say that the 'place' of an action is the opportuneness of the occasion . . . that is, of the fitting occasions for doing something" (1.142).[106] Orderliness applies everywhere and requires fitting "all the parts of our life" together. Cicero offers several examples to explain his point:

> For it is dishonorable and a great failing to introduce into a serious matter something worthy of a dinner party, or some frivolous conversation.[107] Pericles and the poet Sophocles were colleagues as praetor and had met about some shared appropriate action. By chance, a beautiful boy went past and Sophocles said, "Pericles, what a lovely boy!" His answer was a good one: "It is proper for a praetor, Sophocles, to abstain not only from touching, but even from looking." But, if Sophocles had said the same thing at an athletes's trial, it would not have been just to criticize him; so great is the significance of place and time. Similarly, if someone who was about to conduct a lawsuit were to practice to himself while on a journey or a walk, or were to reflect deeply on some other matter, he would not be criticized. If, however, he were to do the same at a dinner party, his lack of awareness of the occasion would make him appear uncivilized. (1.144)

What is most interesting here is Cicero's management of the Sophocles example. While the example seems to cite his role as praetor, suggesting that a *persona* is at stake here,[108] Cicero rather clearly glosses it as an issue of the occasion rather than an issue of a role. Accordingly, even though orderliness may compliment a role-bound action, it appears to be more a general appeal to circumstantial fitness.

In light of these instances, it seems clear that 1.126–149 concerns criteria for propriety that fall outside of Cicero's *persona* theory. In each of the three cases, Cicero presents the criterion in such a way that it applies more broadly than a role does. And, this result should not surprise us, for if *persona* theory is a tool for calculating what is proper, as I have argued, nothing rules out the possibility that there are *other* such tools. Although Cicero's *persona* theory has, as it were, arrested our attention on the stage, it nonetheless is joined by a supporting cast of Roman Stoic maxims about *decorum*.

CICERO AND EPICTETUS: PLAYS OF A DIFFERENT SORT

Although I intend to employ chapter 9 to globally assess Epictetus against Cicero, I want to close this chapter by reiterating several main differences between their treatment of roles. Above all, Cicero's (and Panaetius's) account of roles is narrow in its ambitions and highly schematic, whereas Epictetus's account is broad and fluid. This general difference yields a number of philosophic differences.

As I have been arguing, Cicero confines his account of roles to the virtue of *decorum* (or propriety) and it is only one of many tools for locating what will arouse the approval of one's fellows. Although Cicero could have given a much larger job to *personae*, he did not do so. If Cicero had wanted his *personae* theory to have wide implications for appropriate action, he could have connected roles with the fact that all virtues are unified (cf. *De Off.* 1.98 and *De Fin.* 2.47). The virtues are linked because "whoever has one virtue has them all" (2.35).[109] He therefore could have argued that, when Socrates fulfills his ironic *persona*, he exhibits not only the virtue of propriety but the virtues of justice, courage, and wisdom. And yet, Cicero does not offer such a claim and he does not reverse the thought so that all virtues locate roles. While a *persona* picks out what has *decorum*, and thus all virtue by extension, it does not appear that all virtues are associated by Cicero with roles.

We can see how Cicero confines roles in his narrow treatment of the role of social standing (the third *persona*). For him, that *persona* is one role, whether it is the role of an aristocrat or a freedman. By contrast, Epictetus does not treat our relations as one role; instead, he employs our relations as a criterion that allows us to identify many sorts of roles that we have at once, from the role of brother (a relation) to the role of neighbor (also a relation). In addition, Epictetus includes more kinds of relational roles than Cicero; for example, Epictetus treats a brother as a kind of role whereas Cicero appears to think that family relations are covered by the virtue of justice and hence are not analyzed within his account of roles (see *De Off.* 1.50–58).

Cicero's account is also highly schematic because we each have exactly four roles. This schematic approach does give some strength to Cicero's account precisely because he is much less ambiguous than Epictetus. In particular, with his fourfold scheme, he is able to guide agents quite directly and he is able to address role conflicts very bluntly: prioritize human fellowship above all. To his credit, Cicero recognizes that role conflicts may occur and he faults Panaetius for failing to consider role conflict (*De Off.* 1.10, 1.152 and 1.161).[110] At the end of *De Officiis* Book I (1.152–161), Cicero takes up the subject of conflicts between duties (1.152 and 1.161) and he argues that such conflicts are either merely alleged (e.g., 1.159), or, where they do actually occur, we should give precedence to social or civic appropriate acts over any other appropriate act. "Let the following, then, be regarded as settled: when choosing between appropriate acts, the chief place is accorded to the class of appropriate acts grounded in human fellowship" (1.160; cf. 1.153).[111]

By contrast, as we saw, Epictetus's account is not only fluid, but we had to work hard both to establish that he recognizes conflict and to suggest ways that such conflicts may be resolved. Nonetheless, Epictetus's fluidity gives his role theory an adaptability that can account for many more kinds of lives. And, for each of these lives, he can underscore the importance of self-analysis and self-knowledge. While Cicero's role theory is nearly algorithmic, Epictetus's patently is not.

Finally, because Cicero limits his *personae* theory to the virtue of *decorum* whereas Epictetus does not, we can see that they are reading the role metaphor in two fundamentally different ways. In one way, we can read a play as a performance in front of an audience. Accordingly, we are actors who must perform in an attractive fashion to our spectators, that is, we ought to act with the virtue of *decorum* (propriety). So, even if I have been given only a minor role, I should make the best of it and not break the illusion by giving a weak performance. I should preserve my role because breaking my role is improper before an audience. The idea behind Cicero's *persona* theory, then, is that we are social agents with an audience, so we must act to arouse the approval of others (cf. *De Off.* 1.98). This social approval appears relevant even when we are alone; for Cicero, it seems that we are always to imagine our actions before an audience and let shame or approval guide us. Indeed, we can even understand Cicero's appeal to the four *personae* as an attempt to organize the world of social approval into genres of action: our humanity, our personality, our social standing, and our career. Cicero's second role, for example, is concerned to ensure a pleasing fit between our temperament and our behavior (*De Off.* 1.107–109). In much the same way, Cicero's third role is concerned to match our social standing to our profession; aristocrats therefore should not engage in such "demeaning" professions as small-scale trade or else they will invite social disapproval (*De Off.* 1.150–151).

On the other hand, we can read a play, not as a performance, but as a story in which each part fulfills a specific function. One actor must be the protagonist by defending a cause, another must be the antagonist by opposing it, still others the chorus. Each part is understood, not in terms of how it will please an audience, but in terms of what it does for the whole (the story). So, even if my role is a "minor" one, I should make sure that I continue to defend my cause as I benefit the whole. I should preserve my role, not because my audience expects it, but because I have a function that must be fulfilled. While Cicero's account is focused on aspects of our performance, Epictetus's account encompasses our whole lives as narratives in a communal story. In Cicero's discussion of the third *persona*, for example, he idealizes the aristocrat who earns income by acting as head of a large-scale farm while he looks down upon manual laborers as unseemly (*De Off.* 1.150–151; cf. 2.89). By contrast, Epictetus appears to have no such aristocratic assumptions. In advising a young interlocutor, he points out that the city needs shoes as much as it needs an amphitheater (*Ench.* 24.4). For Epictetus, there is no shame in a manual profession so long as it matches our talents and the needs of our city. As a result, no Epictetean role is unimportant or demeaning because each role has a job that benefits the whole.

NOTES

1. Although I will indicate some places of disagreement, my account of Cicero in this chapter is indebted to Dyck 1996. The translations of Cicero's *De Officiis* are taken from Griffin and Atkins 1991. However, in the translation of *decorum*, I have substituted "proper" and "propriety" for "seemly" and "seemliness." Moreover, I have substituted the terms "appropriate act" and "appropriate action" for "duty" and "duties." I have done so in order to create consistency and in deference to the arguments that the English term "duty" is not ideally matched to the Greek Stoic term *kathêkon* (appropriate action). The challenge of consistency is compounded by the fact that Cicero is attempting to express Greek Stoicism in Latin. Cicero translated the Greek term *kathêkon* with the Latin term *officium* (obligatory service), though not without controversy. Some modern commentators have objected to Cicero's translation and there is evidence to suggest that, in Cicero's own day, his Greek-speaking friend Atticus also raised objections (Dyck 1996, 3–8). However, it is evident that Cicero is trying to talk about the same sort of actions as his Greek predecessors, so it is fair to translate his Latin term and the Greek term with the same English expression. In addition, a number of scholars argue that the English term "duty" is ill-suited to capture the Greek term *kathêkon*. For apt (but brief) criticism of translating *kathêkon* as "duty," see Bonhöffer 1996, 203 and 232. As Bonhöffer says, "the Stoics had no notion at all of this concept of duty in the strict, imperative sense . . ." (288). Cf. Long 1974, 208.

2. In July of 44 B.C.E., the year of Caesar's assassination, Cicero set out for Athens from Rome to visit his son, Marcus. Before Cicero reached the tip of southern Italy, he was summoned back to Rome for a crucial senate meeting that was to be convened by Antony (*De Officiis*, 3.12; Dyck 1996, 8–10 and Griffin and Atkins 1991, xiv–xv and xviii).

3. *De Officiis* 1.1; see citations from Cicero's letters in Griffin and Atkins 1991, xvi.

4. Cf. 2.45 and Dyck 1996, 16, and Griffin and Atkins 1991, xvii.

5. E.g., Dyck 1996, 82–83; Griffin and Atkins 1991, xix; and Miller 1913, xiv.

6. Long 2002, for example, is notable for the fact that it does *not* rely on this strategy. Instead, Long rightly surmises that Epictetus looks to Socrates as his forefather. Although Long is receptive to the claim that Epictetus may have been influenced by Panaetius, he does not utilize Cicero's fourfold list to structure his account of Epictetus. Instead, Long structures his account primarily around the themes of orthodox Stoicism, treating Epictetus's discussion of our human role as the Stoic obligation to preserve our *prohairesis* (volition) and to adopt a cosmopolitan outlook. In turn, Long treats our "secondary roles" (232) such as son or councilor as contexts to express our human obligation to preserve our *prohairesis* under any circumstance, to treat our relations as a matter of preferred indifference, and to play well whatever role in the cosmos that we have been given (233–244). While I take the view that Long's general approach is a step in the right direction, his treatment remains brief and my aim in this book has been to provide a substantially fuller treatment of Epictetus's account of roles, both universal and specific.

7. See Brunt 1975, 16 fn. 45. Indeed, as he stresses, "I can thus see no fundamental difference in Epictetus' use of πρόσωπον . . . from that of Panaetius" (34 note 9).

8. Richard Sorabji 2006, 160–161. Dobbin 1998, 80–81, seems to be in the same camp.

9. Frede 2007, 166–167.
10. De Lacy 1977, 167.
11. Gill 1988, also seems to follow this strategy, but I would suggest that his case is warranted; the focus of Gill's article is Cicero's account of roles. Naturally, he treats Cicero's account as a model by which he evaluates the claims of Epictetus.
12. The subject of personhood and personality has been somewhat popular in the literature on Epictetus. Readers interested in Epictetus's place within the development of our notion of personhood should look to Gill 1995 and Sorabji 2006.
13. E.g., De Lacy 1977, 168.
14. These four terms represent my own summary of Cicero's four roles, although others have summarized them similarly. See Gill 1988. Cicero himself generally does not supply a one- or two-word summary for his roles. The fourth role, for example, is variously described as the role "which we assume for ourselves by our own decision [*nobismet ipsi iudicio nostro accommodamus*]," as the role "that we want [*velimus*] ourselves" and "that proceeds from our own will [*nostra voluntate*]" (1.115).
15. It is difficult to find an English translation for *decorum* that works well in both adjectival and noun form. The *Oxford Latin Dictionary* offers "becoming, fitting, seemly, proper, suitable, decorous" for adjectives and "that which is seemly, suitable; seemliness, fitness, propriety, decorum" for nouns. Moreover, as Cicero describes it, the term *decorum* must pick out both "what is fitting" and "what is pleasing to others." To cover those senses while employing a neutral translation, I have opted to translate *decorum* as "proper" (adjective) and "propriety" (noun).
16. An unsurprising move, given the aesthetic overtones Cicero finds in *to prepon*. Cf. Brunt 1975, 13–14.
17. As Dyck 1996 neatly points out, in the 1.97 reference to "loud applause," there is a concern with approval (248).
18. By contrast, Dyck 1996 sees the move, not from art to virtue, but from nature to art so that art is a sign of nature: "The implicit premise is Aristotle's conception of poetry as imitation (*Poet.* 1447a13 ff.), so that the characters should conform to what would be expected from such a character in real life; cf. De Lacy, 1948 ['Stoic Views of Poetry'], 256–7" (255). I would be persuaded by Dyck's reading if Cicero had not declared, immediately before the passage quoted, that we are able to see that propriety (as a virtue) exhibits certain features from "that propriety to which poets aspire" (1.97).
19. Cf. the limitations placed on the craft-analogy by Plato and Aristotle. See Plato *Republic* 333e–334b, *Hippias Minor* 375d f., and Aristotle *Nicomachean Ethics* II.4 and 1140b21–28.
20. Of course, Stoic philosophy of nature provides Cicero with the resources to argue against the existence of evil roles, but he does not here appeal to them.
21. De Lacy 1977 worries about whether it makes sense for Cicero to term our humanity a role: "All the other *personae* are to some extent individuating, whereas the first is common to all human beings. The stage analogy breaks down, unless the aim is to differentiate the role of a human being from that of a lower animal or a god. This may in fact be Cicero's intention, since the passage in which he introduces the first *persona* (*De Off.* i.107) follows closely on a discussion of the difference between men and animals (i.105). Cicero's extended use of the term is therefore not altogether unreasonable" (165).
22. Dyck 1996, 1–2 and 8–10.
23. De Lacy 1977, 165, agrees; indeed, because of its (implicit) identification with moderation, De Lacy wonders whether the idea of a universal role adds anything new to the discussion of moderation. Griffin and Atkins 1991 seem to read 1.100–106 as pertinent to the universal role (xlix). Dyck 1996 allows this as a possibility, but wavers: the discussion at 1.100–106, he says, "would have been expected under the first virtue [*prudentia*] (which Cicero accords very short shrift . . .) or could have been accommodated under the first *persona*, that of the human being as such, on grounds that human beings, as opposed to animals, subordinate the appetites to reason . . ." (239–240; but cf. 250 and 259). Gill is ambiguous; in his 1988 article, he confines Cicero's account of role theory to 107–121, but, in explaining the makeup of the first *persona*, he footnotes 1.100–102 and his 1994 article casts a wider net by saying that role

theory is covered in 1.93–121. But, in neither case does he explicitly declare moderation as a topic for role theory.

24. Some scholars believe that Cicero's description here is implicitly in tension with more standard Stoic psychology. By describing moderation as the rule of reason over impulse, Cicero may have committed himself to the unorthodox claim that the soul is divided into two halves, reason (*ratio*) and impulse (*hormê*; *appetitus*) (1.101) with one part standing in opposition to the other. But, this implication runs contrary to orthodox Stoic doctrine that the soul is undivided and that impulses and passions are mere extensions of judgment. Chrysippus and Zeno held that the various faculties (or "parts") of the soul are simply qualities of a single underlying substrate (L&S, 28F. Cf. 321). Cf. Griffin and Atkins 1991, 40 fn. 1, and Dyck 1996, 260–261 and fn. 146; they note the same difficulty in Cicero's formulation. However, this view was not universal among the Stoics. Dyck points out that Cicero's implication is consistent with the views of the middle-Stoa (ibid., 259). Posidonius embraced the pluralistic model of Plato (L&S 65K, M, and P) and Panaetius may have accepted Aristotle's bipartite model (ibid., 53J). Thus, if Cicero's implication is intentional, he may have been following Panaetius (his avowed model for the *De Officiis*). Read charitably, we can say that Cicero did not intend to make a claim about psychology; rather, he intended to assert that moderation means living by reason, not passion, and that *decorum* is founded on our nature as rational beings.

25. This passage has been the subject of textual dispute (see Dyck 1996, 261–263) but not in ways which affect my reading here.

26. Cicero adds that acting from a persuasive justification is "practically the definition of appropriate action" (1.101), a remark that refers to his larger argument that propriety is both a feature of all of the virtues as well as a special virtue unto itself (1.93–101). However, his argument about the two dimensions of propriety falls outside the aims of our discussion of his *personae* theory. All we need see here is the connection between propriety and the theory of the four *personae*.

27. Outside of the discussion here, Cicero frequently appeals to seeking the mean. For other instances of the mean as a proportion, see 1.93, 129, 130–131, 133, and 140. See also 1.124 where the mean even makes its appearance in how Cicero characterizes the appropriate acts of a private person.

28. Dyck 1996, 264–264, charges that Cicero's brief discussion of humor and gravity is "not introduced or connected to the preceding argument." Instead, he believes Cicero takes up these topics because they are especially relevant to his own son; but, as Dyck himself points out (ibid., 265), Cicero's topic structure here parallels Aristotle's analysis of temperance and leisure at *Politics* 1333a16 ff.

29. Note that Cicero also describes pleasure in terms of keeping things in place (see above), suggesting that he is perhaps unwittingly switching between the two characterizations of moderation.

30. To a certain extent, Cicero will go on to do some of the latter with his account of the second *persona*, but this still leaves the universal role bereft of any such elaboration.

31. Kamtekar 1998 agrees (148 fn. 42).

32. In this way, I think De Lacy 1977 incautiously summarizes this as based on "our individual natures" (163; cf. 165) and as referring "precisely to the distinctive features that identify the individual and separate him off from other individuals. Far from being external, it is what makes him what he is" (164). Indeed, if Cicero were to hold to an individual role, it would have to be some sort of unique combination of the last three *personae*: personality, circumstance, and choice. Taken together, these perhaps could make up an "individual" role.

33. Gill 1988, I think, gets this issue right but, independently, refers to this role as one which is "specific to us as individuals" (174). But, he is not explicit about the fact that these roles capture classes of individuals rather than being special to just one individual. Accordingly, at least one scholar has interpreted Gill to be making just the error I suggest that he avoids (Kamtekar 1998, 149).

34. Dyck 1996, asserts that this list can be compressed into "only two sets of contrasting qualities: (1) *lepos/hilaritas* : *severitas/gravitas/ambitio* and (2) *calliditas* : *simplicitas*" (272). While this schema has merit, it compresses a bit too much because ambition does not seem to contrast properly with jollity. And, perseverance does not seem to fit the dyad at all.

35. Brunt 1975, 14; cf. 16 and 19. In fn. 32, he cites I 107 ff.; 119 f.

36. Stephens 1998, 115. Reydams-Schils 2005, 27, seems to have a similar interpretation.

37. Similarly, Gill 1994 says that this role takes into account that each of us is "a human being of a specific kind, with distinctive talents, attitudes, and personal style . . ." (4604).

38. Hijmans 1959, 26, also takes this position.

39. In setting up his objection, Gill 1988, 179, unfairly castigates P. A. Brunt for quoting "Polonius' memorable advice to Laertes" (Shakespeare, *Hamlet*, I.3) as a way of capturing the second *persona*: "This above all: to thine own self be true" (Brunt 1975, 14). Gill takes this to be a romanticization of Cicero's interest in personality. But, Brunt does not cite the *Hamlet* quote in the context of the second *persona*; instead, he cites it as an epilogue to his entire discussion of role theory, signifying that he means the advice to capture something of role theory as a whole. In light of Gill's own 1994 article, "Peace of Mind and Being Yourself: Panaetius to Plutarch," there is a sense in which it is perfectly appropriate to say that role theory tells us to "be true to yourself."

40. Gill 1988 suggests that this feature may have arisen by the Panaetian and Ciceronian drive to incorporate conventional mores, but he leaves it only as a possibility (184–185).

41. It appears as though Kamtekar agrees. See Kamtekar 1998, 148 fn. 42.

42. Cf. Brunt 1975, who glosses these examples by saying that Cicero "illustrates this role somewhat maladroitly, by the diversity in the character of certain historic figures of whose morality he can hardly have approved" (34 fn. 6).

43. The priority here resembles the one offered by Cicero at the end of *De Officiis* Book I (1.152–161).

44. Dyck 1996: "The formula *tenenda sunt sua cuique* has, of course, been transferred from the treatment of justice (cf. *ad* § 21)" (279). But, it is important to stress that the object of "one's own" has been shifted from property to one's own nature.

45. On these grounds, I think Dyck 1996 overstates the issue when he compares this passage to Aristotle's use of the "image of the rule (κανών) . . . applied to the good man (σπουδαῖος)" and says that, in Cicero, "*nostra natura* has replaced the good man (σπουδαῖος) as the standard . . ." (279).

46. Cf. 1.113–114 and 1.145–146. This maxim, suggests Dyck 1996, is "evidently modeled upon that of the sage," whose correct actions are self-consistent (281).

47. However, when Gill 1994 speaks of being "one person" he is also thinking of consistency between *personae*: "all four *personae* have to be integrated with each other if we are to achieve personal coherence and life-long consistency . . . (98, 110, 114, 120)" (4604; cf. 4605). While Cicero does believe that roles should be made consistent, he does so by creating a hierarchy of the *personae* so that, in any conflict, the first *persona* wins out over the others, the second over the third, and so on. In addition, he makes no reference to consistency between roles here. So, as I read him, Cicero's maxim of consistency is limited in focus; it is concerned exclusively with consistency over time.

48. This is not to say, however, that Cicero believes that there are no universal standards about humor in conversation. See 1.103–104 and 132–136.

49. Homer, *Odyssey*, Book 1, line 1; Sophocles, *Ajax*.

50. Rist 1969, 240; Rist cites Plutarch *De Stoicorum Repugnantiis* 1039d and 1042d.

51. Although I will go on to disagree with Rist, his chapter on suicide is quite useful.

52. Griffin and Atkins 1991, agree that Cato committed suicide in order to preserve his moral freedom (a Cynic-type reason), but they puzzlingly add that that was specific to him: "Cato himself felt that what he did was not appropriate for his companions in the same external situation of being defeated by Caesar at Utica (Plutarch, *Younger Cato* 65.4; 66.4), but that, as accepting pardon would be dishonourable *for him*, death would secure his moral freedom" (44).

53. Brunt 1975, 15, interprets Cato's constancy (*constantia*) in an unusual manner: Brunt believes that Cicero is not praising the constancy of Cato's temperament as much as he is the constancy with which Cato held his hostile view of tyranny. Thus, while Brunt believes that Cato's decision *is* based on his *persona*, what features in that *persona* is not an issue of personality but rather of rigidity of political belief. That said, Brunt is more concerned with Plutarch's analysis than Cicero's, and Plutarch's analysis may be more adaptable to the point Brunt is making.

54. Accordingly, I disagree with Gill 1988 when he faults Cicero for failing to discuss the case of Regulus, who honored his oath to Carthage at the cost of his life, in terms of the *personae* theory (187; cf. 199). Although Cicero certainly admires the unyielding Regulus just as he admires Cato (1.39 and 3.99–113), Cicero grounds Regulus's decision in Regulus's own oath, not his personality.

55. This way of understanding Cato's suicide mirrors what I suggested earlier about how the second *persona* is subordinate to the first and how *decorum* is subordinate to the demands of *honestum*.

56. Presumably, this means that they found the idea of death distasteful but still tolerable. Indeed, we can imagine, for example, cases of individuals whose *persona* demands that they confront tyranny with cloak-and-dagger sarcasm, as in the later fictionalized versions of Petronius.

57. Cf. *De Officiis*, 1.71. My remarks here are inspired by the thoughtful discussion in Gill 1994 contrasting *personae* theory with greatness of spirit (4610; cf. 4619).

58. See above.

59. As the *Oxford Classical Dictionary* (Third Edition) puts it, "Suicide was neither wholly approved or wholly condemned: everything depended on the motive, the manner, and the method" (1453). For example, see how a graceful and ungraceful suicide are handled in *Tacitus's* Annals at 15.60–64 and in the *Letters* of Pliny the Younger at 3.16.3–6. Cf. Seneca the Younger, *Letters* 70.19–23.

60. We could also say that Cicero wrongly employs the *personae* theory in a desperate *apologia* for his own failure to commit suicide. Whether or not such a biographical explanation is true must be left to the historians, for it is not a philosophical explanation of the doctrine.

61. My account is, of course, highly abbreviated and details have been left out.

62. The only instance where Epictetus seems to take something like mood into account is at 1.29.31–32, but the incident is trivial, and, of course, Epictetus still advises the listener "to hold your peace."

63. Cf. 1.110, 1.111, and 1.113: "Each person should hold on to what is his . . ." (1.110); "You cannot preserve that [evenness of life] if you copy someone else's nature and ignore your own" (1.111); "Reflecting on such matters, everyone ought to weigh the characteristics that are his own, . . . not wanting to see how someone else's might suit him; for what is most proper for a man is the thing that is most his own" (1.113).

64. Which is possible, given what we saw earlier about him implying a divided soul, a position inconsistent with orthodox Stoicism.

65. See Gill 1988, 174; cf. Gill 1994, 4604–4605. See also Dyck 1996, 285, 287, and 295–296.

66. That is, concerned with moral action; Gill 1988, 191.

67. Gill 1994, 4606. By implication, Brunt 1974, 12, too agrees when he discusses the two roles here as a natural evolution from orthodox Stoic precepts (*praecepta*; moral advice or rules of thumb).

68. E.g., many of these views are summarized in Aristotle's *Physics* II.4. See also Polybius, who counterpoises chance and natural explanations in his historical narrative (xv.34 and xxxvi.17) and Tacitus, *Annals*, 6.22.

69. De Lacy 1977 fascinatingly notes that there is a parallel "to Cicero's third *persona* . . . in the Cynic tradition. Teles (third century B.C.E.), in his work *On Self-Sufficiency*, gives Bion as his authority for the statement that τύχη, like a poetess, assigns at one time the *prosôpon* of πρωτολόγος, at another time δευτερολόγος, at one time the *prosôpon* of king, at another of wanderer (ἀλήτης); and Teles remarks that just as the good actor must play well whatever role the poet gives him, so the good man must play whatever role fortune has given him" (165). De Lacy cites *Teletis Reliquiae* 2, p. 3 Hense = Stobaeus, Vol. III, pp. 37–38 Wachsmuth-Hense.

70. Although Cicero is quite clear that there are four *personae*, his analysis is sometimes rather haphazard and digressive, making it necessary for us to piece together some of its components.

71. Gill 1988 appears to doubt whether 1.124–125 should be connected with *personae* theory, even though he clearly grants that it concerns social roles (191–194). His doubt arises from the fact that role theory, especially the first *persona*, does not feature in Cicero's reason-

ing in 1.124f. (ibid., 191–192). However, my interpretive principle is to give Cicero the benefit of the doubt—where a passage appears relevant to role theory, include it. Dyck 1996, 239, appears to agree since he interprets 1.124f. as applicable to circumstantial roles (cf. 295).

72. They also observe that the "omission of the last two [*viz.*, clients and patrons] is indicative of Cicero's general lack of interest in obligations towards recognized social inferiors. Though he notes that we have obligations even towards the lowest, i.e., slaves (I.41, cf. II.24), we hear nothing, not only of appropriate acts to clients (ties that may have been weakening in the late Republic), but of the relationship of patron to ex-slave" (Griffin and Atkins 1991, xxii–xxiv; see also 24 n. 3).

73. Cf. Gill 1994, 4604; Brunt 1975, 14.

74. Dyck 1996, 295–296, also airs this thesis, but he remains uncommitted.

75. Cf. 3.1–4.

76. I owe this observation to Dyck 1996, 295.

77. See also 2.89.

78. However, note that Cicero does not attempt to distinguish the deceptive *irony* of Socrates, which he praises (1.108), from what he calls the dishonesty of tradesmen, which he condemns (1.150).

79. Cicero also seems to think it important that trading happen by land (at home?) rather than by port (overseas?), but this strange and cryptic qualification is neither explained nor justified. Cf. Dyck 1996, 337.

80. I owe this latter criticism to Dyck 1996, 333. What may explain Cicero's distinction is the fact that large-scale traders act more like corporate managers than shopkeepers, but, even so, such an explanation fails to justify Cicero's distinction between them in terms of goodness.

81. Griffin and Atkins 1991 take this as evidence that the material here must go back to "more general discussions of how to earn a livelihood such as Chrysippus' *On Lives* . . ." or to Panaetius (58 fn. 1). But, the attribution of this material to Panaetius has been the source of disagreement. See Dyck 1996, 331–333.

82. See Griffin and Atkins 1991, 59 fn. 1.

83. If Cicero thinks that the lowest class remains improper even in their fated professions, he would effectively condemn as debased the very physical labor that he himself believes is necessary for securing the basic goods by which we survive (2.13–15).

84. I am here bypassing how Cicero's inclusion of choice would fit with more Stoic claims about determinism and fate, but I take it that Cicero regards choice as unproblematic. For discussion of choice and determinism, see Dyck 1996, 288, and Bobzien 1998.

85. Curiously, Dyck's 1996 commentary does not connect this aspect of the *persona* to Panaetius; cf. Dyck 1996, 288, where we would expect Dyck to notice.

86. L&S 63G = Panaetius fr. 109 = Stobaeus *Eclogae* II.63, 25–64, 12 = *SVF* III.280.

87. This is the one line in Cicero of which Epictetus sounds strangely reminiscent. See *Discourses* 3.23.1–2: "Tell yourself, first of all, who you wish [*theleis*] to be; and then act accordingly in what you are doing."

88. At 1.119, Cicero will grant that there are individuals who are intelligent enough and educated enough to decide their own course, but such people are, as he says, "extremely rare." See below.

89. Cicero does not explain why we are likely to succeed in the same ventures as our forebears, but Dyck 1996 suggests that "Presumably the reason for this counsel is that one is likely to have inherited some of the same *ingenium* [talent]" (293). If Dyck is right, it seems that our own nature features more prominently than Cicero implies or realizes when he treats this as the *persona* of choice.

90. Cicero also says of our ancestors that we should "not imitate them in their faults" (1.121) but this seems irrelevant to career choice, unless he is thinking of imitating unsavory professions.

91. Given how Cicero invokes nature here, he is evidently thinking of one's own nature in terms of talents or capacities. Accordingly, I disagree with the attempts by some commentators to treat this maxim as a reduplication of the second *persona* and its context. Dyck 1996, for example, believes that this final *persona* "could have been described equally well as the result of the action of the second *persona* within limits imposed by universal human nature (the first

persona) and external circumstances (*necessitas* or the third *persona*) . . ." (285; cf. Griffin and Atkins 1991, 47 fn. 1). But, as I argued earlier, the second *persona* concerns our temperament, so it seems implausible that Cicero would pin our career choice simply on personality rather than on capacities more broadly. Nature, as it is being cited here, seems far broader than the examples posited in the second *persona* which concerns whether to be gregarious or taciturn. Cf. Stephens 1998, 115–116, who seems to agree.

92. On the issue of the place of fortune in Stoic determinism, see Dyck 1996, 285–286. However, I disagree with Dyck's implication that, for Cicero (and Panaetius), fortune is "a construct that covered human ignorance of causal relations" (286; but cf. 288). As the language of the passage indicates, Cicero indeed associates fortune with unsteadiness and inconstancy—hardly features of a deterministic chain of causes.

93. Cf. Dyck 1996, 286.

94. Dyck 1996, 293 and 337, says that 1.151 supplies an example of this career change when Cicero advises that traders move their operations from the sea to the land. But, that example fails to qualify as a change in *career*.

95. Of course, there are still questions about the scope of that choice. As Stephens 1998 puts it, "Does Cicero mean that if one has roughly equal talent for two different professions (or virtues), then one is free to select either in assuming one's fourth *persona*? Or perhaps with this fourth *persona* Cicero wants to make room for exceptions to the second: so long as I am not naturally awful at oratory, it is allowable for me to devote myself to it even if philosophy is my stronger talent" (115–116).

96. It is puzzling that Cicero's review of the foregoing sections does not match up more neatly with his fourfold account of role theory. Perhaps, as Dyck says 1996, the disjunct between the summary and what it summarizes "has no particular significance" (299).

97. Moral advice offered to non-sages. On *praecepta* and *decreta* in Stoic ethics, see Mitsis 1993, 285–312; and, Kidd 1978, 247–258.

98. Editors of the text have made different attempts to organize the text here. See Griffin and Atkins 1991, xlix, and Dyck 1996, 240, 299–300, and 315.

99. Cicero explicitly cites this by the Greek term. Other minor criteria also appear (such as an appeal to beauty at 1.130), but they are invoked so briefly it is difficult to limn the scope of the concepts. He also appeals to the mean (at 1.129–132 and 1.140) in order to discover what is proper in a random array of examples and these appeals could straightforwardly apply to the first *persona* (as I have construed it), but his account merely provides further examples of the mean without extending the notion of a *persona*.

100. Of course, the Cynics took their position to be grounded in nature, but, while Cicero signals some awareness that Cynicism derived its arguments from Zeno, he does not confront them. See Dyck 1996, 300–301.

101. Dyck 1996 traces the presence of this criterion back to "the simile of the playwrights (§§ 97–98a)" where the exhortation for "*approbatio* of one's fellow humans was . . . first made" (301). Dyck has a point, but it is equally likely that Cicero is influenced by his own conception of *honestum*, the highest good. As Dyck himself notes, "*Honestas* or, more commonly, *honestum* . . . derives . . . from the sphere of public standing . . ." (ibid. 69; see above; cf. Miller 1913, 10–11).

102. But, cf. 3.93 where Cicero imagines an extreme and unique scenario where a man could be required to dance in the forum!

103. Of course, Cicero should not be taken to be advocating that one pretend to have virtue. Instead, he seems to believe that one's external behavior reflects the state of one's soul. Thus, if we act so as to cause condemnation, this likely indicates a defect of spirit. See 1.131, 134, and 146 and Dyck's comments on this passage, 309, 313, and 325, respectively.

104. Dyck 1996: "in Cicero's day Stoicism could be a sharp tool for criticizing Roman practices. This tool becomes dull, however, in Cicero's hands . . ." (35). But, to his defense comes Brunt 1975: ". . . in fact Stoics seldom recommend acts that would have violated conventions. . . . The good man does not change the rules but obeys them more strictly" (13; cf. 12 fn. 19).

105. Cicero allows that certain extraordinary individuals, like Socrates, may break custom, but he stresses that they "acquired such freedom on account of great, even divine, goodness"

(1.148). Dyck, 330, complains that Cicero here provides no criteria for admission to this category," but I take it that Cicero believes he has provided it in citing Socrates's remarkable virtue.

106. Editors have found the text of 1.141 difficult but not in ways that affect my point. See Dyck 1996, 320–322.

107. See also 1.134–137.

108. Cf. Dyck 1996, 326.

109. Thus, while virtue has parts, Cicero can affirm the orthodox Stoic position that virtue is unified (see L&S 61B).

110. Ironically, Dyck 1996, 269, faults Cicero for only once noticing the possibility of role conflict!

111. For a discussion of these passages, see Dyck 1996, 338–352, especially 338–340.

Chapter Nine

Epictetus's Role Ethics: The Unfolding Script

I wrote this book in order to explain what Epictetus means by a role without conflating his role theory with Cicero's. Towards that end, we examined an interwoven set of topics: Epictetus's two kinds of roles, the universal human role and specific roles (as indicated by our nature, our relations, our choices, and by divine signs); how roles indicate what is appropriate by establishing what actions are reasonable and follow upon our roles; roles as the centerpiece of Epictetus's theory of education so that individuals train to be truly good by fulfilling their roles rather than becoming sages; role conflict and resolution; and Cicero's four *personae*: humanity, personality, social standing, and career choice.

I now seek to put all of these pieces together by directly differentiating Epictetus's role theory from Cicero's. I shall argue that Cicero conceives of roles merely as a means to determining the requirements of the gentlemanly virtue of propriety (*decorum*), whereas Epictetus intends his role theory to be a comprehensive ethics for all persons. I shall further argue that Cicero's roles are based on social approval and one's personality, while Epictetus's roles are more broadly based on our placement within a community and are bounded by our own capacities.

THE AIM AND SCOPE OF ROLES

Epictetus is readily distinguished from Cicero in his treatment of the universal, human role. Cicero's human *persona* is virtually co-extensive with the virtue that is concerned with social approval (*decorum*). According to our human *persona*, then, it is attractive for us to act reasonably rather than brutishly. By contrast, Epictetus's human role is far more robust because it requires that we be reasonable and pious, that we preserve our capacity of volition by valuing virtue instead of externals, and that we respect our sense of shame.

The scope of Epictetus's human role is striking because it does not concern propriety nor does it seem concerned with the canonical virtues. Although Epictetus surely thinks that justice, courage, wisdom, and moderation are human virtues, he surprisingly does not give them much attention. Instead, Epictetus seems to associate our human role with a wide variety of desirable traits (such as self-control and indifference to preferred externals) and thus with practices that are intrinsic to each of the four virtues. We cannot have courage unless we treat preferred externals, including our own life, as a matter of indifference. We also cannot have courage unless we are pious because we will experience equanimity rather than fear when we trust the designs of providence. We can practice justice only if we recognize that preferred externals are not worth a fight. And so on. Accordingly, Epictetus's human role not only includes the canonical virtues but seems to be reframing those very virtues and what they require.

This central difference between Epictetus and Cicero has further repercussions for the ethics of Epictetus. Because Epictetus has effectively invented a new ethics by means of roles, he must reconfigure what constitutes an ethical ideal. For standard Stoicism, this ethical ideal is the sage because the sage is perfectly wise, just, courageous, and temperate. For Epictetus, the ethical ideal must instantiate some exemplary role and be filled by an unusually good person, but the ideal must also allow that roles may differ from person to person. To accomplish that, Epictetus offers the role of the extraordinary individual. In addition, since roles differ from person to person, Epictetus is compelled to supply parameters for roles in order to indicate when we do and do not have a given role. I suggest that, when we add up the material of the previous chapters, we can see that Epictetus offers two distinctive parameters: the communities to which we belong (an external parameter) and the various capacities we have for action (an internal parameter). Taken together, these factors further differentiate Epictetus from Cicero and represent the most distinctive features of Epictetus's roles. I shall discuss those features in the next three sections: (i) exemplary roles in practical reasoning, (ii) the external parameter of community memberships, and (iii) the internal parameter of capacities.

i. Exemplary Roles in Practical Reasoning

Both Cicero and Epictetus posit specific, exemplary roles that serve as idealized instances for their respective role theories, whether Cato in Cicero or the purple-in-the-white toga in Epictetus, but their examples compel us to ask what relationship, if any, ordinary agents should have to "elite" roles. Are these roles to act as objects of imitation? If so, in what sense? In the section ahead, I want to examine this issue and argue that Cicero and Epictetus each envisage a different relationship to exemplary roles. I will argue that although Cicero resists making an archetype out of figures like Cato, his third role (*persona*) (social status) speaks against generalizing that resistance. In particular, the third *persona* equates the Roman social hierarchy of Cicero's day with an ethical hierarchy; I shall base my argument on how Cicero handles the subject of money-making. By contrast, I shall argue that Epictetus implies that exemplary roles must *not* be imitated as archetypes, but rather they must be reformulated for each of us; I shall base my argument on Epictetus's replacement of the sage with a new kind of ethical ideal.

Despite Cicero's insistence that we should not follow Cato's example if our second *persona* (personality) is not the same as Cato's, Cicero's third *persona* idealizes a form of money-making that is available only to the very wealthy. In particular, I want to suggest that Cicero seems to arrange the professions according to how well they approximate the *decorum* found in an aristocratic means of making-money: owning a farm. If we extrapolate from Cicero's example, it seems that owning a farm merits the highest approval because it produces beneficial products, it requires prudential oversight, it avoids the "ugliness" of manual labor, and it affords leisure time for the owner. As Cicero says, "there is no kind of gainful employment that is better, more fruitful, more pleasant and more worthy of a free man than agriculture" (1.151).

By extension, Cicero appears to assign *decorum* to other professions in so far as they can participate in those features. For example, if one has the career of an architect, one has a job that is beneficial even though it may require such pedestrian activities as collecting payments, visiting job sites, or haggling with stone merchants; hence, it affords a good (though not maximal) degree of social approval. Similarly, one can have a career as a teacher of honorable subjects because it requires prudential oversight of one's pupils and it produces benefits; hence, it, too is afforded a moderate degree of approval. Beneath such moderately esteemed professions, individuals of the lowest social strata are also required to approximate the model of owning a farm (where possible). Thus, while a baker cannot avoid working with his hands and it is unlikely that he oversees many people in his operation, he can at least produce a beneficial product if he dedicates himself to producing staple goods like bread and he avoids the wasteful delights of pastries. Although such a baker will not be as "proper" as the farm owner or the architect, it seems that he can have a defective or incomplete propriety since he is afforded at least some approval for the kinds of things he decides to bake.

In this way, when Cicero puts forth *decorum* as the aim of his role theory, he describes this *decorum* as what is generally pleasing to others, but his third role consistently measures this social approval by reference to the tastes of the Roman elite. Since this elite approval is so narrow, Cicero must measure all other roles against aristocratic instances of roles. However, although this limitation seems to imply a firm line between what is approved and what is not, Cicero at least blurs it by treating the ownership of a farm as a paradigm for earning a living. We are measured against that paradigm, not absolutely but by degree. To the extent that we share the features of an aristocrat who owns a large farm, we share in social approval. To the extent that we do not, we are socially diminished. In effect, the third *persona* equates Roman social hierarchy with an ethical hierarchy.

Against such a singular scale, Epictetus does not treat exemplary roles as ideals that we must approximate; he treats them as proof of the fact that each of us can keep making progress. In this way, Epictetus does not use Cicero's model of approximation. Instead, Epictetus downplays the sage and replaces that ideal with the role of extraordinary individuals, an ideal that we relate to in a manner different than we do to the sage. Being a sage is not a role but rather is a perfection that is independent of any role that we might play, whether slave or Cynic. In order to idealize roles, then, Epictetus needs a figure other than the sage, and he creates that ideal out of individuals who have roles that appear extraordinary or exceptional. These extraordinary individuals include figures as diverse as the philosopher Socrates who baits the Athenian jury into executing him, an unnamed Olympic athlete who chooses death over medical castration, and the senator Helvidius who risks torture (or worse) for refusing an order of Caesar. Significantly, these individuals are known for their roles, just as the rest of us are; their special role arises from the fact that they have exceptional capacities relative to the rest of us, making them the "bulls in the herd."

Because extraordinary individuals have talents which differ from ours, we must relate to them in a manner different than we do to the Stoic sage. With sages, we aspire to be exactly like them, to have perfect knowledge and, given the same circumstances, to perform the same actions that they would. With extraordinary individuals, we do not aspire to have the same epistemic state as they do. Moreover, we do not aspire to perform the same actions as they do, even under the same circumstances. That difference is the implicit point of *Discourses* 1.2: our actions must differ from extraordinary individuals because extraordinary individuals have the special talents needed to play the role of being "the purple stripe in the white toga." The ordinary senator should obey Caesar's command to stay silent while the extraordinary Helvidius (who also happens to be a senator) should refuse to obey. The ordinary senator should not aspire to imitate Helvidius by speaking out but instead should be inspired by Helvidius's example to gracefully keep his peace without heaping any praise upon the tyrannical Caesar. In this way, extraordinary individuals operate as ideals in the sense that they fulfill challenging obligations. On the basis of these challenges, we are challenged to exercise our own capacities to meet the obligations of our own specific roles. We do not imitate the actions of extraordinary roles; we instead imitate extraordinary individuals by always seeking to improve the performance of our own specific roles.

In order to make this relationship possible between our ordinary roles and the roles of exemplars, Epictetus must uphold one of the most striking features of his account of roles: he must hold that genuine goodness is not restricted to the sage. Epictetus identifies goodness with fulfilling our universal and specific roles, and this fulfillment includes the roles of every sort of person, whether slave or philosopher. This identification explains why we do not need to be exactly like extraordinary individuals. Since ordinary individuals can be fine and good, the role of extraordinary individuals do not serve as archetypes for ordinary people. Exemplary roles are roles that must be fulfilled *only* by individuals endowed with the talents to fulfill them.

It seems, then, that Cicero and Epictetus posit a very different relationship between ordinary and extraordinary roles. For Cicero, the relationship is ambivalent; while he seems to be pluralistic about most *personae*, his third *persona* implies a monistic ideal that we should all seek to approximate. For Epictetus, the relationship is not one of approximation but rather is indicative of a pluralistic ideal that justifies each of us fulfilling our universal and specific roles.

ii. The External Parameter of Roles: Community Memberships

Epictetus's roles include every kind of relation between agents, personal and public, familial and political. I suggest that what underlies this "external" parameter of Epictetus's roles is the priority of our memberships in communities. I shall here argue that the concept of community membership explains a number of important features of Epictetus's account of roles. It bolsters Epictetus's division of roles into two kinds (universal and specific), it explains why our roles are neither infinite in number nor unique in kind, and it supports his claim that we each have many roles.

In terms of the division of roles, the universal role and specific roles are commensurable because both entail membership in a community but each is differentiated by the scope of that community. Our human role is our membership as rational agents in the vast community composed of all rational beings. Our specific roles, whether that of brother or that of citizen, entail memberships in particular communities, whether the family or the state.

Given that our human community and our more specific communities are commensurable, it is striking that Epictetus implies any division for roles at all. Indeed, it seems that Epictetus could have divided our communities in many different ways; he could have grouped them into public and private, natural and acquired, and so on. Why does Epictetus not treat our universal role as the specific role that we have when the community is maximally expanded? I want to suggest that Epictetus divides our community memberships into human and specific because that division is a practical way to divide communities and the obligations that they entail. In particular, Epictetus has grouped our community obligations into those that can be managed as a unit (our universal ones) and those that must be managed on a case-by-case basis (our specific ones). Our human community is worthy of being a class unto itself because Epictetus wants to give precedence to our community with God while leaving all other communities equal to each other in importance. Thus, in any conflict between our divine community and our local ones, the divine relation must take precedence; in any conflict between our local communities, no community will necessarily have priority. Epictetus's account of roles thereby gains a flexibility lost to Cicero's rigid fourfold scheme.

While Epictetus seems to resist imposing a taxonomy onto roles, he also seems to resist the claim that agents have an infinite number of roles. In Epictetus's view, when we contemplate a course of action, we need only consider a small number of roles. I suggest that we do not have an infinite number of roles because we are not members of an infinite number of communities. In locating roles, we first identify the various groups of people around us who work and live together, whose actions affect each other, and who have jobs to do for each other. We must then determine which of those communities have *us* as a member, that is, those in which we are a functional part. Therein we locate our various roles. Should any random collection of people entail roles, we would indeed have an infinite number of roles; but, as limited by our communities, our roles are finite. For example, should a Roman meet a stranger in the market while waiting in line to buy bread, he must ask himself if he is in a community with this stranger. The short-lived line of strangers itself does not appear to be a community so it does not generate a role. However, the membership of these individuals in the city and in the cosmos *are* memberships in a community; they thus have the specific role of fellow citizens and the universal role of fellow human beings. In this way, while our membership in these communities may change as we join new ones (e.g., marriage) or others are dissolved (e.g., exile or even death), the number of such communities remains definite and so do our roles.

In much the same way, we can appeal to our community memberships to explain why our roles will never be *sui generis*. To have a *sui generis* role, an agent would have to have a part within some community that can only be filled by numerically one individual for all time. Such an exclusive role is at odds with the very nature of a community (as Epictetus conceives it) since communities are functional associations that are formed to use talents and meet needs. Each member is there to do some type of useful job and so our membership in any community will always be a token of some class type. Agents, then, do not have individual roles but rather have specific or class type roles.

Aside from underscoring roles as a finite set of class types, our community memberships also help to account for why we have many roles. Because we are members of several different kinds of communities and each membership constitutes a role, we have several different roles and these roles may conflict. Epictetus treats each community to which we belong as distinctive, and he holds that our obligations arise simply from the place and function we have *within* each community, not simply from within our human community. To see the plurality of these communities, I want to consider an analogy which posits roles for non-humans, that is, for animals. While Epictetus is concerned with human roles, this analogy is not farfetched since Epictetus himself uses animal roles as an analogy (e.g., the "bull in the herd" for extraordinary roles), and the Stoics recognized that we can provide a reasonable defense for an animal's actions. On this analogy, then, if an animal gives birth to an offspring, it creates the community of a family; this relationship entails the role of parent and offspring and therefore makes it appropriate for an animal parent to care for its young. Similarly, cattle form a kind of community and the strong bull of that herd must therefore take up a leadership role in which it is appropriate for the bull to defend the herd against a lion. Such instances make clear that it is our place within a specific community that generates a role and obligation, not our humanity or the animals' mere membership in the class of cattle. Certainly, our humanity makes possible various roles that animals do not have (such as teacher or shoemaker), but that human community does not create our specific roles. It is because Aeneas is a member of many communities that he has many roles; and, it is his membership in a community with other Trojans that conflicts with his membership in a community with Dido and the Carthaginians. In this way, the animal analogy suggests that he has separate and potentially conflicting roles.

iii. The Internal Parameter of Roles: Capacities

If we look to the internal features of roles, Epictetus's account of roles also differs from Cicero's in its multifaceted use of capacities as a feature of roles. I shall argue that Epictetus equates our capacities with our nature, that capacities explain the need for training in roles, and that Epictetus maps our capacities in order to harmonize them with our community memberships.

Compared to Epictetus, Cicero's list of approved roles (*personae*) is notable for what little place is given to our distinctive capacities. Cicero does admit that we should look at our talents when we consider our careers, but he does not seem to think that our talents can override the very limited set of socially approved careers. Should a young aristocrat find himself ill-equipped for philosophy, law, or rhetoric but well-equipped for playwriting, it seems that Cicero's *personae* theory would deem the latter course to be less proper. In so far as Cicero recognizes that individuals may be equipped with extraordinary talents, he seems to accommodate such talents only for careers that will win us glory, whether as a military general or as the "new man" (*novus homo*) who breaks with his father's humble career path.

Against Cicero, Epictetus makes our capacities foundational to our roles and he treats our capacities as constitutive of our nature. To determine our capacities *is* to determine our nature. This "internal" parameter determines our roles by excluding those roles that we are unable to fill (as in the case of the bad "singer") and sometimes by necessitating a role that requires a special capacity which we happen to possess (as in the case of the Cynic). By equating our nature with our capacities, Epictetus tacitly excludes Cicero's second role (the *persona* of personality) from counting as a role because personality traits are not capacities. Of course, Cicero's personality traits could be taken as capacities but only in the sense that personality governs what we can or cannot do with *decorum*. The taciturn man is able to tell a joke, but his joke will not please us. Epictetus's roles, however, do not recognize social finesse.

Moreover, Epictetus portrays capacities not only as faculties to be exercised but as faculties that admit of, and even require, training. In *Discourses* 1.2, for example, Epictetus closely joins the subject of capacities to the subject of training. He emphasizes that, even though the "bull in the herd" is indicated by its special talents, its talents must nonetheless be developed by a "winter's training." Without such training, the bull may be unfit for the very role its capacities require. In much the same way, when Epictetus describes his plan for ethical education and makes roles the subject of the central subject for study, his plan is as much a system for training us in our roles as it is a course of study. This training is essential to ordinary agents who seek to fulfill their roles because Epictetus ascribes to them an epistemic state that can be overturned, a state consisting of right beliefs (*ortha dogmata*). Since right beliefs can lead to virtuous action, what becomes important for Epictetus is *how* we maintain them, that is, how we prevent them from being overturned—we do so through practice and training.

Even though capacities are foundational, our capacities alone may not be sufficient to indicate Epictetus's roles since we have many capacities, and some of them do not entail a role. I have the capacity to curl my hands into a fist, but that is not a role nor does it make me a boxer. Instead, Epictetus implies that, in order to properly locate our roles, we must understand the function that our capacities can fill for a particular community. I take this idea from Epictetus's imagined account of the heavens; as he sees it, the heavens are orchestrated so that the sun does its part because it has the power to generate light, the moon has its part because it can reflect light, and so on (3.22.3–8). If we extrapolate from Epictetus, what seems relevant is not just the fact that the sun has the capacity for heat and light but the fact that the *other* heavenly bodies do *not*. Other bodies have the capacity to reflect sunlight but not to generate light; so, the capacity for light (the sun) is placed in one position and role while the capacity to reflect light (the moon) is placed in another position and role. If all heavenly bodies had similar capacities to the sun, the sun's role would likely be different. As one among many such bodies, this alternate sun joins a chorus of light and its role is not to outshine other stars, to provide supporting light, to be evenly placed in the sky, and so on. Alternatively, if all heavenly bodies shared the power to give light but the sun retained a special power to give heat, the sun might take on yet another role, one which must balance the need to keep from outshining other bodies with the need to provide sufficient heat for our cosmos.

Applied to our own roles (both universal and specific), it is apparent that they count on a capacity that should be understood within the confines of some community. The role of father, for example, depends upon the capacity to care for one's children in virtue of the fact that children cannot care for themselves and they are one's own offspring. The role of a doctor is generated since one individual has the capacity to practice medicine and others in the community have the need and capacity to be healed. Indeed, even the human role (as Epictetus fashions it) is a capacity that must be understood within a community: we have the ability to admire God as a thinking creature and God should be admired; we have the power to organize or domesticate animals for our own ends while animals have the limited capacities to be used in that way; hence, the human role is born.

Epictetus unites functionalism (implied by capacities) with the idea of playing a part (as implied by communities). This may be understood as a modification and extension of Aristotle's function argument. Epictetus modifies Aristotle's function argument because he seems to understand these functions in relational terms whereas Aristotle understands them in absolute terms. Epictetus extends Aristotle's function argument for human beings to include our functions as individuals within a community. While Aristotle seeks our function as human beings, Epictetus seeks our more specific functions within various communities, from civic functions to our family functions. And, just as Aristotle appeals to our essential human nature in order to limit the functions we should make into virtues (removing, for example, our animal functions), so Epictetus appeals to our capacities relative to a community in order to limit what roles we possess.

In this interplay between capacity and community, Epictetus seems to be balancing two kinds of capacities and to weigh them differently against the needs of the community. One type is specific and the other is general. In the first instance, Epictetus treats capacities as talents for doing specific sorts of activities, whether wrestling in the Olympic games or living the life of a Cynic. Epictetus seem to think that such talents carry a distinctive application and therefore suit individuals for specific roles. The Olympic wrestler, for example, finds that his talents not only suit him for the life of an athlete but particularly for the life of a champion wrestler. He would also find that his talents did not earmark him to be a foot messenger, even if such a role utilized his strong legs. Moreover, as Epictetus sees it, the Olympic wrestler does not determine his athletic role by measuring his talents against the talents of others; he knows his role simply by introspection, regardless of the talents of others.

What is interesting about these special capacities is that they entail roles that talented agents should adopt even if they conflict with membership in a specific community, whether the family or the state. Those who have the special talents to be Cynics, for example, must take up that role even though they must leave behind the community of their family. Moreover, although Epictetus implies this privileged status only for the role of Cynics, I want to suggest that his account is consistent with admitting the same status for many other sorts of roles. Since Cynics are released from their family obligations because their talent is divine, rare and indicative of a specific role, it stands to reason that any role with unique talents should not be weighed against the needs of the local community, whether it is the role of the exemplary senator who causes a commotion in the senate house for refusing the orders of Caesar or the gifted artist who refuses to leave his work at home in order to go to war. Of course, Epictetus would likely want to limit the number of such roles and he would surely criticize individuals who make any role into one that can be practiced regardless of the community, but it is nonetheless an important feature of Epictetus's role theory that some roles do not accommodate the local community; it is the local community that must accommodate them.

In the second type of capacities, Epictetus treats capacities as broad in their scope and applicable to many different roles. If I have a capacity for working with my hands, it may apply to smithing, shoemaking, or perhaps even to manually driven professions like surgery. No special role is indicated; at most, these general capacities merely rule out those roles for which we may be particularly disqualified. With these kinds of capacities, Epictetus gives precedence to the communities to which we belong; our community attachments determine what capacities we must exercise because the community determines what roles we must fulfill. In this way, if I have the intellectual skills to be a pedagogue or a civil servant, I should look to my community and determine what role needs to be filled. Similarly, if I have the role of a younger brother in my family, I must fulfill that role even if I am perhaps more able than my older brother to do the work of a steward (as befits the elder sibling). Only if my older brother is strictly unable to fill his role, it seems, would I play the part of his steward.

What stands out about these more general talents is the fact that Epictetus seems to manage them in order to remove any tension between our capacities and the communities to which we belong. This tension arises because it is possible that I may have talents that the community has no need for; I may be suited to become a rhetorician in a community that has too many rhetoricians and not enough doctors. And yet, if Epictetus treats most capacities as applicable to many different roles and he requires ability rather than the special skill of social grace, then Epictetus resolves this potential tension by favoring those roles needed by the communities to which we belong (cf. *Ench.* 24.4). Accordingly, while our own nature is indeed foundational for roles, nature should appear first in our reasoning only as a check to determine if we have exceptional talents. If we have such talents, then we should accept the signs of providence and choose to fulfill the relevant special role. If not, we should analyze the communities to which we belong and take up whatever needed roles we are capable of filling.

Finally, Epictetus further harmonizes capacities and communities because he tacitly understands the self not as an atom but as a set of relationships that we have with others. To discover our roles, Epictetus advises that we examine ourselves; but, to examine ourselves, it turns out that we have to measure our capacities in the context of the communities to which we belong in order to determine what roles apply to us. Using Epictetus's sun example, we can say that the sun would call itself "the sun" only if it were the sole source of heat and light in the heavens; if not, the sun would call itself "a star" or some other such designation. To declare who it is and determine what it can do, the sun must situate itself among the other bodies in the heavens.

TOP-DOWN AND BOTTOM-UP

In light of the foregoing distinctive features of Epictetus's role theory, I want to close by speculating that Epictetus arrived at those features because he seems to be synthesizing two different approaches to ethics, what may be called a top-down and a bottom-up approach. Both approaches constrain his role theory. Epictetus constrains role theory with a top-down approach when he inherits the doctrines of Stoicism and he asserts their principles concerning indifference, choice, virtue, and cosmic nature. This inheritance is top-down because Epictetus often treats Stoicism as philosophically established and so he spends less time arguing for Stoic doctrines than applying them. When Epictetus does argue for Stoicism, he argues narrowly against philosophic opponents (usually Epicureans or Skeptics) or he argues swiftly and generally with ordinary agents. With Stoicism as a given, Epictetus has immediate solutions to many ethical questions. If you are unhappy, it must be that you treat preferred externals as having worth because nothing makes us unhappier than to wish for goods that do not come to pass; and so on. Epictetus proves more interested in discussing *how* to put that doctrine into practice and how to meet the puzzles that it raises. Thus, when he discusses preferred externals in *Discourses* 2.5, he does not argue for their indifference but rather takes up an interesting and difficult puzzle about what it means to be indifferent. His puzzle concerns the worry that indifference requires us to be careless about externals, and he argues at length that indifference is consistent with carefulness.

It is this top-down approach that gives role theory some of the orthodox Stoic features that it has. Particularly, Epictetus is concerned to make roles do the work of Stoic ethics rather than just the work of *decorum* (as in Cicero). Thus, Epictetus explicitly says that universal and specific roles determine what is appropriate, and he makes the universal role of humans largely co-extensive with the standard Stoic conception of virtue. Although Epictetus reframes Stoic ethics through the human role, it is nonetheless true that the practitioners of the human role will behave very much like the Stoics who are making progress in virtue. Not surprisingly, then, Epictetus tends to treat reasoning from our roles as though it would produce the same kinds of obligations as reasoning from nature in general. On this view, if I determine that I have the role of a younger brother, I will recognize that I ought to be obedient. If I determine that the process of appropriation has attached me to my family and that my brothers and parents are preferred externals, I will similarly recognize that I ought to be obedient to my brothers and parents. In both cases, the obligation to obey is what follows from an account, whether an account of a role or an account of the teleology of nature.

Yet, Epictetus is equally constrained by a bottom-up approach to ethics because he gathers fresh observations about the practical reasoning of ordinary persons. In *Discourses* 1.2, for example, Epictetus seems to notice that real agents struggle with their obligations in life and, at times, they even find conflicts among their obligations. These agents, who are not sages, sometimes hesitate before an action that they rightly believe is good and this hesitation is little quelled by Stoic lessons on logic, preferred externals, or the sage. As Epictetus sees it, what explains the actions of these agents is what they find reasonable and unreasonable. Interestingly, Epictetus does not take a top-down approach and force upon these agents an account of Stoic epistemology. Instead, he makes the startling observation that these agents base their sense of what is reasonable on their specific roles in life. Thus, Epictetus rather strikingly addresses these agents' conflicts by discussing with them their specific roles.

It is from these sorts of observations that Epictetus seems to create his account of roles and utilize it to serve as an ethics for ordinary agents.

Epictetus is thus committed to fashioning these roles so as to accurately reflect how real agents employ roles in their practical reasoning *and* to ensure that roles do indeed establish satisfactory obligations. These roles must be part descriptive and part normative. Epictetus accomplishes that objective by building on the fact that real agents treat roles as an answer to the question "Who am I?" and he shows how roles are an expression of both the (internal) capacities and the (external) community memberships of the agent. Roles, therefore, are made to join together what we can do with what we ought to do; that is, roles incorporate the very foundation of an ethics.

Because Epictetus designs roles to meet the doctrines of his top-down approach and to include the observations of his bottom-up approach, he accomplishes what his role theory evidently set out to do: to maintain his Stoicism while addressing the practical reasoning of ordinary agents. Although scholarly attention has tended to focus on the extraordinary individuals in Epictetus's *Discourses* because these figures initially appear similar to the sage, the preceding chapters and the above analysis affirm that Epictetus equally addresses the needs of ordinary agents. Epictetus is evidently concerned with both ordinary and extraordinary figures because his role theory treats both figures as truly good so long as they have chosen the proper balance between their capacities and their community memberships, that is, so long as they have realized their proper roles. To both these individuals, Epictetus's message remains the same as what he says to the anonymous slave who must hold the chamber pot (1.2.8–11) and the father who arrived at his school and confesses that he ran away in anguish from his gravely ill daughter (1.11): your roles constitute who you are, so in order to know your role, you must know yourself (1.2.11; cf. 3.22.53); armed with that self-knowledge, go back to the world, fulfill your roles, and thereby realize yourself as a virtuous human being.

Bibliography

Annas, Julia. 1981. *An Introduction to Plato's Republic*. New York: Oxford University Press.

———. 1993. *The Morality of Happiness*. New York: Oxford University Press.

———. 1995. "Reply to Cooper." *Philosophy and Phenomenological Research* 55 (3): 599–610.

———. 2007. "Epictetus on Moral Perspectives." In Scaltsas 2007, 140–152.

Anscombe, G. E. M. 1963. *Intention*. 2d ed. Oxford: Blackwell.

Aristotle. 1984. *The Complete Works of Aristotle: The Revised Oxford Translation*. Bollingen Series. Edited by Jonathan Barnes. Vol. 71:2. Princeton, NJ: Princeton University Press.

Asmis, Elizabeth. 2001. "Choice in Epictetus' Philosophy." In *Antiquity and Humanity: Essays on Ancient Religion and Philosophy: Presented to Hans Dieter Betz on His 70th Birthday*, edited by Adela Yarbro Collins and Margaret Mary Mitchell, 385–412. Tübingen: Mohr Siebeck.

Barnes, Jonathan. 1997. *Logic and the Imperial Stoa*. New York: E. J. Brill.

Barney, Rachel. 2003. "A Puzzle in Stoic Ethics." *Oxford Studies in Ancient Philosophy* 24: 303–340.

Billerbeck, Margarethe. 1978. *Epiktet: vom Kynismus*. Leiden: E. J. Brill.

———. 1996. "The Ideal of the Cynic from Epictetus to Julian." In *The Cynics*, edited by R. Bracht Branham and Marie-Odile Goulet-Cazé, 205–221. Berkeley and Los Angeles: University of California Press.

Bobzien, Susanne. 1997. "The Stoics on Hypotheses and Hypothetical Arguments." *Phronesis* 42 (3): 299–312.

———. 1998. *Determinism and Freedom in Stoic Philosophy*. New York: Oxford University Press.

Bonhöffer, Adolf Friedrich. 1890. *Epictet und die Stoa*. Stuttgart.

———. 1894. *Die Ethik des Stoikers Epictet*. Stuttgart.

———. 1996. *The Ethics of the Stoic Epictetus: An English Translation*. Translated by William O. Stephens. New York: Peter Lang Publishing.

Bradley, F. H. 1962. *Ethical Studies*. Oxford Paperbacks, no. 39. London: Oxford University Press.

Branham, R. Bracht, and Marie-Odile Goulet-Cazé. 1996. *The Cynics*. Berkeley and Los Angeles: University of California Press.

Brennan, Tad. 1996. "Reasonable Impressions in Stoicism." *Phronêsis* 41 (3): 318–334.

———. 2005. *The Stoic Life: Emotions, Duties, and Fate*. New York: Oxford University Press.

Brennan, Tad, and Charles Brittain, trans. 2002a. Simplicius' *On Epictetus' "Handbook 1–26."* Ithaca, NY: Cornell University Press.

———. 2002b. Simplicius' *On Epictetus' "Handbook 27–53."* Ithaca, NY: Cornell University Press.

Brunt, P. A. 1975. "Stoicism and the Principate." *Papers of the British School at Rome* 43: 7–35.

———. 1977. "From Epictetus to Arrian." *Athenaeum* 55: 19–48.

———. 1986. "Cicero's *Officium* in the Civil War." *Journal of Roman Studies* 76: 12–32.

Cooper, J. M. 1995. "Eudaimonism and the Appeal to Nature in the Morality of Happiness: Comments on Julia Annas, *The Morality of Happiness*." *Philosophy and Phenomenological Research* 55 (3): 587–598.

_____. 1996. "Eudaimonism, the Appeal to Nature, and 'Moral Duty' in Stoicism." In Cooper 1999. Originally published in *Aristotle, Kant, and the Stoics*. Edited by S. Engstrom and J. Whiting. Cambridge: Cambridge University Press.

_____. 1999. *Reason and Emotion: Essays on Ancient Moral Psychology*. Princeton: Princeton University Press.

_____. 2007. "The Relevance of Moral Theory to Moral Improvement in Epictetus." In Scaltsas 2007, 9–19.

———. 2007. "The Relevance of Moral Theory to Moral Improvement in Epictetus." In Scaltsas 2007, 9–19.

Crivelli, Paolo. 2007. "Epictetus and Logic." In Scaltsas 2007, 20–31.

Cullyer, Helen. 2003. "Paradoxical *Andreia*: Socratic Echoes in Stoic 'Manly Courage.'" In *Andreia: Studies in Manliness and Courage in Classical Antiquity*, edited by Ralph M. Rosen and Ineke Sluitter (Leiden: Brill): 213–233.

De Lacy, Phillip H. 1943. "The Logical Structure of the Ethics of Epictetus." *Classical Philology* 38: 112–25.

———. 1977. "The Four Stoic *Personae*." *Illinois Classical Studies* 2: 163–172.

Diogenes Laertius. 1925. *Lives of Eminent Philosophers*. The Loeb Classical Library. Translated by Robert Drew Hicks. New York: G.P. Putnam's Sons.

Dobbin, Robert F. 1991. "Προαίρεσις in Epictetus." *Ancient Philosophy* 11 (1): 111–135.

———, trans. 1998. *Epictetus: Discourses, Book I*. Clarendon Later Ancient Philosophers. New York: Oxford University Press.

———, trans. 2008. *Epictetus: Discourses and Selected Writings*. New York: Penguin Group.

Dyck, Andrew R. 1979. "The Plan of Panaetius' *peri tou kathêkontos*." *American Journal of Philology* 100: 408–416.

———. 1996. *A Commentary on Cicero, De Officiis*. Ann Arbor: University of Michigan Press.

Engberg-Pedersen, Troels. 1986. "Discovering the Good: *Oikeiosis* and *Kathekonta* in Stoic Ethics." In *The Norms of Nature: Studies in Hellenistic Ethics*, edited by Malcolm Schofield and Gisela Striker, 145–183. New York: Cambridge University Press.

Falconer, William Armistead, trans. 1923. Cicero's *De Senectute, De Amicitia, De Divinatione*. The Loeb Classical Library. New York: G. P. Putnam's Sons.

Erler, Michael. 2007. "Death is a Bugbear: Socratic 'Epode' and Epictetus' Philosophy of the Self." In Scaltsas 2007, 99–111.

Frede, Michael. 2007. "A Notion of a Person in Epictetus." In Scaltsas 2007, 153–168.

Frankfurt, Harry G. 2003. *Necessity, Volition and Love*. Cambridge: Cambridge University Press.

Gill, Christopher. 1988. "Personhood and Personality: The Four-*Personae* Theory in Cicero, *De Officiis* I." *Oxford Studies in Ancient Philosophy* 6: 169–199.

———. 1990. "The Human Being as an Ethical Norm." In *The Person and the Human Mind: Issues in Ancient and Modern Philosophy*, 137–161. Oxford: Clarendon Press.

———. 1994. "Peace of Mind and Being Yourself: Panaetius to Plutarch." *Aufstieg und Niedergang der römischen Welt* 36 (7): 4599–4640.

———. 1995. *Personality in Greek Epic, Tragedy, and Philosophy: The Self in Dialogue*. Oxford: Clarendon Press.

Griffin, Miriam. 1984. *Nero: The End of a Dynasty*. New York: Routledge.

———. 1996. "Cynicism and the Romans: Attraction and Repulsion." In *The Cynics*, edited by R. Bracht Branham and Marie-Odile Goulet-Cazé, 190–204. Berkeley and Los Angeles: University of California Press.

Griffin, Miriam, and E. M. Atkins, trans. 1991. Cicero's *On Duties*. Cambridge Texts in the History of Political Thought. New York: Cambridge University Press.

Graver, Margaret. 2007. *Stoicism and Emotion*. Chicago: University of Chicago Press.

Hadot, Pierre, and Arnold Ira Davidson. 1995. *Philosophy as a Way of Life: Spiritual Exercises from Socrates to Foucault*. Translated by Arnold Ira Davidson. New York: Blackwell.

Hard, Robin, trans., and Christopher Gill, ed. 1995. *The Discourses of Epictetus*. The Everyman Library. Rutland, VT.: C. E. Tuttle.

Hershbell, J. B. 1989. "The Stoicism of Epictetus: Twentieth-Century Perspectives." *Aufstieg und Niedergang der römischen Welt*, edited by W. Haase, 36.3, part 2: 2148–63.

Hijmans, B. L. 1959. ΑΣΚΗΣΙΣ: *Notes on Epictetus' Educational System*. Van-Gorcum: Assen.

Hock, R. F. 1992. "'By the gods, it's my one desire to see an actual Stoic': Epictetus' Relations with Students and Visitors in His Personal Network." *Semeia* 56: 121–142.

Inwood, Brad. 1985. *Ethics and Human Action in Early Stoicism*. Oxford: Clarendon Press.

———. 1999. "Rules and Reasoning in Stoic Ethics." In *Topics in Stoic Philosophy*, edited by Katerina Ierodiakonou, 95–127. Oxford: Clarendon Press.

———. 2005. *Reading Seneca: Stoic Philosophy at Rome*. Oxford: Clarendon Press.

Inwood, Brad, and Pierluigi Donini. 1999. "Stoic Ethics." In *The Cambridge History of Hellenistic Philosophy*, edited by Keimpe Algra, 675–738. New York, NY: Cambridge University Press.

Irvine, William B. 2009. *A Guide to the Good Life: The Ancient Art of Stoic Joy*. New York: Oxford University Press.

Jagu, A. 1989. "La Morale d'Epictète et le christianisme." In *Aufstieg und Niedergang der römischen Welt*, edited by W. Haase, 36.3, part 2: 2164–2199.

Johnson, Brian Earl. 2012a. "Socrates, Heracles, and the Deflation of Roles in Epictetus." *Ancient Philosophy* 32 (1): 125–145.

———. 2012b. "Ethical Roles in Epictetus." *Epoché* 16 (2): 287–316.

Kamtekar, Rachana. 1998. "ΑΙΔΩΣ in Epictetus." *Classical Philology* 93: 136–160.

Kidd, Ian G. 1955. "Stoic Intermediates and the End for Man." In Long 1971b, 150–172. First published in *Classical Quarterly* n.s. 5: 181–194.

———. 1978. "Moral Actions and Rules in Stoic Ethics." In *The Stoics*, edited by John M. Rist, 247–258. Berkeley: University of California Press.

Korsgaard, Christine M., and Onora O'Neill. 1996. *The Sources of Normativity*. Cambridge; New York: Cambridge University Press.

Lidell, H. G., R. Scott, and H. S. Jones. 1968. *A Greek-English Lexicon*, 9th edition. Oxford: Oxford University Press.

Long, A. A. 1968. "Aristotle's Legacy to Stoic Ethics." *Bulletin of the Institute of Classical Studies* 15: 72–85.

———. 1970. "The Logical Basis of Stoic Ethics." *Proceedings of the Aristotelian Society* 91: 85–104. Reprinted in Long 1996b: 134–155.

———. 1971a. "Freedom and Determinism in the Stoic Theory of Human Action." In Long 1971b, 173–199. London: Athlone Press.

———, ed. 1971b. *Problems in Stoicism*. London: Athlone Press.

———. 1974. *Hellenistic Philosophy*. London: Duckworth.

———. 1983. "Greek Ethics after Macintyre and the Stoic Community of Reason." *Ancient Philosophy* 3: 184–197. Reprinted in Long 1996b: 184–197.

———. 1989. "Stoic Eudaimonism." *Proceedings of the Boston Area Colloquium in Ancient Philosophy* 4: 77–101. Reprinted in Long 1996b: 77–101.

———. 1996a. "The Socratic Tradition: Diogenes, Crates, and Hellenistic Ethics." In *The Cynics*, edited by R. Bracht Branham and Marie-Odile Goulet-Cazé, 28–46. Berkeley and Los Angeles: University of California Press.

———. 1996b. *Stoic Studies*. Cambridge: Cambridge University Press.

———. 1997. "Stoic Philosophers on Persons, Property-Ownership and Community." In *Aristotle and After: Bulletin of the Institute of Classical Studies*, edited by Richard Sorabji, suppl. 68: 13–31.

———. 2002. *Epictetus: A Stoic and Socratic Guide to Life*. Oxford: Clarendon Press.

Long, A. A., and D. N. Sedley. 1987. *The Hellenistic Philosophers*, vols. 1 and 2. Cambridge: Cambridge University Press.

Lutz, Cora E., trans. 1947. "Musonius Rufus: The Roman Socrates." *Yale Classical Studies* 10: 3–147.

Mates, Benson. 1953. *Stoic Logic*. Berkeley and Los Angeles: University of California Press.

Millar, Fergus. 1965. "Epictetus and the Imperial Court." *The Journal of Roman Studies* 55: 141–148.

Miller, Walter, trans. 1913. Cicero's *De Officiis*. The Loeb Classical Library. New York: The Macmillan Company.

Mitsis, Phillip. 1993. "Seneca on Reason, Rules and Moral Development." In *Passions and Perceptions*, edited by J. Brunschwig and M. Nussbaum, 285–312. New York: Cambridge University Press.

Mueller, Ian. 1978. "An Introduction to Stoic Logic." In *The Stoics*, edited by John M. Rist, 1–26. Berkeley: California University Press.

Nussbaum, Martha C. 1986. *Fragility of Goodness*. Cambridge: Cambridge University Press.

———. 1994. *The Therapy of Desire*. Princeton: Princeton University Press.

———. 2002. "The Incomplete Feminism of Musonius Rufus: Platonist, Stoic, Roman." In *The Sleep of Reason: Erotic Experience and Sexual Ethics in Ancient Greece and Rome*, edited by Martha Nussbaum and Juha Sihvola, 282–326. Chicago: University of Chicago Press.

Oldfather, William Abbott, trans. 1928. *The Discourses as Reported by Arrian; the Manual; and Fragments*, Vols. I and II. The Loeb Classical Library. Cambridge, MA: Harvard University Press.

Oliver, James H. 1970. "Arrian and the Gellii of Corinth." *Greek, Roman, and Byzantine Studies* (11): 335–338.

Panaetius. 1952 *Panaetii Rhodii Fragmenta*. In *Philosophia Antigua*, edited by Modestus van Straaten. Collegit iterumque ed. Vol. 5. Leiden: E. J. Brill.

Pembroke, S. G. 1971. "*Oikeiôsis*." In Long ed. 1971, 114–149. London: Athlone Press.

Plato. *Complete Works*. 1997. Edited by John M. Cooper, D. S. Hutchinson. Indianapolis: Hackett Publishing.

Pomeroy, Arthur J., trans. 1999. *Arius Didymus: Epitome of Stoic Ethics*. Atlanta: Society of Biblical Literature.

Reydams-Schils, Gretchen. 2005. *The Roman Stoics: Self, Responsibility, and Affection*. Chicago: University of Chicago Press.

Rist, John M. 1969. *Stoic Philosophy*. New York: Cambridge University Press.

———, ed. 1978. *The Stoics*. Berkeley: University of California Press.

Ross, W. D. 1988. *The Right and the Good*. Indianapolis: Hackett Publishing.

Sandbach, Francis Henry. "*Ennoia* and *Prolêpsis* in the Stoic Theory of Knowledge." In Long ed. 1971, 22–37. London: Athlone Press, 1971. First published in *Classical Quarterly* 24 (1930): 45–51.

———. 1985. "Aristotle and the Stoics." *Cambridge Philological Society*, supplementary volume no. 10: 1–88.

———. 1989. *The Stoics*. 2nd ed. Indianapolis: Hackett Publishing.

Scaltsas, Theodore, and Andrew S. Mason, ed. 2007. *The Philosophy of Epictetus*. Oxford: Oxford University Press.

Schofield, Malcolm. 2007. "Epictetus on Cynicism." In Scaltsas 2007, 71–86.

Schofield, Malcolm, and Gisela Striker, eds. 1986. *The Norms of Nature: Studies in Hellenistic Ethics*. New York: Cambridge University Press.

Sedley, David. 1999. "The Stoic-Platonic Debate on *Kathêkonta*." In *Topics in Stoic Philosophy*, edited by Katerina Ierodiakonou, 128–152. Oxford: Clarendon Press.

Shelton, Jo-Ann. 1988. *As the Romans Did*. Oxford: Oxford University Press.

Sorabji, Richard. 2006. *Self: Ancient and Modern Insights about Individuality, Life, and Death.* Chicago: University of Chicago Press.

———. 2007. "Epictetus on *Prohairesis* and Self." In Scaltsas 2007, 16–25.

Stadter, Philip A. 1980. *Arrian of Nicomedia.* Chapel Hill: University of North Carolina Press.

Stanton, G. R. 1960. "The Cosmopolitan Ideas of Epictetus and Marcus Aurelius." *Phronêsis* 13: 183–195.

Star, Chester, Jr. 1949. "Epictetus and the Tyrant." *Classical Philology* 44: 20–29.

Stephens, William O. 1998. "Masks, Androids, and Primates: The Evolution of the Concept of 'Person.'" *Etica and Animali*: 111–127.

———. 2007. *Stoic Ethics: Epictetus and Happiness as Freedom.* London: Continuum.

Striker, Gisela. 1991. "Following Nature: A Study in Stoic Ethics." *Oxford Studies in Ancient Philosophy* 9: 1–73. Reprinted in *Essays on Hellenistic Epistemology and Ethics.* Cambridge: Cambridge University Press, 1996.

Syme, Ronald. 1982. "The Career of Arrian." *Harvard Studies in Classical Philology* 86: 181–211.

Tsekourakis, Damianos. 1974. *Studies in the Terminology of Early Stoic Ethics.* Wiesbaden: Steiner.

White, Nicholas P., trans. 1983. *The Handbook.* Indianapolis: Hackett Publishing.

Wirth, Theo. 1967. "Arrians Erinnerungen an Epiktet." *Museum Helveticum* 24: 197–216.

Woolf, Raphael, trans., and Julia Annas, ed. 2001. *On Moral Ends.* Cambridge Texts in the History of Philosophy. Cambridge: Cambridge University Press.

Xenakis, Jason. 1968. "Logical Topics in Epictetus." *Southern Journal of Philosophy* 6: 94–102.

———. 1969. *Epictetus: Philosopher-Therapist.* The Hague, Netherlands: Martinus Nijhoff.

Index

Printed in February 2023
by Rotomail Italia S.p.A., Vignate (MI) - Italy